AF572423

ABORIGINAL CULTURE TODAY

ABORIGINAL CULTURE TODAY

EDITED by

ANNA RUTHERFORD

DANGAROO PRESS – *KUNAPIPI*

Aboriginal Culture Today is a special double issue of the International Arts Magazine *Kunapipi*, a journal which specialises in the literature and culture of the post-colonial world. *Kunapipi* is published by Dangaroo Press and is edited by Anna Rutherford. This special issue is Vol. X, Nos. 1 & 2, 1988.

Kunapipi receives assistance from the Literary Arts Board of the Australia Council, the Federal Government's Arts Funding and Advisory Board.

This special issue was published with the assistance of the National Aboriginal and Torres Strait Islander Bicentennial Programme.

ACKNOWLEDGEMENTS

The editor wishes to thank the following writers and publishers for permission to reprint material.

Oodgeroo of the Tribe Noonuccal, Custodian of the land Minjerribah (formerly Kath Walker) for 'Paperbark' from *Stradbroke Dreamtime*, Angus and Robertson Publishers, 1972, and for the poems 'Dawn Wail for the Dead' and 'No More Boomerang' from *My People: A Kath Walker Collection* Jacaranda Wiley Ltd, 1970; Sally Morgan and Fremantle Arts Centre Press for extracts from *My Place*; Pat Torres and Magabala Books for the story 'Gurrewayi' from *Jalygurr: Aussie Animal Rhymes*, Glenyse Ward and Magabala Books for extracts from *Wandering Girl*; Archie Weller for 'One Hot Night' from *Going Home*, published by Allen & Unwin, Sydney, 1986. I would also like to thank Sally Morgan for permission to use 'Taken Away' for the cover.

Many people helped me to complete this special issue and I am grateful to all of them. But there are two people I would like to thank in particular, Carolyn Osterhaus and Mona Andersen, both of whom helped to make what at times looked like an impossible task, possible.

Cover 'Taken Away' Sally Morgan

Typeset in Baskerville by Lighthouse Data.

This book is copyright. Apart from any fair dealing for the purpose of private study, research, criticism or review, as permitted under the Copyright Act, no part may be reproduced by any process without written permission. Enquiries should be made to the publisher.

First published in 1988 by Dangaroo Press
Australia: G.P.O. Box 1209, Sydney, New South Wales, 2001
Denmark: Pinds Hus, Geding Søvej 21, 8381 Mundelstrup
UK: P.O. Box 186, Coventry CV4 7HG

© Dangaroo Press – *Kunapipi*, 1988 ISBN 1 871049 55 5

For
Oodgeroo of the Tribe Noonuccal
A Tribute

TABLE OF CONTENTS

EDITORIAL

This volume is a tribute to the Aboriginal people who, in spite of the terrible atrocities committed against them and their land over the past two hundred years of white settlement, have still managed to survive. The volume makes no attempt to hide the wrongs that were and still are being perpetuated by white society. But the overall tone of the essays by the Aboriginal contributors is, I believe, a positive one. The emphasis is not just on survival but on a determination to 'walk tall', to assert pride in their Aboriginality, to take control of their own culture through the establishment of Black presses, Black record labels, media; to present their own images in film, literature and the visual arts. All stress the need to introduce Aboriginal studies into Australian schools so that both black and white Australians may become aware of Aboriginal culture and history.

I regret very much the absence, through no fault of mine, of an article on the work of Jack Davis. However, I hope to have an article on Jack Davis in a forthcoming issue of *Kunapipi*. I would also have liked to include some poems by Joy Williams in this issue. For ideological reasons which I respect, she declined permission. However, I am pleased to say that she has agreed for them to be published in the next issue of *Kunapipi*.

In his article in this volume Mudooroo Narogin (Colin Johnson) writes: 'The celebration is not for the birth of white Australia, but for the survival of the Aborigines over the last two hundred years; of their coming together in Sydney; of the bringing down of the ancient ceremonies from the North, and of the laying to rest of the corpse of the past. It is a celebration of hope for the future'.

My hope is that this volume will contribute in some small way to this celebration.

Anna Rutherford

Restoring a Future to a Past

Yet nothing fluctuates more than the notion of 'past'; it depends actually on a decision, or a pre-decision, which can always be surpassed by another decision which restores a future to that past.

Henri Corbin, 'The Man of Light in Iranian Sufism'

The Bicentenary is often viewed as the commemoration of an invasion and the destruction of Aboriginal Australia, defined by Eric Willmot as the place of 'the beginning, the place of becoming human'.

The executive officer of the Foundation for Aboriginal and Islander Research Action, Robert Weatherall, in the most recent issue of Social Alternatives put forward the following popular analogy:

> It is impossible to ask Aboriginal people to participate in Expo '88 and Bicentennial celebrations, because it would be like asking the Jewish community to celebrate the holocaust that occurred against them. It would also be impossible to ask the Japanese people to celebrate Hiroshima. You wouldn't get the support.

Notwithstanding this it has proved possible to ask the Aboriginal community to become involved in the Bicentenary – to the extent that in response to the Australian Bicentennial Authority's National Aboriginal and Torres Strait Islander Program several hundred communities and individuals indicated they wished to be involved.

Another approach to the Bicentenary which has wide appeal has been outlined by Galarrvuy Yunupingu:

> If you want us to join you in a celebration for all Australians, 1988 should be the year when you come to us with a real recognition of who we are and a positive vision of our place in this Australia. It should be the year when we sit down together around the negotiating table and work out a treaty to rewrite the constitution, to set the right course as a truly just society for Australia's next 200 years and beyond.

Many of the Aborigines and non-Aborigines who marched in the contra Bicentenary event on 26 January 1988 would have agreed with Yunupingu's sentiments. The march itself was considerably broader in its cultural implications than a straightforward boycott. One Aboriginal leader's speech, following the march, would not have been out of place coming from an advocate of the 'Living Together' theme of the Bicentenary and the striking news photographs of the march and its individual participants point to a victory of the spirit over historical circumstance.

In England on the day of the march, Burnum Burnum, an Aboriginal ecologist and actor, laid claim to that country and among other things, solemnly undertook not to souvenir, pickle or preserve English heads or make a quarry of England and agreed to teach the natives Pitjantjatjara and how to have a spiritual relationship with the earth. Burnum's irony in part exemplifies his refusal to be imprisoned by history or to accept a moral or a political dimension of the Bicentenary as being the only one. Speaking of his own Bicentennial grant to prepare a traveller's guide to Aboriginal Australia (to be published by Angus & Robertson later this year) Burnum has sometimes said that he is celebrating 250 Bicentenaries.

European settlement in Australia meant the end of a world and its effect was as devastating as the Mongol conquest of Islamic civilisations during the 12th Century. The psychological and physical brutality which attended the expansion of European interests in Australia into the 20th Century is being documented in increasing detail and thoroughness in contemporary histories. These facts in the modern world assume an importance which overrides all other values.

A parallel is often drawn between the Aboriginal and American Indian experiences. In the 1930s, Black Elk, an American Indian elder who had lived through the wars which culminated in the massacre at Wounded Knee, in summary of his life and the experiences of the Indian people, said:

> I did not know then how much was ended. When I look back now from this high hill of my old age, I can still see the butchered women and children lying heaped and scattered all along the crooked gulch as plain as when I saw them with eyes still young. And I can see that something else died there in the bloody mud, and was buried in the blizzard. A people's dream died there. It was a beautiful dream.

Similar traditions in Australia not only depict the events which accompanied the subjugation of a nation but also in Eliade's terms introduce 'history' into Aboriginal life. The process happens not without struggle and Eliade writes:

> Hence it is...probable that the desire felt by the man of traditional societies to refuse history, and to confine himself to an indefinite repetition of archetypes, testifies to this thirst for the real and his terror of 'losing' himself by letting himself be overwhelmed by the meaninglessness of profane existence.

Side by side with dreaming traditions, oral histories are preserved, detailing the experiences of European contact. As well as being a record of the experience of Aboriginal/non-Aboriginal contact the histories introduce Western historicism into even the most traditional communities and increasingly Aboriginal Australians begin to define themselves by the experience of 200 years.

Out of this dialectic develop concepts such as Aboriginal sovereignty and land rights and their attempted satisfaction within the ambit of Western law and affirmed by Government aid programs which legislate to improve material conditions and which are often perceived as de facto compensation.

There has been a marginal attempt to classify the Bicentennial Aboriginal Program as compensation, but it has not been a consideration for those Aborigines implacably opposed to the Bicentenary. For them the question of adequate compensation is irrelevant compared to the moral issue of a bicentenary and with regard to compensation, the question of land rights is the issue. The Bicentennial Aboriginal Program is usually accepted for what it is – a creative forum for the Aboriginal community in the Bicentenary year. In comparison to the health, welfare, economic development and employment creation programs administered by the major bodies in Aboriginal affairs, the Bicentennial Aboriginal Program is comparatively modest – with a total budget of $7.46 million.

- Guidelines for funding applications were purposefully as broad as possible. To be eligible for consideration projects had to:
- Commemorate Aboriginal or Torres Strait Islander life, people, events or customs.
- Celebrate some aspect of Aboriginal or Torres Strait Islander life or achievement.
- Preserve or develop Aboriginal or Torres Strait Islander life, custom or society.
- Create a better understanding of the Aboriginal and Torres Strait Islander presence and experience in Australia.

• Promote greater social harmony and understanding in Australia.

Tom Thompson, the Australian Bicentennial Authority's publisher, has pointed out that we are witnessing a major cultural event in the movement of an oral tradition to a written form. This is born out in the number of literary/historical projects in the Bicentennial National Aboriginal and Torres Strait Islander Program. As well as names like Sally Morgan, hitherto unknown authors such as Ruby Langford are being published under the program. If there is one quality which distinguishes the Aboriginal writers being published, it is their authenticity, the borrowed polemics of sixties' radicalism are replaced by a search for an individual and genuine Aboriginal voice.

Traditional communities are involved in this process through organisations such as the Western Desert Puntukunuparna and Broome based Magabala Books. The Western Desert Puntukunuparna on behalf of the Western Desert communities is undertaking a massive Aboriginal oral history of the non-Aboriginal Canning Stock Route, the last venture in non-Aboriginal Australia's quixotic 'exploration' of Australia. A recent progress report on the oral history describes the different approach to history taken by Aboriginal society. The Canning Stock Route was seen as a

> quite marginal episode in the history of the desert. Gradually the significant themes became clearer: country, movement, autonomy and the joys of the hunter-gatherer economy.
>
> There was, of course, much discussion about first contacts with the whitefellas and their tucker but it seemed incidental to the main themes, it took the form of anecdotes about a different world which was not readily perceived as a threat to their own. The stories about country confirmed their unshakeable confidence in the integrity of their culture...

The Bicentennial National Aboriginal and Torres Strait Islander Program has been open-ended enough to reflect changes taking place in Aboriginal culture and its symbiotic relationship with non-Aboriginal culture.

Following the success of *Mayi*, Magabala Books has published three other titles in 1988, *Wandering Girl, Story of Crow* and *Jalygurr. Wandering Girl's* promotional poster evokes the power of the book by quoting a few lines, 'Soon as I opened the door all the chatter and laughter stopped. You could hear a pin drop as all eyes were on me..."Tracey dear, is this your little dark servant?" I just stood there smiling. I thought it was wonderful that at last people were taking notice of me...I turned to the lady who did all the talking and said, "My name is Glenyse". She was quite startled; she said, "Oh dear, I didn't think you had a name."'

Magabala Books will also be publishing the Bunuba's retelling of the story of the Aboriginal resistance leader in the Kimberleys, Jundamurra, who fought only 90 years ago. Reading the first proofs of this historical novel it is hard not to relive the beauty and clarity of the Kimberley landscape or to sympathise with the metaphysic which inspired the Bunuba. Oral traditions from the Bunuba people provide completely new perspectives on Jundamurra's motives and personality – a person who converted from something of a renegade to a committed law man during the period of war with settlers.

The establishment of Keeping Places, the preferred Aboriginal term for museum/cultural centres which carry out the dual function of preserving and renewing Aboriginal culture, is also expressive of a development in the outward form of Aboriginal culture. Historical information which once would have been individual becomes recorded and stored in accessible forms for the total community. Dreaming traditions and the heritage of the law collected and memorised over a lifetime are also recorded on video or audio cassette for selected community use.

Granted cultural evolution happens regardless of specific programs, but having a program sensitive to the needs of the community accelerates and provides the material supports which encourage this process. Further examples of this translation of value and culture include Australia's first Aboriginal television station which is being established in Alice Springs with a transmission range of approximately one-third of the Australian land mass and a computerised dictionary of Aboriginal languages being established for use by all Australians. At Yuelamu, in a variation of traditional practice, a secret/sacred ground painting previously done on open ground to be eventually dispersed by the elements, will be constructed by elders in a Keeping Place for permanent ceremonial use.

The interplay between Aboriginal and non-Aboriginal culture is most clearly seen in a Jimmy Pike work to be included in the Bicentennial Aboriginal Program's art poster series. Entitled *Kartiya Boat*, the artist engages in an active interrogation of European culture with his representation of a clipper ship approaching the Australian coast. The work could almost be the definitive Bicentennial picture, having been done by a major artist, an Aborigine, and dealing with the crucial event of the Bicentenary. In the act of creating, Jimmy Pike transforms the 'chaos' of non-Aboriginal Australia into a 'cosmos' understandable by all Australians, but quietly from a sovereign Aboriginal position.

Stephen Muecke has pointed out the serpentine relationship between Jimmy Pike's work and non-Aboriginal Australia via shared cultural needs and high fashion:

> Jimmy Pike's traditional symbolism, a statement of belongingness to the country, answers a need on the part of the metropolis for an ethical direction which is placed outside of the infinite proliferation of information, media technologies and representations. The fact that his work is of the highest artistic order, and that it has found a vehicle in design and fashion is a tribute to his traditional practice of 'moving culture along' and to the sensitive and creative entrepreneurial work of Desert Designs (the artist's agent).

Perhaps a researcher examining the official Bicentennial Aboriginal program in 50 years' time will recognise the first signs of an Aboriginal renaissance, popular and cultural and unconditioned by political didactics or popularisations of traditional Aboriginal spirituality. They might also acknowledge that the first steps in the Aboriginal repossession of Australia began as a cultural movement. Further to this they might find the hermeneutic Jimmy Pike engages in when he paints a sailing ship, a more useful and integrated attempt at understanding the Bicentenary than some of the crude dissections of contemporary critics.

The process might be summed up in the words of Corbin:

> To integrate a world, to make it one's own, also implies that one has emerged from it in order to make it enter into oneself.

Oodgeroo of the Tribe Noonuccal Photo Gerry Turcotte

'Recording the Cries of the People'

AN INTERVIEW WITH OODGEROO (KATH WALKER)

INTRODUCTION

Kath Walker was born in 1920 on Stradbroke Island. She is a member of the Noonuccal tribe, custodian of the land Minjerribah ('Aborigines don't *own* the land, we are merely its custodian'). When the government of Australia set up a welfare system on the island in the 1920s, the medical superintendent decided he wanted the Aboriginals close enough to 'keep an eye on', but not too close to intrude upon him. Kath Walker's tribe was moved to the 'One Mile' settlement at that distance from Dunwich where they remain today. The whites of Dunwich, however, are presently trying to move them out in order to develop the waterfront area for tourism.

Kath Walker recently adopted the name Oodgeroo, after the old woman from one of her own legends. In that story, Oodgeroo, so named because of the paperbark tree on which she writes her stories, travels the land recovering the history of her people. It is a fitting title for a woman who has spent close to thirty years recording the voice of Aboriginals. Kath was one of the leaders of the Civil Rights Movement which led to the 1967 referendum which finally allowed Aboriginals to vote. Through poetry, prose, essays, and recently, artwork, Kath Walker has articulated the concerns of Aboriginals, and has protested against the many injustices which still beset her people in modern day Australia.

Kath has also been one of the leading members of the Queensland Aboriginal Advancement League; The Federal Council for the Advancement of Aborigines and Torres Strait Islanders (FCAATSI); and later of the Aboriginal Tribal Council. When the FCAATSI Movement collapsed in 1970, Kath retired to Moongalba, where she attempted to gain the title to her tribal land. It has been denied her by the Queensland Government. She has since turned the area into an educational centre which has hosted well over 25,000 young students, both black and white.

In 1964 her first volume of poems, *We Are Going*, was released by Jacaranda Press. It sold out before it could be launched and soon went into seven editions in as many months. Her second book, *The Dawn is at Hand,* published in 1966, was equally popular. This was followed in 1970 by *My People* which collects her previous work and includes additional poetry and prose pieces. *Stradbroke Dreamtime,* her first complete work of prose, features both autobiographical material as well as modern Aboriginal legends of her own creation. This was published in 1972. It was followed, almost a decade later, by a personally illustrated children's book, *Father Sky and Mother Earth,* which tells the story of creation from an Aboriginal perspective. In 1985, Ulli Beier released a book entitled *Quandamooka: The Art of Kath Walker* (Robert Brown and Associates), which features a series of Kath Walker's illustrations, accompanied by her brief commentary on each work.

This interview was conducted at Kath Walker's Sydney home, on 28 January 1988, two days after the Australian Bicentennial Celebrations which saw the country's largest ever civil rights protest march. The following is an edited version of this interview.

Gerry Turcotte

Could I ask you first how you started writing?

I was always fascinated by words. I was at a mixed school in Stradbroke which we call Minjerribah and I always topped the class in English and art. I used to make 'jiggly' rhymes at school but I took writing seriously in the sixties. I realized there had always been story-tellers in our world before the white man ripped the guts out of us, and what really got me seriously into writing was listening to the voices of my people. I thought, My God, we should be writing this down. Our story-tellers would stand for three days just creating stories, and I thought it's time to get back to it. Because the only book that the Aboriginals were allowed to be literate about was the Bible. And whenever they tried to express themselves – right up to the sixties – was to say, like Samuel, or, like Noah, in order to compare, to put their message over, to be understood. And whenever the old men would come into the meetings they would always have the Bible under their wing, you see. And I thought, My God it's time we recorded the cries of the people and gave them a book they could call their own. So I wrote *We Are Going*. The

Aboriginal people don't see it as my book, they see it as theirs, and it's true, it is their book, because it's their voices, their hopes, their inspirations, their frustrations, their aspirations. And it sold mainly out of curiosity value. The first edition sold in three days. Then it went into seven editions in seven months. And its success was inevitable, I think, not because I'm a good writer, but because for the first time the Aboriginals had a voice, a written voice. I'm the highest selling poet in Australia.

Who has been your audience?

Decent people.

Blacks or whites?

Oh, whites as well as blacks. The humanitarians – who wanted to know more about the Aboriginals – welcomed it with open arms, because in the early stages, the whites were kept very effectively away from the Aborigines. And whites will tell you quite blankly, I've never met an Aborigine in my life, so how could they know about us, how could they feel for us? It was done deliberately. They didn't want friends of the Aborigines coming out and upsetting the jolly old white Australian apple cart you know, rocking the boat.

When you first started writing you were criticized as being a didactic writer – your poetry was dismissed by some as propaganda. How did you respond to these criticisms?

I agreed with them because it *was* propaganda. I deliberately did it.

There is no such a thing as non-political writing, is there?

That's right! If you talk about a hole in the street up there that's politics. And this old clichéd business of saying we are non-political. If you're non-political, man, you're dead, you're not even thinking. So this was another 'fear' thing that they put into the unenlightened to keep them from rocking the boat. Australia is full of boats that are so still it isn't even funny.

You have recently adopted the name Oodgeroo...

Oodgeroo, of the Noonuccal tribe, custodian of the land Minjerribah, which is Stradbroke Island. Yes.

I believe this is the name of an old woman who records the history of her tribes on bark. She is her culture's historian.

I wrote that story in the *Stradbroke Dreamtime.* Pastor Don Brady, now deceased, gave me that name when we were demonstrating against the Queen having *dared* to come across to Australia to celebrate Captain Cook's 'DISCOVERY' of Australia. What rot! And we were down at La Perouse, throwing wreaths into the water then, and while we were waiting for the rest of the people of FCAATSI (which was a civil rights movement) to turn up, Don said, Gee whites are buying your book as well as blacks, Kath, and he was surprised about that because anything pertaining to blacks up until then was 'they don't exist because you actually can't see them'. He and a lot of the Torres Strait Aboriginals were very, very surprised that whites were actually buying the book. And he said, Kathy, if we had our own way of life, if we could decide our own destiny, the tribal elders would have called you Oodgeroo, because you couldn't do it without your sister, the paperbark tree. You need the paperbark. Which was quite logical. And so when I went home I wrote the story of Oodgeroo who had lost her tribes and was trying to get back to them, and it's only lately that the people who've read the story have realized that I was writing about myself.

Were you always accepted by your people in your role as spokesperson?

From 1960 they saw me as someone they could trust, who was honest and tolerant. I'm very rich because I'm loved by all my people, it's a very beautiful thing. No money could surpass that. The love that my people feel for me is just so tremendous. It's a lovely feeling.

In your first book, We Are Going, *there is a decidedly hopeful note to your poems, such as in 'Son of Mine' and 'United We Win'. In the first you speak of 'men in brotherhood combine', and in the second, you seem to refuse to blame whites for the situation of Aboriginals.*

Oh, I'm not refusing to blame the whites for what's happened. I'm saying that there are some whites who want to rectify the wrongs. Not all of them, but there are some.

You were one of the leaders of the Civil Rights movement which fought for and won the right to hold a referendum in 1967, an event which Aboriginals believed would mark a positive change in their lives.

So did non-Aboriginals believe that. (Although a lot of them voted that way to ease their consciences, I might add.) But it was really believed that the moment we gave the federal government a clear mandate to act on behalf of Aboriginals, we could resolve the problem. But we didn't reckon with the federal government who didn't have the guts to step in and take this responsibility because they were afraid of losing the votes from the states, so they played politics against us.

Two days ago the largest gathering of Aboriginal and white protesters in Australia's history gathered to protest against the Australia Day celebration and its implications. With Black deaths in Custody rivalling those of South Africa: with living conditions for Aboriginals shamefully inadequate; all the signs seem to suggest that things have got worse for the Aboriginal people, not better. Do you feel a sense of despair after all the work you've done?

No. I can't afford the luxury of despair or pessimism. We still have to hope. We're a timeless people, we've lived in a timeless land. We have suffered the invasion of two hundred years, and we'll go on suffering. But we are going to survive. And what we have to do now is find, in the white Australian scene, the true humanitarians. And we found a lot of them on that march. That was brilliant, how the whites stood with us. And there were a lot of them. It's the biggest march in Australian history.

What strikes me about your collection My People, *is that there are two very different voices speaking. One which says 'Gratefully we learn from you. / The advanced race. / You with long centuries behind you'; the other says 'Take care! White racists! / Blacks can be racists too. / A violent struggle could erupt / And racists meet their death'. Is one of these voices truer than the other?*

No, I think they're on a level par. I think what you have to look at is that I'm not talking about the humanitarians, I'm talking about the real racists. There are racists and non-racists in the white Australian scene. I'm saying join up the non-racists and to hell with the others, we want nothing to do with them.

Anyone reading your work can't help but notice an incredible sense of humour underneath it all. Poems like 'Nona' and 'Jarris' Love Song' are filled with good humour and an obvious love for your characters. How do you maintain that sense of humour in the midst of current racial realities?

That's easy to answer. In the Aboriginal world we give way to all emotions. In the 'British', the present white generation of Australian people have been told that to cry is weakness, and if a ten year old boy gets up and cries they say, My goodness! But in the Aboriginal world, to cry is a beautiful thing. To us it's compassion. The most beautiful thing I've ever seen is an old Aboriginal man crying for his dead grandson, and unashamedly letting the tears roll down his cheek. Now if you suppress emotions you've got problems. When anger comes you've got to kick something. Let's hope they kick trees, not human beings. All these emotions must be brought out and dealt with outside, because if you suppress them, you're in trouble. You get what has happened in Melbourne where obviously these young people could not find anyone to talk to and get that out of their system, so they picked up a gun and went on a rampage.[1] That's a terrible indictment against his friends and his relatives, that he couldn't speak out. But in the Aboriginal world if we are worried, or if we are sad, or lonely, we'll find someone and we'll cry on their shoulder – and their shoulder is always there to cry on. And so we use all our emotions. When I'm in a happy mood, the humour comes up, and when I hear about a death, down I go to that level of the emotions. This is why Aboriginals have survived, because they use all their emotions. This stiff-upper British lip – let the British have it, I want nothing to do with it, it suppresses too many things.

You once said, 'I felt poetry would be the breakthrough for Aboriginal people because they were story-tellers and song-makers, and I thought poetry would appeal to them more than anything else'.[2] *That was before you wrote* Stradbroke Dreamtime *and*

Father Sky and Mother Earth, *and found you could express yourself just as well through prose. Despite this do you still think poetry is the major literary genre for Aboriginals?*

Yes. I can give you an example. I was at Lismore, New England, and we were having a conference. This old man came in with the Bible under his arm and he was trying to express himself with the Bible. And then after my book, *We Are Going* came out, the next year round, here he was standing up there with *my* book under his arm. And he was quoting my poetry and this amazed me further because I knew he could not read nor write. When he got down, I went over to him and said, Old One – in our world that is an honourable name, no connotations of anything else but respect – I said how come you can recite my poetry I know you cannot read nor write. He said, Oh that was the easy part, girl. I would take it to all my white friends and to our own people who could read and write and I would make them talk it over and over until I got it in here. And he got it into his head. It was an amazing, wonderful thrill to see that old man up there quoting Kath Walker.

It seems to me that your most successful poems are those that don't use 'White-European' poetic forms.

That's right. Back to my culture. Well, I'm in my own culture there. When I'm dealing with a rotten language that's supposed to be a *pure* language ... it's been pinched from the French, the Germans and everyone. It's a bastardized language the English language and it's a terrible language to work with. Terrible!

But you did find that you had to imitate traditional 'white' poetic forms at first, until you could break through into your own rhythms and approaches to writing?

Well, if you're going to be a successful writer you're forced into using the English language in order to be published. And I do not know the Aboriginal – the Noonuccal language. It was flogged out of us at school. It was forbidden, it was classed as a pagan language. You get rid of that pagan language and you learn the king's English. Which is a *Christian* language. In the name of Christianity! look at what they did to us.

In two recent books, Father Sky and Mother Earth *and* Quandamook *you reveal an entirely different and quite considerable talent as artist. Do you see your art work as an extension of your writing?*

As a matter of fact I was an artist long before I became a writer. I dropped my artwork when I saw the need of my people wanting a book. And then I stuck with my writing and have belatedly gone back to the art. But the need for the book was more important than my art. You know how *Quandamooka* came about? I hid it for years because it was the way I saved my sanity during the civil rights years. I used to go home and just go back to my art. It was Ulli Beier who came to me one day concerning something totally different to that. I happened to be checking up on my art stuff, and they were in boxes everywhere, you know ten years saving them up. He wanted me to edit a book, or to be part of the editorial board on a magazine he was bringing out on writers in the Pacific. When he saw my stuff he said, this should be on walls, and I said, leave them alone. That's the only privacy I've got. Don't take my privacy off me. Anyway, he talked me into having an exhibition down at his place, and that's the reason for the book. So my last little bit of privacy is gone; everyone knows everything about me.

I'm curious to know why the illustrations for My People *were done by a New Zealander, Mollie Horseman, instead of by an Aboriginal artist – or by you?*

Because my white Australian publishers didn't even ask me to do it. They got a New Zealand artist – who was a Kiwi, she's not a Maori – to do it and she's been educated in the English form of art and I ended up looking like a silly little imitation *Alice in Wonderland.* Although the art is beautiful, it's not Australian. It's not suited and I was very upset about it when I saw it. Strangely enough people say it looks lovely. But it looks like a send up of *Alice in Wonderland.* I'm very disappointed about it.

In Quandamooka, *the artwork is very much influenced by Aboriginal motifs, forms and myths. And yet in one, which you called your 'interpretation of a spaceship 3,000 years A.D.', we suddenly have the coming together of two entirely different worlds and times – a fascinating fusion of space-age technology and age-old artistic constructs.*

Do you know what inspired that? I was in America and was horrified at all these space things all over the place and it took over my whole thinking and writing and whilst I was in America all I was doing were things about space. So that's how that happened. I was feeling the tension of the people about the space things that were everywhere.

And how do you reconcile those two visions?

You don't. I wasn't ... I'm not trying to bring anything together, I get an urge to do something I put it down. There's no rhyme or reason. If I'm in the field looking at all these nuclear reactors, naturally my mind is going to go to space. What is man doing anyway cluttering up everything? We've already got to the stage where there's no return. This madness to conquer everything they see. The Americans are worse then everybody else in this. No, the Russians are just as bad. I was very uptight about it. As a matter of fact I was in Harrisville and Los Angeles, and a month after I came home there was that leak there. So I escaped it by a month. What upsets me is that there have been many leakages but when Chernobyl went up, the whole world condemned them. But America has had at least nineteen disasters like that and they covered them all up. The truth is not getting out. So this is what inspired me to ... it was a form of protest I suppose.

This particular art piece does suggest how Aboriginal artists might conceptualize the future and appropriate it for themselves.

Well they haven't been brain-washed, like in the white field, by all the top artists, starting from Rembrandt right down. When they're studying. We didn't *study* art, we just picked up the pen and did it. So it's original art, therefore it has not been fouled up by teachers of art.

What struck me when reading your prose – especially the second part of Stradbroke Dreamtime *was how closely you link your stories with ideas of conservation, culture and so forth. Do you write your work primarily to educate?*

You're talking about the legends in *Stradbroke*. They're modern, twentieth-century legends out of my head. The standard legends were lived by the people themselves and those are all well and truly in the minds of the people. But I feel that there's a need now for the present generation of artists to create a twentieth-century Aboriginal art form, both in writing and in art work. So this is very contemporary art work, only I'm still using the Aboriginal way of doing it. It's a beautiful fusion of the worlds. And in the case of my writing new legends it was because I'm a conservationist. It's a religion with me. And my politics, of course, are humanitarian. I felt that if I were to tell the children the Aboriginal names of all the trees and draw a story around them then they would see them as I do and not chop them down. It's sort of a blow for conservation.

Let's change tack for a moment. In many ways the Bicentennial has been very valuable for the Aboriginals hasn't it?

Oh, it's the year of the Aborigine. It's marvellous. And we're utilizing every moment of it. We'll mourn, but we'll take advantage of it. The spotlight of the world is on us, we'd be fools if we didn't.

So you feel the protests on the twenty-sixth of January were a success?

Oh! my goodness yes! And there's more to come. We've just had theatre at the Belvoir where it played to packed houses. Brilliant theatre. Unfortunately we haven't got enough money to take it anywhere else. That's what we lack, you see. That's why we're going overseas and asking other countries to support us. Especially to support us in the Aboriginal Theatre Trust. We put it on through them. But the government of Australia does not want us to create these things, it doesn't want us to have a platform. Now, I would rather have my people on stage using a gun with blanks and putting their protests across that way, than to have them going in the streets and indiscriminately killing people. So theatre is a must for the Aboriginal people. And with or without the government's help I will be with a lot of others, and we will build that theatre. It will be done.

What do you think of Jack Davis's work?

Jack Davis is superb! Superb! He's an established playwright now. But he's always had to go begging. And yet, when he went to Canada, the first thing he did was say half price for pensioners, all Indians in free, and it hit the headlines. But we do that. Because these people can't afford it. And where we felt that people just could not afford it, well, we said all right. We save so many free tickets, you see. We'll always do that. How dare the white Australians say, if you haven't got the money you don't go. How dare they. How *dare* they. White Australians have got a lot to learn. I hope that we will be tolerant enough to teach them.

Jack Davis has claimed that the Aboriginal lobby is fragmented by too many 'pseudo leaders' who are 'not capable of leadership'. Do you agree?

Yes. Unfortunately. When the dingo pup wants to become cock of the walk he's usually about sixteen when he tries it. But he mellows as he grows older, and after a while the 'pseudo leaders' drop out into oblivion. It's the dedicated leaders who stand the test of time.

Has the Aboriginal lobby ever recovered from the break-up of the FCAATSI and the later demise of the Aboriginal Tribal Council?

It's never recovered, but then, it wasn't meant to go on anyway. It was full of Labor party people who helped us build it. I was ten years as state secretary on that thing. But when we asked our white friends not to vote but to support us on our decisions, they refused. What they said to us was, We have no confidence in you shaping your own destiny. It had to go. The moment we realized that the whites were in to clear their own consciences, we said not on. And we broke it up. What will reform again is a new group of people. They're fragmented at this stage, but they'll finally get together. You know, you have to build the little pockets first, and then one day it'll all come together. And it'll be run entirely by Aboriginals. The FCAATSI movement was manipulated by the Australian Labour Government, who supported it and gave it every help. But they wanted to control it. And this is when we woke up to it. We thought, Oh no this is not what we've been fighting for all these years. That we do as we're told, by white Australia again, be they socialist or otherwise. So it was a dead horse, and we buried it deep.

It was largely the young people who originally rebelled and who requested that whites not vote, wasn't it?

Yes. The young people were saying to Doug Nicholls and myself that these whites are in it to make themselves look good and to pat themselves on the back, and we said, Oh come on, come on. And so, people like my young son said, All right, I'm going to move a motion asking the whites not to vote, so that we can hear the clear voice of the Aborigine. And the whites did not want to throw the vote. Doug and I stood with the young people. We said, Right, you're correct, they are in here for their own benefit. They are wanting to keep control over the Aboriginals. Then of course we tried to get the Aboriginal Tribal Council going, but without money from the government ... and the government wasn't going to back us. But one day it'll work. Aboriginals have survived terrible odds, with the strychnine in the flour bags, and the scalping. Men would go out and shoot us and bring the scalps back and get three pound for it. The murder, the rape. We survived all those things. Whites look at me and say, Look, you're not a full blood, you're half white. And I'll say, The reason for that is that our great, great grandmothers were raped by whites. We're not responsible for that white blood, the white man forced it upon us. And that stops the argument.

There are no full blood whites anyway!

Well, that's it! When someone comes to me and says, Are you a full blood, I say, NO, are you? I beg you pardon? they say. Are you? Oh, I see what you mean. No. It's the rudest thing. They don't realize they're being rude. Australians are very rude people. Very thoughtless, tactless, they have an inbuilt racist attitude which is rather sad.

How do you feel about Bicentennial grants to Aboriginal writers, dancers, film-makers and so forth? Do you feel that Aboriginal artists should have refused them on principle, or are they right to use the money?

My advice to the Aboriginals – they say we're picking up blood money, I answer we've been picking up blood money for two hundred years – whatever comes from whites is blood money. I say pick it up and run with it and use it against them. I'm all for it. Whatever money they can get off white Australia go for it.

I wonder if you could describe some of your work at Moongalba and some of the problems you face because of the Queensland government's refusal to hand over the land to you.

They still refuse to hand it over to Aboriginals. I'm there on a peppercorn lease. One peppercorn per year on demand. They're waiting for me to die so that they can take it back. But I'm going to fool them, I'm not going to die. There have been 27,800 children there in the last seventeen years who come, all children, to learn about how the Aboriginals lived and how they hunted. It's ideal to go hunting on Stradbroke Island, because you pick up shellfish, you don't have to go chasing wallabies or anything. You don't have to pick up a gun. We give them the best of food, because shell fish and crabs and lobsters are on the menu up there. But they have to go and get it themselves, and they have to learn to do it the Aboriginal way. So it's an insight into the beautiful free life of the Aboriginal people. Kids love it. They keep coming back.

At one time the Queensland government wanted to put in a bridge between the mainland and Stradbroke Island. *Have they done so yet?*

They keep wanting to, but it won't be put in, no way. Eighty-two percent of the people on Stradbroke – black and white – don't want the bridge put in. It's only the greedy politicians who want the bridge. They want to turn it into a little Manhattan for tired politicians when they retire. A stately home away from home. There's been a big backlash reaction against it from the people on the island. We don't want to be part of the mainland. They'd ruin it if they put a bridge across. She's only twenty-three miles long. Well, she *was* thirty-*two* miles long until the civic fathers of the early days came in. A ship came aground. When they boarded it they found it was full of dynamite. Those silly white people decided the most sensible thing to do with wet dynamite was to take it away from civilization and blow it up. So they took it to the Island. They thought, Stradbroke Island, they're uncivilized, so it doesn't matter if we get them. They took it there and blew it up on the Island.

And they cut the Island in two! So we now have North and South Stradbroke! And that's how they did it. Boy. Very strange people, whites. Especially Australian.

As a final question, I wonder if you could discuss some of your future artistic projects.

My last book is a hodgepodge of art and storytelling and poetry. When I went to China I wrote seventeen poems about the place. I was really inspired over there. When I came home the Chinese people were just so thrilled by me doing that that they appealed to my publisher to let them be part of the publication of it. They also asked if I would allow it to go into Mandarin as well as English. And I agreed to this. So at the present time it's up in Beijing being translated into Mandarin. Hopefully it will be in front of the public this year. But I don't know if it will. Publishers always put you on a deadline, but they always go over theirs.

NOTES

1. On 9 August 1987, a nineteen-year-old, Julian Knight, went on a rampage in Melbourne which became known as the Hoddle Street Massacre. Using a high-powered M-14 semi-automatic rifle, Knight killed seven people and injured another eighteen. This attack preceded by ten days the Hungerford killing in England in which sixteen were killed. On 9 December 1987, another Melbourne massacre took place. Referred to as the Queen Street Massacre, this occasion saw nine people shot dead and five injured. The twenty-two year-old Frank Vitkovic fired an M-1 rifle indoors, then leapt eleven storeys to his death.
2. Kath Walker, interview (by Jim Davidson), *Meanjin: Aboriginal Issue*, Vol. 36, No. 4 (1977): 428.

Oodgeroo

PAPERBARK-TREE

In the new Dreamtime there lived a woman, an Aborigine, who longed for her lost tribe, and for the stories that had belonged to her people; for she could remember only the happenings of her own Dreamtime. But the old Dreamtime had stolen the stories and hidden them. The woman knew that she must search for the old stories – and through them she might find her tribe again.

Before she set off, she looked for her yam-stick and dilly-bag, but Time had stolen these, too. She found a sugar-bag that the ants had left and which Time had forgotten to destroy, and she picked it up and carried it with her wherever she went. Time laughed at her efforts; he thought her new dilly-bag was useless.

One day, as she searched, the woman came upon the ashes of a fire her own tribe had kindled long ago. Tears came to her eyes, for she yearned for her tribe, and felt lonely. She sat down by the ashes and ran her fingers through the remains of the fire that had once glowed there. And as she looked at the ashes, she called to Biami the Good Spirit to help her find her tribe.

Biami told her to go to the paperbark-trees and ask them to give her some of their bark. The paperbark-trees loved this woman who had lost her tribe, and they gave her their bark. They knew she was not greedy and would not take more than she needed. So she put the bark in her dilly-bag.

Then Biami told the woman to return to the dead fire of her tribe, collect all the charred sticks, and place these, too, in her bag – and to do this each time she came upon the dead fire of any lost tribe.

Time did not understand what the woman was doing, so he followed her.

She travelled far and wide over the earth, and each time she came upon the dead fire of a lost tribe, she would gather the charred sticks, and when at last her bag was filled with them, she went to the secret dreaming-places of the old tribes. Here she rested and again called to Biami, and asked him to help her remember the old stories, so that through them she might find her tribe.

Biami loved this woman, and he put into her mind a new way in which she might find those stories and her tribe. The woman sat down and drew from her bag the charred pieces of stick she had taken from the dead fires, and placed the paperbark flat upon the ground. She drew the sticks across the paperbark, and saw that they made marks on its surface.

So she sat for many years, marking the paperbark with the stories of the long-lost tribes, until she had used up all the charred remnants she had gathered and her bag was empty. In this way she recalled the stories of the old Dreamtime, and through them entered into the old life of the tribes.

And when next the paperbark-trees filled the air with the scent of their sweet, honey-smelling flowers, they took her into their tribe as one of their own, so that she would never again be without the paperbark she needed for her work. They called her Oodgeroo. And this is the story of how Oodgeroo found her way back into the old Dreamtime. Now she is happy, because she can always talk with the tribes whenever she wants to. Time has lost his power over her because Biami has made it so.

Dawn Wail for the Dead

Dim light of daybreak now
Faintly over the sleeping camp.
Old lubra first to wake remembers:
First thing every dawn
Remember the dead, cry for them.
Softly at first her wail begins,
One by one as they wake and hear
Join in the cry, and the whole camp
Wails for the dead, the poor dead
Gone from here to the Dark Place:
They are remembered.
Then it is over, life now,
Fires lit, laughter now,
And a new day calling.

No More Boomerang

No more boomerang
No more spear;
Now all civilized –
Colour bar and beer.

No more corroboree,
Gay dance and din.
Now we got movies,
And pay to go in.

No more sharing
What the hunter brings.
Now we work for money,
Then pay it back for things.

Now we track bosses
To catch a few bob,
Now we go walkabout
On bus to the job.

One time naked,
Who never knew shame;
Now we put clothes on
To hide whatsaname.

No more gunya,
Now bungalow,
Paid by higher purchase
In twenty year or so.

Lay down the stone axe,
Take up the steel,
And work like a nigger
For a white man meal.

No more firesticks
That made the whites scoff.
Now all electric,
And no better off.

Bunyip he finish,
Now got instead
White fella Bunyip,
Call him Red.

Abstract picture now –
What they coming at?
Cripes, in our caves we
Did better than that.

Black hunted wallaby,
White hunt dollar;
White fella witch-doctor
Wear dog-collar.

No more message-stick;
Lubras and lads
Got television now,
Mostly ads.

Lay down the woomera,
Lay down the waddy.
Now we got atom-bomb,
End *every*body.

Paperbark

Perhaps before I get into the main channel of this paper which will be menandering like the Brisbane River, though I trust it will have spots of note, of beauty and sacred significance, as well as clumps of paperbark trees along its banks, I should explain the title. Paperbark signifies the paper on which writers write,and hence I shall be discussing, or analysing written Aboriginal writing, rather than the rich oral traditions. This may seem a simple symbol easily understandable, but getting deeper into the symbol, or going from the paperbark to the paperbark tree, the dreaming symbol of the symbol, we reach Oodgeroo Nunaccul, or if you wish Kath Walker, the noted Aboriginal poet.

During the coming together of the tribes in January 1988 in Sydney, I spoke to Oodgeroo, and she explained to me that her name Oodgeroo means *paperbark* and that as creative writers our totem, or dreaming should be the Paperbark tree. This seemed logical as the paperbark tree, or whitefella name *maleleuca*, or my country name, Mudrooroo, has always had an important place in Aboriginal life in that it has been used for *Myas*, roofing materials, for bandages and for drawings. And so, this has become our *Dreaming*, or our secondary totem,or our functional dreaming. Thus Kath Walker has taken, or changed her whitefella name to Oodgeroo Nunaccul, and I have changed my name to Mudrooroo Naragin. Kath Walker's last name refers to her tribal name, the Nunaccul tribe of Stradbroke Island, but in regard to my last name it refers to my place of birth in Western Australia. I have used a place name rather than a tribal name in that it is difficult to isolate the particular name of the tribe which owns that part of Western Australia, as we have coalesced into one people, the *Nyungar* and possibly one tribe, the *Bibbulmum* which I think refers more to the Swan River basin than to my area.

Now with paperbark out of the way, but not forgotten, for as it is the symbol of our dreaming, it grows within this paper so that it may take the shape of a paperbark tree, or the trunk, or the branches, or the leaves, or the twigs, or the bark itself. *Dreamings* are potent forces and as the sap passes through the entire tree with the exception of the outermost bark, so the sap of the dreaming permeates this lecture and flows much like water in the channel of a river.

Firstly, I would like to start off with creative writing itself. I start here, at the root, because so much bullshit has been put forth on this subject, usually from a Western perspective beginning with the ego existing in splendid solitude and from this divine monad comes the great work. I, instead of seeing the ego as splendidly isolated, see it as being social, that is that man or woman is a social being and that the ego of man or woman is not only formed by society or by the community, but extends out from the head or beyond the skin, the bark, to thrust back into the community. There is really no inner or outer isolation, and the tree of the ego is swayed and moved more by what is happening around, the breezes, the earth, the touching hands of a human being, than by say, the sap rising from the roots and up the trunk and permeating each branch, twig and leaf. Naturally, if we did concentrate on the inner sap of the tree, its essence so to speak, we would find that it too is determined by outer things, the soil and its content, the rain, or moisture and so on. So it seems that this isolation, sometimes put out as being the abode of the writer and his ego, this splendid isolation is an illusion, or if you want, a man-made construct.

Now as to the creative act, which sounds so fine, if we ignore the fact that the creative act is often plagiarism which has to be explained away. I remember writing a paper on an example of deliberate plagiarism as method in the African writer Yambo Ouloguem's, *Le Devoir De Violence*, and the critics' reaction to this and to a further case of plagiarism by the white Australian writer, Thomas Keneally. Naturally, if you accept the concept of intellectual property this is stealing; naturally, if you accept the basis of the creative act as lying in 'Intertextuality' you don't. A plagiarist is someone who is found out. Now here, taking this a step further, before dropping it, or rather using it as the beginning or root of an analysis of a piece of my own writing, I would like to quote from the French theorist, Roland Barthes:

> that a text is not a line of words releasing a single 'theological' meaning (the 'message' of the Author – God) but a multi-dimensional space in which a variety of writings, none of them original, blend and clash. The text is a tissue of quotations drawn from the innumerable centres of cultures.' ('The Death of the Author,' in *Image-Music-Text*, Glasgow, Fontana, 1977, p. 146.)[1]

This quotation should be kept in mind. Now first of all perhaps what all of us have been getting this year is *Celebration of a Nation*, which has two distinct meanings, or significations to what may be broadly separated into two centres of culture in Australia: the European – specifically, the Anglo-Celtic – and the Aboriginal.

Now these are not two binary oppositions, separate and distinct, but spill over into each other. A reading of a map of any suburb in the city of Brisbane shows an intermixture of these two cultures. Street names, road names, for example: *Burbong Road. Burbong* is a signifier of Aboriginality; *road*, of Europeanness, and if we extend this further both constitute a signifier of Australianness, and in a deeper reading may extend into the super-structure of Australian society to reveal the overall position of Europeans and Aborigines, for in Burbong Street or Road few Aborigines live, there are few signs of Aborigines, the roadside is divided into blocks holding European houses and so on. There is a marked absence of Aboriginality in the area except for that name, and perhaps a few names of houses, or intersecting roads. The indigenous people have gone away leaving only isolated words of their language to signify their absence. Now, I turn to my written text, rather than the text of a map, or the text of a suburb, though we must remain aware that any system of signs form a text which may be read, and by reading I mean only the deciphering as much as we are able to of a system of signs.

CELEBRATION OF A NATION.

Cockatoo folds down to the ground beside a tall broken-trunk tree emptied out by a long ago bushfire. Dark interior gleams in soft morning light breaking it wide open into the cubed edging of wood turned charcoal in that long ago fire, in that long ago burning into hollow log formed for this occasion, for cockatoo, yellow-sulphur crest, seeking to ignite that flame, to excavate that hollow, to fill it with the broken honeycomb of bones pulverised into broken cells oozing with honey, dripping with honey from the far north as a cry resounds, hoarsely like the craw-crawing of crow biding his time, but missing his time as cockatoo takes the sound and unfolds, stealing the air with white wings as he circles in a heavy lazy floating of hot wings, once, twice and up into a green tree not too far away and green-lush with the hot sun baking earth brown, waiting for the gift of the north in that hoarse cry, that crow-call clawing at the fire bubbling with the blackened heavy drum filled water brown with the swirl of leaking tea stains, swirling with leaves edging into the hot morning, reaching out a smell to cockatoo residing with this caravan, this righteous camp of souls urging hope regained in the ceremony. But the call comes again, clawing through to where Cookalingee dances her mock dance of despair in a show revealing death and survival, life and hope all suited-up and short-panted for a new dawn to commence.

Cookalingee, lithe young dancing body evading hard masculinity of occasion by partnering a chair. Inert fissures performing less a hopeful change than the eroded squares of charcoal fashioned fully for this occasion as Cookalingee whirls out her female dance of unable to endure yet enduring this time of mourning, this time of sadness, this time of celebration of youthful litheful dancer's body enduring a swirling of the air, of atonement, of past meals being prepared and discarded with no thought of this latter day engraved in the motions of her body encircling the chair, thrusting motion towards, receiving it back. Her dress fluttering, her hair fluttering, her arms eroding the urgency of cook house fire. Her energy, her youth seeking to engulf that chair. Heavy inertness, less than the tree charcoal under the hot sun of voices preparing bodies for the ceremony. Cookalingee sinking down in a crying at her lot, in a crying at the lot of her people responding to the calling, crow-calling, craw-crawing from that camp site far from her dreaming place where now feet stamp out an encircled belief around the stillness of the body waiting for honeyed tree, crushed-bone tree, life-long tree oozing with honey dripping from the ruptured body cells.

Far north homeland green with many urgencies of plants flows down and withers into dry yellow dusks and air drained of moisture and life-giving ceremonies such as this being stamped out, performed sacred and entire, secret and meaningful beyond clicking camera booms and pens whispering words into black boxes re-arranging magnetic particles to record unknown records. Feet stamping, knees bending thudding the feet down, thudding the feet down. How, pow, puffs of dust rising, lingering on the crow call. Cockatoo watching safe in his near but far away tree as Cookalingee suffers her fate without knowing that she is suffering her fate in the dance, of feet thudding up particles of dust to manacle the magnetic re-arrangement of the atoms into an American voice questioning: 'Say, why do you think it's called Bennelong Point anyway?': To manacle the magnetic arrangement of the atoms into an American voice replying: 'Guess, because it's bin a long time since they owned it.'

And as the feet thud, and as a dancer stops to catch a still position on one thin black leg, then gives a quick convulsion simmering into discontent a black queen in a white queen's paraphernalia of long white gloves extruding to the elbow a nasalised unhoneyed voice duly commanding a royal performance of the particles to cease, then start again in ordered lines of:

'My loyal subjects and all de men, I range over your faces and recall your pleasing vanities in selecting my husband and my royal self to be here, thus evading any unpleasantries in not only not being at home, but in being here in a somewhat darkened form, though smeared with the whiteness of my gloves as befitting the occasion dealing with the smearing of pipe clay somewhat resembling the sails of flocks of cockatoos circling overhead and tugging at dark bodies, sublime and horizontal of these my first ships touching these, our shores with the rotten hulks of despair and future crime. Do I hear the craw-crawing of crow, is that the screeching of vivid livid sails? Sulphurous fumes decorate our heads. Our diadem glitters with the calling eyes of this, our day of mourning being celebrated in our subject, Cookalingee's dance. God bless her female heart and dishpan hands. Her warm body and subdued meant-for-better-things mind. It's in the gloves, the white gloves, cockatoo's crest, and the craw-crawing of our subject, crow. Let them dance, coffin awaits them – but, but before then, a pause, a pause, magnetic particles record, this our refrain:

A youthman was found hanging in his cell
On this our day, when everywhere the Aborigines
Were dancing, everywhere the Aborigines were marching.
They're just like us, is our quaint refrain,
They like balls and footy and songs and beer:
We ignore their call for Landrights!

On Australia's day, a youthman strangled in a cell:

Who killed him; who were his murderers?
Not I, said the cop, I only took him in.
Not I, said this town, I never spoke his name,
It's no fault of mine that he has to die –
We treat them as we do our own,
There's no racism in our town.

On this, our day a youthman dies while his people
Camp nearby trying to recover stolen land.
They daub this town with white and raise high

The Red, the Black and Gold.
The red is his blood,
The black his skin,
The gold our cause as bright as sun:
We want our land and there is no turning back.'

A waving wink of a hand behind a smile as the ceremony continues with black bodies and faces gleaming behind the stains of white clay mourning the absence of ceremony at the site burdened with the tree excavated by the sulphurous crest of cockatoo lifting a gnarled claw to scratch out the rhythm of clap-sticks calling him away from pursuing didgeridoo droning out his place in the proceedings as Cookalingee gives a swirl light years away from the heavy stamp of heels scattering the dust particles and arousing the bees to spread out in a thick line of nectar-laden flight as the bones are crushed, hu,hu,hu,hu, into honeycomb slices as Cookalingee sinks down embracing her beloved chair heavy and inert, slippery with the scented sweating polish of her limbs aching and clutching in mourning the rounded body of the tree trunk, light and grey and quivering with the heated air as didgeridoo squawks cockatoo into a belated arrival of folding down right on the very ragged, blackened splinter of poor, fella tree: him gone along with that fella; him dead one now; him honey one now; him honeycomb now; him secreting the sweetness of Cookalingee – she little one, one time big with her hollow tree trunk filled with honeycomb, filled with honeycomb, sweet sap honey dripping. Her son, him bin hanged in that jail. Him bin died in that jail cell just yesterday time. Bub,buh,buh,buh,buh – didgeridoo calling crow lounging as Cookalingee stirs her loins all atremble to make the magnetic particles align themselves again American-wise.

'Say, what is this? Is this what you call a corroboree? Hey, you guys, this is a dinkum corroboree! And we can stay? And we can take pictures? Say, our folks back home will just love this!'

WARU, WARU! Attention, attention! Hey, hey, Cookalingee leaping to the rhythm of Warumpi Band dissipating the cries from the past. Cockatoo screeches the last of his didgeroo sounds. Tree quivers and becomes inert as the bones are laid to rest and the white clay soothes his sulphurous wounds and makes him whole enough for the bees to enter through his skull and plaster his insides with wax dripping with the yellow nectar of their flight. WARU, WARU, clak-crak, clak-crak, clak-crak, clak – measured rhythm of clap-sticks falter into syncopation. Mourn-ing, mourn-ing, mourn-ing, didgeridoo murmurs before picking up on the rhythm, cel-e-bration, cel-e-bration, cel-e-bration. And their skins shine darkly under the full sun light and their skins shine whitely in the full sunlight as their bodies dance to cel-e-bration, cel-e-bration, cel-e-bration; ofa, ofa, ofa, ofa; nat shun, nat shun, nat shun – shunit, shunit, shunit, shunit...

THE END

Now what are we to make of my first paragraph, rather long and bereft of city signs. How are we to read it? Cockatoo is but a bird, or is he, and what is his relationship to the hollow tree, to fire? How are we to take this bird? How are we to take his role? If we seek to come to grips with this sign, it breaks open into an icon, as in the Mac computer, and this icon is symbol. Cookatoo as symbol. A blonde-haired white man with all that that entails for an Aborigine, but further, if we take into account Barthes' quotation in which he sees the texts as multi-dimensional and from numerous centres of culture, if we know that this piece of writing, this text is from an Aborigine we might look beyond the obvious, go into the icon to elicit further meanings. We must remain aware of the intertextuality of the text, and of the centre of Aboriginal culture, specifically localised here as northern. And again if we are or have been aware of the events of January, 1988, *Celebration of a Nation*, and of the caravan of people, traditional Aboriginal people travelling down to Sydney, this will make us consider that our icons may owe a great deal to Arnhem Land Culture, and again with the Aboriginal view of the celebration as being a celebration of survival, of an escape from genocidal practices added to media reports of an old man dying on the way to Sydney and ceremonies being conducted, we might make the connection that cockatoo is a bird associated with the funeral services in Arnhem Land, and if we know of the Djambidj cycle of ceremonies, we will be aware of this. Cockatoo is connected with funeral ceremonies and in our text this is brought out by a further icon of the hollow log, or hollow tree, and pulverised bones, referring to the method of finally laying to rest the deceased in Arnhem Land. Another icon in the text is crow, again a bird interested in everything about death. Crow is a bird who is a familiar of death. He does not hesitate to come close to it, whereas cockatoo prefers to keep his distance. Other icons remain to be deciphered, but I leave these with the comment that the caravan refers to the people travelling down from the north with their ceremonies to fertilise what they see as a land barren of Aboriginality. I stress that we are not so much interested in whether this is true or not, but it is an ideological position held by people in Arnhem Land.

The last sentence of the paragraph introduces an icon as a character: *Cookalingee*. Here, there is a shift in that the traditional symbols or icons give way to one signifying Urban Aboriginal culture. The icon infolds a poem of Oodgeroo's, 'Cookalingee'. And the sign is meant to signify her poem and all that it contains, plus more, but we'll get to that. First, I'll give Oodgeroo's poem.

'COOKALINGEE' (For Elsie Lewis).

Cookalingee, now all day
Station cook in white man's way,
Dressed and fed, provided for,
Sees outside her kitchen door
Ragged band of her own race,
Hungry nomads, black of face.
Never begging, they stand by,
Silent, waiting, wild and shy,
For they know that in their need
Cookalingee give them feed.
Peering in, their deep dark eyes
Stare at stove with wide surprise,
Pots and pans and kitchen-ware,
All the white-man wonders there.
Cookalingee, lubra still
Spite of white-man station drill,
Knows the tribal laws of old:
'Share with others what you hold;'
Hears the age-old racial call:
'What we have belongs to all.'
Now she gives with generous hand
White man tucker to that band,
Full tin plate and pannikin
To each hunter, child and gin.
Joyful, on the ground they sit,

With only hands for eating it.
Then upon their way they fare,
Bellies full and no more care.

Cookalingee, lubra still,
Feels her dark eyes softly fill,
Watching as they go content,
Natural as nature meant.
And for all her place and pay
Is she happy now as they?
Wistfully she muses on
Something bartered, something gone.
Songs of old remembered days,
The walkabout, the old free ways.
Blessed with everything she prized,
Trained and safe and civilized,
Much she has that they have not,
But is hers the happier lot?

Lonely in her paradise
Cookalingee sits and cries.
(Oodgeroo Noonuccal)

There is one *last* thing to add about the final words of my first paragraph. These, 'a new dawn to commence' signifies Oodgeroo's second book of poetry: *The Dawn is at Hand.* (Brisbane, 1966)[2]

Cookalingee signifies urban culture, modern dance as opposed to traditional dance. The chair signifies dead wood, a manufactured article. Sydney or any city with its hardness of manmadeness: roads, and buildings, cars and life itself. But she is an Aborigine, and as she dances her city dance, the crow calls her to the camp site where the people from the north are conducting proper ceremonies. In Aboriginal dance, the feet stamp; in European dance, feet are but points and dancing appears to be an attempt to evade the solidity of gravity.

The third paragraph refers back to the camp site and the ceremony revitalising the south. Urban and Country come together. The reporters and television crews that accompanied the caravan are referred to and encapsulated in Cockatoo in his near but far away tree. They are separated from the ceremony by not having the cultural knowledge from the Aboriginal centre. This is stressed by the American voices. Outside participants, though not unsympathetic, they cannot read the obvious, cannot make the connection between sign and signifier.

The ceremony is magical, is Aboriginal, and evokes a white response, strange and as distant to many people as the ceremonies of Aborigines' are. Directly, it is an intrusion, or a fragment of intertextuality, from Jean Genet's *The Blacks*; indirectly, it may refer, or be a referent to Roland Barthe's quotation. Death enters directly in a welter of icons or symbols, as the Drag Queen gives a version of the celebration and the invasion of Australia from black and white perspectives. It is her/his right as a complex icon. Beyond blackness and whiteness, beyond maleness and femaleness, partaking of both and of both, and of the original crime, and as perpetrator and victim, he/she re-iterates present crime and death. The poem she/he recites is from my collection: *The Song Circle of Jacky* (1984). The central stanza is built around the children's rhyme, *Who Killed Cock Robin,* which has been used for a number of folk songs including *Who Killed Norma Jean,* by Pete Seeger, and as such folk songs signify music in good standing with the Left, we have another icon or sign signifying the alliance, or support of the Aboriginal cause by the left. Nothing is simple it seems, though the last stanza is made up of direct signs signifying the meaning of the colours of the Aboriginal flag, though personalised in an individual dying a jail death.

The colour *white* as white pipe clay, or ash signifies mourning, a time of mourning, or in mourning. White in this text signifies this, among other things, for as I have said signs are icons which are symbols of things. They are complexities which may be broken down or built up just as texts may be built up or broken down. The perceiving of these signs is an act of reading with a reader who brings his own readability to the sign and the sign-system. Now when the icon of the queen disappears, the ceremony re-appears, though at a place marked with an absence of ceremony in the sense that the ceremonies that once belonged to this southern land have been forgotten and are no longer performed, though there is Cookalingee dancing out her dance in a theatre which is considered to be the remnants, or the evolution of the old magic circle, the *bora ring* from the Aboriginal centre, or the *amphitheatre* from the European centre. Ceremonies and theatrical performances are magic, that is they are magic-invoking rituals, and so magic is present in my text. The funeral ceremony continues, the bones are crushed and as happens in the Djambidj ceremony, either symbolic or actual bees begin flying to make their hive in the hollow tree now filled with the pounded bones of the deceased.

It might be appropriate now to talk about some of the icons I have used:

Hollow tree, hollow log signifies a coffin. The bones are interred therein.

Bones: Skeletal human bones pounded into pieces. Reformed to serve as the cells for honey.

Honey: a complex icon. Meanings shift and signifiers disappear into the spiritual. It can signify a strong and potent food, mead, the buildup of a new body different from the old, even the vanished internal organs and flesh. In fact with the honey and the bees, the tree is reincarnated into the living. It more or less takes death away from death, and serves as a symbol of sweet endurance, rejuvenation, rebuilding, rebirth. Thus with the ceremony, a time of mourning, a time of sadness is rejuvenated into a time of gladness. The funeral ceremony is at the same time an increase ceremony, and is necessary for the continuation of the species.

This is shown in the paragraph after the poem and with the vanishing of the Drag queen, Cookalingee is seen as the mother of the young man who was killed in the jail cell. It is his funeral service we are witnessing and Cookalingee's dance is also a funeral service and both combine: country and urban, though all this is unseen by the iconic tourists. They see only what they are able to see.

In the last paragraph, the theme of celebration is taken up. The sense of this is that in Aboriginal culture death is an occasion for communities having the same moeity or Dreaming to come together in a ceremony, perform the rituals properly, then conduct any other business. It is a time of retying old ties and strengthening community links. An Aboriginal band, *Warumpi Band*, begins playing at the end of the funeral service. The whole rhythm changes. Mourning becomes celebration; but this is a celebration of increased hope. It is not for an actuality and so the rhythm continues *shunit, shunit, shunit*. For the celebration is not for the birth of white Australia, but for the survival of the Aborigines over the last two hundred years; of their coming together in Sydney; of the bringing down of ancient ceremonies from the north, and of the laying to rest the corpse of the past. It is a celebration of hope for the future.

Traditional Aboriginal culture is a complexity which does not separate out a literature from ceremony or society. Literature is sung and any prose serves only as a commentary on the songs, though this is changing under the contemporary pressures of the modern world. Songs are to be sung and experienced in ceremonies or rituals, and the meanings vary to the degree as to how far a participant has entered into the complete spirituality of the community. Thus signs have changing signifiers with the significations depending on the knowledge of the recipient, or the reader. In the new Aboriginal writing, and by new Aboriginal writing, I signify writings by such writers as Lionel Fogarty, there has been a shift away from what has been a simple plea, or a writing slanted towards white people. A tool useful for understanding. This early writing did not result in a return of understanding, but an outrage of critics directed at such writings as being puerile and essentially not as good as European writing. Naturally, this attitude has always been directed at writing which tends towards the straight forwardness of propaganda, and at writing which is meant to be recited publicly, rather than pondered over in the quietness of a person's study. Aboriginal writing is often meant for public consumption in a public act such as before a crowd of people at a political meeting, and this makes for misunderstanding on the part of those critics who emphasise the aesthetic at the expense of the content, or message. Now, since the works of early Aboriginal writers who emphasised message and accessibility, Aboriginal writing has developed towards a spirituality interested in using and exploring the inner reality of Aboriginality in Australia. Naturally in doing this, there are problems in that there may be no readership for such a writing, or that those critics who dismissed Aboriginal writing for accessibility may now dismiss it for obscurity. A hope lies in the fact that literary criticism has developed new techniques in working with texts which may appear on the surface obscure. It is refreshing to find that we are far from the dreariness of the conventional: it doesn't rhyme, it doesn't scan, it's not grammatical, it's not poetry, it's not prose etc. etc.

When the Victorian English critic, Mathew Arnold formulated his question for the critic, he did not stress conventional grammar and sentence structure as criteria for what is good and what is not, though he most likely accepted this as being beyond comment.

He formulated three questions:

1. What is the writer trying to do?
2. How well does he succeed in doing it?
3. Is it worth doing?

So what is the Aboriginal writer trying to do? Naturally, this varies according to the writer, and many critics and book reviewers still disparage a writer because they don't like what he or she is trying to do, or because he or she is not trying to do something else. This happened when Oodgeroo Nunaccul published her first books and it still continues among some critics and reviewers, though others have come to accept Aboriginal literature as a strong and vibrant Australian literature in its own right.

The second question demands creative reading from the reader. In fact there might not be a definite answer, or you may have to know something of modern critical practice to formulate an answer. One block which occurs here is that the reader when shown how he or she might change his or her reading habits, feels that such an approach destroys the pleasure of reading. Then we must ask what is this *pleasure*, and what are we reading for?

The third question: *Is it worth doing?* Art makes us aware of what we know and don't know that we know. Our conscious awareness, our ego, often seems to support the idea that we know all that we should know, or all that should be known. I see the ego as a master or mistress of illusion, and art and literature might help us to be aware that there is more to the ego than our heads, just as there is more to literature than standard sentences, standard grammar, standard modes of coping with reality. If it is impossible for us to, for example, change the colour of our skins, or even our sexual preferences, we can come to some understanding of other ways of being by reading about them. And when we begin formulating ideas on exactly why we are reading, why we want to put ourselves in the less than passive position of the reader, we then might begin growing and querying some of the things around us. The act of reading is important, and can be extended beyond books to the many texts surrounding us. Reading is a creative act, and may even extend into that of the creative writer, for after all a creative writer is usually a creative reader, which brings us full circle to the quotation I began the body of this paper with, and which now with another reading might render up other meanings.

> that a text is not a line of words releasing a single 'theological' meaning (the 'message' of the Author – God) but a multi-dimensional space in which a variety of writings, none of them original, blend or clash. The text is a tissue of quotations drawn from the innumerable centres of cultures.'

NOTES

1. Roland Barthes, 'The Death of the Author' in *Image – Music – Text* (Fontana, Glasgow, 1977) p. 146.
2. Kath Walker (Oodgeroo), *The Dawn is at Hand* (Jacaranda, Brisbane, 1966).

Butcher Joe (Nangan)

12 inches by 9 inches. Pencil and watercolour on paper

True story: eighteen centuary people aboriginals from
Beagle Bay crossed the Desert came out Fitsroy River
where telegraph line crossed before, That's before langgee
So this woman from Beagle Bay. this. one woman
middle aged went away across the desert that was
soaked water some place dry anyway that women
crossed the Plain she had enough water, she also had
a sore head and she came to the telegraph line
line before langgee. and she see's water right over
the river. full river too langgee. That women she
knows where water hole in river. sea water drys
up women came down dia water hole she drank
and she was tired and went to sleep under a tree.
she didn't care who come's turn over

STORY NOT FINISHED

she was that sound asleep and at the same time
her hands and legs were weak and tired. all of a sudden
alligator see's her come in then drops off to sleep again
alligator comes real close to her alongside the woman
throw his hands over his shoulder. That old woman
she had a dream about his boyfriend she thinks
then she throw her hand over his shoulder. Then when
she looked properly she saw the alligator
she tried to escape but couldn't the alligator dragged
her into the water. The alligator dived deep into
the water still holding the leg of the woman. then
they swam up to the alligators home. Then that
woman was living with the alligator, he was a good man
fed her on raw meat. So that woman
watch now alligator go so she got
away to yeda station.

STEPHEN MUECKE

Two Texts (and one other)

In hommage to Butcher Joe (Nangan) of Broome, Western Australia

I insert myself, here, in between these two texts by Butcher Joe: Stephen Muecke, his friend? Perhaps. In a field of ambiguous relationships of both work ('research') and pleasure,always at several removes from any possibility of a 'true' or 'real' contact.

I sign myself here in sydney, in your absence, a signature which accumulates as style, a specific sort of trace like your own, coming at the end of a life of being written by 'others', all stylistically gesturing their appropriation of a social project which for the moment bears your name, Butcher Joe, but extends beyond all possible ambits of that name. Butcher Joe *and* his paintings. Butcher Joe *and* Aboriginal art. Butcher Joe *and* Aboriginal music. Butcher Joe *and* traditional Nyigina knowledges, etc.

In how many ways are we removed from each other's concerns, he and I? In age, in language/culture, coloniser/colonised, metropolitan and rural, rigid and nomadological.[1] And then I was always working with Paddy Ore, which made Butcher Joe into a kind of marginal character in the story that Paddy and I were telling each other.[2]

And perhaps one needs to distinguish between art and science, as if Butcher Joe were always already 'artist', somehow in excess of all disciplinary constructions of knowledges, a fluid, empty, ab-original incoherence of drifting 'facts' waiting to be stratified. But we know this will miss the mark, because of science's discursive regularities, which carry with them their own points of disappearance. Most significantly, of course, in the unsaid of *origins* which became part of the Aboriginal name at a time when the notion of origin stood at the heart of Western epistemologies, as in Darwin, whose ship, the *Beagle*, finally sank in a bay near the mission of the same name where Butcher Joe first learnt to paint.

Let us conceive of artistic production as a kind of machine, something comprised of different parts which fit together and move in sequence. For instance, there is no artist without a market – they are symbiotic – and the romantic idea which says that the artist comes first, that he or she is in fact 'aboriginal' is no doubt part of the sales pitch which helps move the paintings.

Let us now oppose the 'Western' art machine with the 'Broome' one. What regularities and discontinuities characterise the two, make them incompatible, or, on the contrary, compatible to the extent that Butcher Joe's art can be said to 'emerge', begin to exist? Frame, key, title, signature, museum, archive, discourse, market ... these are some of the 'Western' ones, to which one may add various other categories which limit and define the artistic project.[3]

To these one may oppose, from the 'Broome machine', the categories of trade route, discourse, series, agent ... and there may be others.

The major differences extend along these lines: the 'work of art' is not individuated in Butcher Joe's country, it is not framed, authenticated by a signature, nor does it form part of an oeuvre. It is not destined to accumulate in a museum or archive so as to build up towards a life's work (paradoxically, that is what is now being done with Butcher Joe's work to make it more compatible with the 'Western' machine). The painting is contingent upon an event, or a specific scene in the countryside, or a narrative. It is always connected with discourse, with the discourse of the dreaming (*bugarrigarra*) or history.

It emerges as part of the traditional demand for two-way 'flow' of artifacts, in that sense the painting or pearl-shell carving forms part of a series of artifacts which might have been made by anyone – they bear the signature of the country of origin at least as much as the signature of the crafter. That is why Butcher Joe always makes a 'book' of paintings. His work doesn't finish until he has completed a Spirex drawing book with his watercolours, and his first step is to get someone to write on the corner of each page a series of numbers, from 1 to 10 or whatever. This is how he always begins teaching someone the Nyigina language also; you have to put down the numbers 1 to 6 on the page, then he declines Nyigina verbs according to a ritual which no doubt emerged through many years of working with linguists.

The *series* is a nomadological feature, like that of travelling through the country, one place after another, and a chain of stories, 'and then ... and then ... and then'. This is *not* a hierarchically constructed narrative of plots and sub-plots, major and subordinate clauses, dominant discourses or logical structures which have a strong *metaphorical* tendency (for which it is appropriate to find interpretative 'keys', as in Western symbolism, for instance). The series is *metonymic*, each painting is a new departure, and it corresponds to a particular place – one cannot be subsumed by the other, each one is a site of renewal and decay, as in the desire to paint and to live, live, that is, according to nomadic techniques.

There are two texts, the watercolour of the woman and the crocodile, and the written text, originally in pencil on two sides of a roughly ruled page of drawing paper, now quite yellowed with age, though it probably doesn't date back much before 1977. That is when Butcher Joe painted the picture. The story was written sometime before, by his granddaughter, to whom he dictated in the camp at Beagle Bay.

The analysis to follow will attempt an approach to an Aboriginal aesthetic, rapidly shifting its gaze between the picture and the written text, avoiding where ever possible the available categories of the dominant 'Western' aesthetic, hoping that certain hints coming from conversations with Butcher Joe and Paddy Row will inform the analysis.

TRUE

The woman who travelled to Langgee has a name, but I will not give it here, she is a dead woman, but from this century, not the last. The citing of the date in the written text is an intrusion from white historiography; it is a realist detail, it puts the story in its historical context. The phrase is anthropological, referring as it does to 'aboriginals' (from the outside).

It is a 'true story', generically distinct from the *bugarrigarra* (dreaming) stories; it is about something that happened within living memory, not something that always already was.

The watercolour is realist also, not abstract in a traditional iconographic manner. It too could be read as anthropologically empirical because Butcher Joe always draws 'scenes from real life' as they were before colonisation. Only native animals, clothing and decorations as they were, specific landforms which are the memory of a place old age prohibits him from visiting any more.

HYPOPTICS

Seeing, in this aesthetic, is glancing, it is not gazing full on so as to possess a scene, take it away and store it. It is an aesthetic of the glimpse where things half seen can be imagined as something *other*, beyond and magical:

> Sometimes we see a woman pass but, when you look again you might say: 'Oh I've only seen a grass'. But it is the woman Worawora, she still lives today.[4]

Stories of the third eye and the *ngadjayi* (spirits) confirm this.[5] Perceptions come in flashes, in disruptions of the steady gaze. Since the country is variably peopled by spirits, ghosts and natural things transformed, there is always the danger that this mystical world will break through into perception, especially if you walk in certain 'danger places'. Gaps can appear in the veil of ordinary looking. 'Clever' men, like Butcher Joe, can look through these gaps and see a 'long way'. He has drawn pictures of *rai* and *balangan*, so he is not too disturbed when they make themselves visible to him. It is not the intensity of his gaze which produces them: if he is at peace with a place they will come. The harder you look the less likely you are to see. You dream, and something good will come to you, like your boyfriend, but when you look again...

EROTICS

There is a widespread myth in the North that crocodiles will never harm a woman, 'only keep her for sweetheart business'. There is no denying the phallic forearm of the crocodile. And in the story, at the point of rupture between pages, before you 'turn over', you are told about the woman's desire, a narrative device anticipating an erotic outcome.

The story is structured in two parts, the trip in to Langgee following a traditional Nyigina track, the sore head, no doubt caused by a dispute in camp which has driven her away (the boyfriend?), the arrival, sleep, the sexual subconscious.

Water is already heavily thematised, and it will be the sexual medium: 'dived deep into the water'. The alligator turns into the boyfriend, and when she can look *properly* (rather than figuratively, seeing him as more than an instrumental phallic effect) it is too late. The irony of 'he was a good man' sits uneasily with the 'raw meat', this is why she has to get away, complete the journey back to her people at Yedda, which achieves closure for the text, she will have a story to tell when she gets home.

EXCHANGE

Contact with Butcher Joe could always produce a market, a point of exchange on a trade route. Being on the spot meant that you were in the line of exchange which would frustrate those in Perth who wanted him to retain his work for them alone. 'Things must go two ways', says Paddy Row about Aboriginal-White relations, and he is reinscribing a traditional trade rule. Once it was only the artifact that was traded, but now the agents trade on Butcher Joe's name. His name, the singularity of his style, these are rarities, and rarity is value in the contemporary production of Aboriginal culture as an archival accumulation, not a lived disposable economy for those producing the artifacts.

The story and the painting go together, they displace each other in a certain direction, and the one cannot move without the other. The story glosses the painting as a supplement of pleasure which can be reiterated by the owner, in a faraway place, who can cite Butcher Joe's name and his exotic location. Butcher Joe was tapped into a market and the trade scattered and amplified, beyond his control.

DRIFTING OUT

Butcher Joe has caught the tide and is moving out, to islands where tastes, perceptions, science and calculation are the ripples his work has become. Texts are formed, paintings will be remembered and reproduced, not all the songs will be forgotten. Sentiment will not always get in the way of understanding that an Aboriginal aesthetic is a material way of life, not something to be preserved. It is something that is being produced differently in different sites. Art to 'go' in shops and airports. Art to stay in museums. Even Butcher Joe's art does not have a true point of origin, since its creativity was its dialogue with Western realism. The conditions for an Aboriginal aesthetic are the conditions for living with the possibility of expansion and transformation, always moving slightly beyond recognition, allowing critics and traders the occasional glimpse of a secret which is both profound and as candidly open as the country in which we walk. We walk until we reach a tidal creek, lying down to sleep, happy to drift out, not caring who comes...

NOTES

1. See 'Strategic Nomadology: Introduction' in Krim Benterrak, Stephen Muecke and Paddy Roe, *Reading the Country*, Fremantle, Fremantle Arts Centre Press, 1984 which borrows from 'Traité de Nomadologie: La Machine de Guerre' in Gilles Deleuze and Felix Guattari, *Nille Plateaux*, Paris, Ed. de Minuit, 1980.
2. *Reading the Country* (op.cit.) and Paddy Roe, *Gularabulu*, Fremantle, Fremantle Arts Centre Press, 1983.
3. Jacques Derrida, *La Verité Peinture*, Paris, Flammarion, 1978.
4. *Gularabulu*, (op.cit.) p. vii.
5. *Reading the Country*, (op.cit.) p. 236 n. 36, p. 138.

TERRY GOLDIE

Signifier Resignified: Aborigines in Australian Literature[1]

If the image of Aborigines in Australian literature is analyzed in semiotic terms, the signifier, the literary image, does not lead back to the implied signified, the Aborigines of 'real life', but rather to other images. This could be seen as simply another version of Jacques Derrida's analysis of semiosis, which might be termed the cereal box view of the sign. The person on the box is holding a box with a picture of the same person holding a box with a picture of the same person holding a box ... etc. The root image cannot exist for there must always be another image on the box being held, no matter how small. In the same way, each signifier can refer only to another signifier. Any implied signified is unreachable.

But the signifier can have a precise value. John Berger's *Ways of Seeing* (1972)[2] states of the visual image:

> An image is a sight which has been recreated or reproduced. It is an appearance, or a set of appearances, which has been detached from the place and time in which it first made its appearance and preserved – for a few moments or a few centuries. (9-10)

A literary representation might seem less absolute but the indigene in literature is similarly a reified preservation, an unusually extreme example of the law noted by Edward Said in *Orientalism* (1978): 'In any instance of at least written language, there is no such thing as a delivered presence, but a *re-presence*, or a representation.' (21) Each representation of the indigene is a signifier for which there is no signified except the Image. The referent has little purpose in the equation. In the context of the indigene the unbreachable alterity between signifier and signified is never what many have claimed, an abstruse philosophical concept with nihilist tendencies, but an important aspect of the 'subjugated knowledges'(81) to which Michel Foucault refers in *Power/Knowledge* (1980). The valorization of the image is defined by a process in which the signified is signifier, in which representation is Image.

Yet there is a significant hidden connection between text and 'reality'. In *Orientalism*, Said suggests that what is important in western representations of eastern culture is not the approximation of presence which seems to be the intention but rather the conformity of the works to an ideology called orientalism. Said studies not the reality which the works seem to represent, the truths which they claim to depict, but the reality of the texts and their ideology, and of the ideology of the authors and their culture. In the case of Aborigines, creative literature is but one reflection of a process which permeates Australian culture, even those aspects which seem most removed from native peoples. In the University of Western Australia, a strangely beautiful example of Spanish colonial architecture, the ceiling of the imposing Great Hall is adorned with Aboriginal paintings. Needless to say, there have been few Aboriginal students to look at them.

This reality of the ideology is shaped by the reality of invasion and oppression. Eric R. Wolf, in *Europe and the People Without History* (1982), comments on the creation of 'race':

> Racial designations, such as 'Indian' or 'Negro', are the outcome of the subjugation of populations in the course of European mercantile expansion. The term *Indian* stands for the conquered populations of the New World, in disregard of any cultural or physical differences among native Americans. (380)

At first, 'Indian' was also often used for the indigenes of Australia but soon the vague 'aboriginal' became the term of choice. Still, this change represented no significant variation in representation: 'Aborigine' still means conquered. Neither are the details or even the major events of the Australian conquest significant factors in the image of the native. History awarded semiotic control to the invaders. Since then the image of native peoples has functioned as a constant source of semiotic reproduction, in which each textual image refers back to those offered before. The image of 'them' is not theirs.

This analysis attempts to reveal the semiotic limitations of various texts, particularly of those which have been said to provide 'positive' or 'realistic' views of native peoples. I seek Pierre Macherey's 'ideological horizon' (132), the concealed but omnipresent ideology controlling the text. Yet in identifying that horizon, in deconstructing that centre of control, I must recognize that I cannot avoid asserting my own centre, as a white Canadian male of a certain age. Like any other critic I must recognize that, in Yeats's words, 'The centre cannot hold'.

The shape of the signifying process as it applies to native peoples is formed by a certain semiotic field, the boundaries within which images can function. A few associations suggest the area: boomerang, myall, black velvet and dusky. The native is a semiotic pawn on a chess board controlled by the white signmaker yet the individual signmaker, the individual player, can move these pawns only within certain prescribed areas. To extend the analogy, the textual play between white and native is a replica of the black and white squares. This basic dualism, however, is not good and evil, although often argued to be so, as in Abdul R. JanMohammed's 'The Economy of Manichean Allegory' (1985):

> The dominant model of power – and interest – relations in all colonial societies is the manichean opposition between the putative superiority of the European and the supposed inferiority of the native. (63)

In some early and many contemporary texts the opposition is between the 'putative superiority' of the indigene and the 'supposed inferiority' of the white. In Xavier Herbert's *Poor Fellow My Country* (1975) the mixed-race Prindy has 'at least a degree of realization that he was not truly Aboriginal, while yet his being yearned for Aboriginal community with his environment, rejecting the patent empty alienness of the non-indigenous.' (464) As for Said's oriental Other, positive and negative images are swings of one and the same pendulum:

> Many of the earliest Oriental amateurs began by welcoming the Orient as a salutary *dérangement* of their European habits of mind and spirit. The Orient was overvalued for its pantheism, its spirituality, its stability, its longevity, its primitivism, and so forth... Yet almost without exception such overesteem was followed by a counter-response: the Orient suddenly appeared lamentably under-humanized, antidemocratic, backward, barbaric, and so forth. (Said, 150)

All of Said's 'overvalued' are present in *Poor Fellow My Country* but even there the 'counter-response' is always implied.

The complications extend beyond racial opposition, as noted in Sander Gilman's *Difference and Pathology* (1985):

Because there is no real line between self and the Other, an imaginary line must be drawn; and so that the illusion of an absolute difference between self and Other is never troubled, this line is as dynamic in its ability to alter itself as is the self. This can be observed in the shifting relationship of antithetical stereotypes that parallel the existence of 'bad' and 'good' representations of self and Other. But the line between 'good' and 'bad' responds to stresses occurring within the psyche. Thus paradigm shifts in our mental representations of the world can and do occur. We can move from fearing to glorifying the Other. We can move from loving to hating. (18)

The problem is not the negative or positive aura associated with the image but rather the image itself. In this passage from Herbert, the focus turns from the 'Aboriginal community' of the character to the 'patent empty alienness of the non-indigenous', white Australians, the normative culture addressed by the text. The Other is of interest primarily as a comment on the self, a judgement that could correctly be applied to the present study, concerned with not native peoples but the image of the native, a white image.

This image is usually defined, as it is in Herbert, in association with nature. The explorers attempted to make their signifying process represent real experience, to create the 'information' text defined in Mary Pratt's analysis of African explorers, 'Scratches on the Face of the Country' (1985):

the invisible eye/I strives to make those informational orders natural, to find them there uncommanded, rather than assert them as the products/producers of European knowledges or disciplines. (125)

Thus, to define the Aborigine as 'natural' seems to be 'natural' in Edward J. Eyre's *Journals of Expeditions of Discovery into Central Australia* (1845) but it continues to be so in contemporary fiction, as in Randolph Stow's *To the Islands* (1982). The field, that uniform chessboard, has continued, particularly in the few basic moves the indigenous pawn has been allowed to make.

At least since Frantz Fanon's *Black Skin White Masks* (1952) it has been a commonplace to use 'Other' and 'Not-self' for the white view of blacks and for the resulting black view of themselves, an assertion of a white self as subject in discourse which leaves the black Other as object. The terms are similarly applicable to the Aborigine but with an important shift. They are Other and Not-self but also must become self. Gayatri Spivak, in 'Three Women's Texts and a Critique of Imperialism' (1985), examines the value of the colonized to the colonizer: 'the project of imperialism has always already historically refracted what might have been the absolute Other into a domesticated Other that consolidated the imperialist self.' (253) Any imperialist discourse valorizes the colonized according to its own needs for reflection.

But in Spivak's area of study, the Indian sub-continent, the imperialist discourse remains admittedly non-indigenous. India is valorized by imperialist dynamics but it 'belongs' to the white realm only as part of the empire. Australians have, and long have had, a clear agenda to erase this separation of belonging. The white Australian looks at the Aborigine. The Aborigine is Other and therefore alien. But the Aborigine is indigenous and therefore cannot be alien. So the Australian must be alien. But how can the Australian be alien within Australia? There are only two possible answers. The white culture might reject the indigene, by stating that the country really began with the arrival of the whites, an approach no longer popular but significant in the nineteenth and early twentieth centuries. Or else the white culture can attempt to incorporate the Other, as in superficial examples such as pseudo-Aboriginal names for aspects of white Australian culture, or as in sensitive and sophisticated efforts such as the novels of Patrick White.

The importance of the alien within cannot be overstated. In their need to become 'native', to belong there, whites in Australia have required a process which I have termed 'indigenization', the impossible necessity of becoming indigenous. For many writers, the only chance seemed to be through the humans who are truly indigenous, the Aborigines. As J. J. Healy notes in *Literature and the Aborigine in Australia 1770-1975* (1978),

> The Aborigine was part of the tension of an indigenous consciousness. Not the contemporary Aborigine, not even a plausible historical one, but the sort of creature that *might* persuade a white Australian to look in the direction of the surviving race. (173)

Of course, the majority of writers have given no, or at most very limited, attention to native peoples but the process of indigenization is complex, as in that Great Hall. Each nineteenth-century reference to the white Australian as 'native', so common in *The Bulletin*, is a comment on indigenization, regardless of the absence of Aborigines in those comments. As Macherey states, 'an ideology is made of what it does not mention; it exists because there are things which must not be spoken of'. (132) In other words, absence is also negative presence, as in the natives not mentioned in Henry Handel Richardson's nation-building trilogy, *The Fortunes of Richard Mahony* (1930). This might be opposed by the 'positive absence' of the decorated ceiling or of many poems by the Jindyworobaks, particularly those in Ian Mudie's *Corroboree to the Sun* (1940). There, the Aborigine is usually neither subject nor overt object of the poems but an aid to 'indigenize' the text.

Said notes a number of what he terms 'standard commodities' associated with the orient. Two such commodities which appear to be standard in the economy created by the semiotic field of the Aborigine in Australian literature are sex and violence. They are poles of attraction and repulsion, temptation by the bit of black velvet and fear of the demonic myall black. Often both are found in the same work, as in Charles Rowcroft's *Brandon the Bushranger* (1846), in which the warrior constantly attacks but the maiden, 'the affectionate Oionoo' (223), is an agent to avoid that attack. They are emotional signs, semiotic embodiments of primal responses. Could one create a more appropriate signifier for fear than the treacherous myall? He incorporates the terror of an impassioned, uncontrolled spirit of evil. He is strangely joined by the Aboriginal maiden, who tempts the being chained by civilization towards the liberation of free and open sexuality, not untamed evil but unrestrained joy. They follow the pattern noted in *Difference and Pathology*: 'The "bad" Other becomes the negative stereotype; the "good" Other becomes the positive stereotype. The former is that which we fear to become; the latter, that which we fear we cannot achieve'. (20) Added to this is the alien's fear of the warrior as hostile wilderness, this new, threatening land, and the arrivant's attraction to the maiden as restorative pastoral, this new, available land. The absent Aborigines in *Richard Mahony* and the Aboriginal resonances of Mudie's poems might also be seen in this context. The sign of fear leads to an indigenization which excludes the indigene. Temptation promises an indigenization through inclusion.

An intriguing yet unanswerable question is whether the subject of the Aborigine causes an emphasis on sex and violence, or desire for the frissons of sex and violence suggests the Aborigine. In Charles De Boos' *Fifty Years Ago* (1867) the image of the Aborigine is at one point noble savage, at another a devil, including a stridently gory scene of the massacre of a pioneer family, in which the Aborigine appears as demonic savage par excellence. The interest seems more in violence than in the Aborigine. Or the motivation might be generic, the historical romance establishing the base for present Australia. The novel presents a vision of the founding of a nation and the Aborigine must fit. Thus before the arrival of the whites the noble Aborigine provides an extended history for the greatness of Australia. After the whites arrive, this arcadian purity is somehow transformed into Aboriginal treachery, which becomes a justification to direct the readers' empathy to the invaders rather than to those recently presented as an indigenous aristocracy. The end of the novel re-establishes the nobility of the Aborigine but only while showing the total decay of his society and personal strength. Nobility before contact, treachery during and nobility as contact fades into memory.

The sexual attractions of the Aborigine are often quite complicated, as in John Mathew's 'The Aboriginal Love-Letter', in *Australian Echoes* (1902). The text states, 'The nymph though dark is fair', (39) an amazing phrase which begins with a mythic signifier of sensuality and follows it with an oxymoron which synthesizes Aboriginality and fragile femininity. Still, while complex, this commodity is usually gender-specific. In Rowcroft, the gentle Oionoo has manifest attractions but when the old chief, Walloo-wombee, who is said to look like 'a very aged baboon', (178) turns his attentions to a white woman it is described as 'unspeakable horror, a fate worse than death itself'. (179) Similarly, Mathew's 'The Black Captor' sees 'My love is bright as the flower' (19) but the object of this love, 'The White Captive', sees only 'My swarthy partner, hated ... hellish scenes, that gall me and defile'. (17-18)

The delicate native maiden, the usual sexual focus in literature of the eighteenth, nineteenth and much of the twentieth century, is most memorably portrayed in the title character of Katharine Susannah Prichard's *Coonardoo* (1929), the archetypal Aboriginal figure in Australian literature. She exists in more ominous forms, such as the violent succubus of Charles Broome's 'The Blood of Marlee' (1939) or the degrading wife in Vance Palmer's *The Man Hamilton* (1928), but she is always very unlike the common repulsive intimidating violence of the demonic male. Until well into the twentieth century the male native was almost always violence, never sex. A major change happens, however, in novels such as John Patrick's *Inapatua* (1966) and Christine Townend's *Travels With Myself* (1976) in which a native male is a sexual attraction which the white female uses in her own attempt at liberation.

A third important commodity is orality, all the associations raised by the indigene's speaking, non-writing, state. The writer's sense of native peoples as having completely different systems of understanding, different epistemes, is based on an often undefined belief that cultures without writing operate within a different dimension of consciousness. In earlier works, white writers often deemed this a symptom of inferiority or, as in Conrad Sayce's *Comboman* (1934), a sign of demonic possession. Both the good and the bad sides of orality are usually presented as aspects of the natural. One Aborigine in James Francis Hogan's *The Lost Explorer* (1890) resorts to a typical rhetorical exhortation of violence and nature:

> I, Wonga, of the swift-speeding spear and the fast-flying boomerang, who vanished from your midst like the star that falls in the heavens at night, have now arisen once more like the sun that comes up out of the stormy sea every morn to give brightness and beauty to our island valley. (146)

Prindy in *Poor Fellow My Country* communes with 'The Voice of the Spirit of the Land'. (669) The philosophical base of the positive representations of natural orality found throughout twentieth century literature is represented by the claims made by Walter Ong in *Orality and Literacy*:

> The fact that oral peoples commonly and in all likelihood universally consider words to have magical potency is clearly tied in, at least unconsciously, with their sense of the word as necessarily spoken, sounded, and hence power-driven. (32)

The orality of the native is seen to provide a connection to the inner world of man, unlike the alienating distance of the literary. In a self-reflexive denigration typical of much contemporary literature, texts such as Thomas Keneally's *The Chant of Jimmie Blacksmith* (1973) express ambivalence about the validity of writing through an elevation of the indigene's orality, represented as Said's 'delivered presence'. The title of Keneally's novel claims a transformation in which white text becomes Aboriginal orality.

The Aboriginal narrator can be an important element of orality, especially in recent fiction. The representation of the text as product of an Aboriginal voice creates 'presence' through appearing to change the Aborigine from object to subject, as in the Aboriginal centre of intelligence of Prichard's story 'Happiness' (1932) or of *Inapatua*. The latter uses the first person to validate the description of an educated 'de-tribalized' Aborigine who undergoes re-indigenization.

Representations of native language from the outside extend orality in a different direction, as in naming. At one level the conflict might just be between true and false, between an Aboriginal name which represents Aboriginal culture and an imposed white name which produces a false identity. A larger import is asserted in *Women of the Sun* (1983) when Ann finds out her Aboriginal name: 'She is Pand-jel's daughter – a sun woman... Lo-Arna... Her name means "beautiful woman", you know...' (221) The reindigenization of the Aboriginal maiden is validated through the semiotic shift.

It is as if a different semiotic field is glimpsed, not the field in which the writer places the indigene but the field in which the indigene places the whites and, presumably, him or herself. This creates a continuum from early texts which use a few native words heavily glossed to Donald Stuart's *Malloonkai* (1976), in which Aboriginal terms are defined only by context. A simple record of indigene language might be considered more limited in its representation of the indigenous consciousness than the indigene as narrator but its apparent absolute adherence to the indigenous semiosis could suggest that an even greater bridge has been touched if not crossed. Unlike the case of the indigenous narrator, the white reader – and perhaps author – can barely penetrate the meaning. This is most clear when a white person is given an Aboriginal honorific, such as 'mullaka' in such disparate works as *Poor Fellow My Country* and Mrs. Gunn's *We of the Never-Never* (1908). The implied value of such names is suggested by the explanation of the title in John Boyle O'Reilly's *Moondyne* (1880): 'They gave him the name of "Moondyne" which had some meaning more than either manhood or kingship'. (14) The texts suggest that the application of indigenous language connects the white figure with the power which the indigene represents.

The inclusion of Aboriginal 'speech' seems to represent a prime example of Michail Bakhtin's 'Discourse in the Novel':

> These distinctive links and interrelationships between utterances and languages, this movement of the theme through different languages and speech types, its dispersion into the rivulets and droplets of social heteroglossia, its dialogization – this is the basic distinguishing feature of the stylistics of the novel. (*Dialogic*, 263)

Bakhtin sees this dialogization as creating an important tension in fiction: 'Every utterance participates in the "unitary language" (in its centripetal forces and tendencies) and at the same time partakes of social and historical heteroglossia (the centrifugal, stratifying forces)'. (272)

This suggests a positive view of the process, in which the 'self' of the white text includes the Aboriginal 'Other' within its vision while at the same time representing the 'social and historical' vision of the Other. Bakhtin goes so far as to call it '*another's speech in another's language*'. (324) In opposition I would suggest that the image of the Aborigine is an example of the negative confluence of the centripetal and centrifugal Other. It is centripetal because always subject to the system of white texts. The Aboriginal voice found in Australian fiction 'lives' only in that fiction. It is centrifugal because that Aborigine always reaches out to a semiotic field which has defined the image before its inclusion in the fluctuations of the individual text. The novel of the nineteen-eighties re-presents the extant Image. The process is 'stratifying' in a particularly pernicious sense.

There are many variants to the power of the oral Aborigine, such as the taciturn Aborigine as the obverse of the inflated diction of the orator. At the beginning of Donald Stuart's *The Driven* (1961), the white Tom observes of the Aborigines: 'Strange, the gift most of them had of silence'. (10) Later, Tom is accepted by the Aborigines because he is able to be similarly wordless: 'Good quiet man, this Tom. Not like some of the whitefellers, wanting to talk all the time...' (57) Stuart's novel, like *Poor Fellow My Country* and many others, links this silence to religious values. It is as though the Aborigine eventually transcends the orality, to become the land, to become presence, and mystically become the silent invocation of the consciousness, the vision, of Other.

But this ultimate transcendence does not deny the holistic nature of the process. The voice is part of the silence is part of the land is part of the vision. In *Reading the Country* (1984) Stephen Muecke asserts, 'There is no basis for seeing the dreaming as a mythological past (as in "dreamtime") while it is alive as a *way of talking*.' (14) The oral is part of the native as a sign of oracular power, either malevolent, in most nineteenth century texts, or beneficent, in most contemporary ones. Many early texts suggest orality to be inferior and indigenous beliefs to be absurd superstitions. If such beliefs did represent a different dimension of consciousness, it was not worth achieving, and certainly not equal to white doctrine. Mrs. Campbell Praed's *Fugitive Anne* (1903) finds her own rendition of *Ave Maria* has an oral power superior to any Aboriginal chant. Her faithful servant Kombo notes: 'By'm by, Missa Anne, you tell me again that fellow "Our Father"', he said, confidentially, to his mistress, 'I plenty forget. Mine think-it that frighten Debil-debil.' (65)

For other texts, however, particularly in the twentieth century, an alien space is attractive. In *Poor Fellow My Country* Jeremy is visited by an Aboriginal spirit and his Aboriginal friend asserts, 'That *Lamala* belong to some old blackfeller before, finish now for good. He lonely. He grab 'old o' you. Now you all-same blackfeller...belong country!' Jeremy himself is convinced by the argument: 'That's what struck me ... if I see things like a blackfellow, then I must belong like one'. (1098) A similar but still more ethereal process is glimpsed in Les Murray's *The Boys Who Stole the Funeral* (1980), in which the rural white Australian meets no Aborigines but is also indigenized by an Aboriginal emanation. In *To the Islands*, the title reflects an Aboriginal belief about where the soul comes to rest. The old Christian missionary, Heriot, is on his own journey 'to the islands' in search of some meaning for his life. As part of the process he sings, 'to a corroboree tune of tearing sadness', 'And Christ receive thy soul' (77), but this synthesis of religions is not successful. Only when he finally approaches 'the islands' and abandons his past beliefs does he achieve something epiphanic: 'My soul', he whispered, over the seasurge, 'my soul is a strange country'. (126) In an interesting semiotic variant, the inadequacies of the author's culture, which offers little 'true' knowledge through its own beliefs, in which the alterity of the signifier leaves divine power beyond reach, is met by an indigenous belief system (usually quite asystemic) which offers a Presence to exceed even the presence of orality.

Spivak has commented on the 'soul-making' agenda of imperialist missionaries (Address). They intended to take indigenous peoples who teetered between the absolute material and the false anti-phenomenal and make new creations who would possess the reality of the Christian noumenal. But in many of the texts in this study, the white needs not to instill spirit in the Other but to gain it from the Other. Through the indigene the white character gains soul and the potential of becoming rooted in the land. An appropriate pun is that only by going native can the European arrivant become native. Often in such narratives the Otherness of the indigene is first heightened, as in the use of an indigenous semiotic field. A similar process is the defamilarization of common aspects of white culture. When Aborigines are presented as having an intricately metaphorical view of white science, such as gunpowder or a clock, the Aborigines become doubly the Other. They are Other because the white perceives them as such and because their own perception is clearly that of Other.

Often, however, as in *The Boys Who Stole the Funeral* or Helen Hodgman's *Blue Skies* (1976), or any of the many works on Truganini, 'the last Tasmanian Aborigine', the Other is not living Aborigines but memories of people long obliterated. Aboriginal presence but no present Aborigines. This temporal split is a fifth commodity in the semiotic field of the indigene, the prehistoric. Historicity, in which the text makes an overt or covert statement on the chronology of the culture, shapes the indigene into an historical artefact, a remnant of a golden age which seems to have little connection to contemporary life.

Golden age assumptions seem to underly the choice of genre in the various Aboriginal epics, such as George Gordon McCrae's *The Story of Balladeadro* (1867). The golden age supports the heroic Aborigine in Henry Kendall's 'The Last of His Tribe' (*Leaves* [1869], 92-93) and the end of the golden age supports the degraded Aborigine of the bush ballads by Kendall and James Brunton Stephens or of the mock epic, *The Raid of the Aborigines* (1875), by William Wilks. Many novels which depict an epic sweep of Australian history, such as Rex Ingamells' *Of Us Now Living* (1952) and Eleanor Dark's *Timeless Land* trilogy (1941-53), show Aborigines as only a beginning of Australia, conveniently dropping off the fictional map of contemporary life. The titles are particularly appropriate: Ingamells' excludes the Aborigines from the us, the now and the living and Dark's replaces the time-less indigenes with the time-full European arrivants.

Robert Drewe's novel *The Savage Crows* (1975) makes a still more specific comment on the prehistoric when the Tasmanian Aborigine William Lanney is said to be treated as a 'living fossil'. (13) Johannes Fabian's *Time and the Other* (1983) states of anthropology:

> It promoted a scheme in terms of which not only past cultures, but all living societies were irrevocably placed on a temporal slope, a stream of time – some upstream, others downstream. (17)

When native peoples, perceived to be of the 'early', remain in present Australian society, the 'late', degradation is shown to be inevitable. A corollary of the temporal split between the golden age and contemporary decadence is a tendency to see native culture as either true, pure and static or else not really of that culture, thus the contrast in Kendall between noble and ignoble savage. *Inapatua* eulogizes the remnants of the 'tribal' culture as a specific contrast with the detribalized hero. As implied by the title of John McGarrity's *Once a Jolly Blackman* (1973), the Aborigine of time present is only alienated despair.

Through the commodities the white acquires Aborigine, 'acquires', not 'becomes'. To 'become Aborigine' is an absurdity or madness. Even in one of the most sensitive of the modern white blackfellow texts, Patrick White's *A Fringe of Leaves* (1976), the Aboriginal experience of the shipwrecked Ellen is a transition, a sea change with a necessary surfacing at the end. 'Go native' is necessary, 'gone native' is not. Some psychologists might diagnose even acquisition as a rejection of self for not-self. The typical narrative pattern must modify such a theory, however. The indigene is acquired, the white is not abandoned. Usually, the connection is made through some form of sexual contact, in earlier works, a white male with a native female, in recent often the reverse. But in the majority of works of both types this is followed by the death of the indigene. In *A Fringe of Leaves*, the process is not sex but cannibalism, as Ellen eats the leg of an Aboriginal girl noted for her symbiotic relationship with nature. Ellen swallows the land. In another historical novel by White, *Voss* (1957), still perhaps the most resonant portrait of white contact with Aboriginal presence, the German explorer recognizes that regardless of his egomania his meal will be reversed: '"If we are not devoured by blacks", Voss replied, "or the Great Snake, then we shall be eaten by somebody eventually"' (379). His Aboriginal guide Jackie kills him, as Voss wills him to perform the sacrificial violence of the land. The white who does not 'surface' from Aboriginality dies.

A variety of factors are involved in incorporating the native for the page but still more are added when the genre requires that the native be corporeally present, in the theatre. There must be presence in the theatre, although the presence is that of the actors and not of the author. If this pawn is played by a white actor in disguise signifying processes are at play similar to those in the novel. If a native actor is used the cross-cultural leap in which the white author creates the lines and the context for the indigene's speech might seem a beneficial erasing of boundaries but it might also be considered a means of hiding some very necessary distinctions. In the published text of Keneally's play, *Bullie's House* (1981), there is a lengthy comment by Bob Maya, one of the Aboriginal actors in the original production. He states that he overcame his rejection of a white-authored script when a young Aboriginal girl pointed out to him, 'if it's true and it's about our people, does it matter who writes it?' (xiii) There are various possible refutations of this statement but one brief quotation from Foucault's 'Two Lectures' will suffice:

> I would say that we are forced to produce the truth of power that our society demands, of which it has need, in order to function: we must speak the truth; we are constrained or condemned to confess or to discover the truth. (93)

The girl's simplistic view of the possibilities of an Aboriginal 'truth' in the theatre shows no recognition of the theatrical power/truth which constrains it within a certain semiotization or of the power/truth of white semiosis which condemns it.

A novel can only attempt the Bakhtinian illusion of representing 'another's voice'. The dramatic text makes it possible for another's voice to speak the other as described by the white self. Maya's role as signifier of 'reality' just made the limits of the image more acceptable, in a play which incorporates all of the standard commodities noted above. It appears that as long as this semiotic field exists, as long as the shapes of the standard commodities change but the commodities remain the same, the chess match can appear to vary but there is still a defineable limit to the board. The necessities of indigenization can compell white players to enter the game but they cannot liberate the pawn.

This chessboard analogy might seem a diminution of the issue. It emphasizes distance between sign, the image of the Aborigine in Australian literature, and referent, the Aborigines of Australia, but it perhaps hides the contradictions of the chessboard of Australian political reality. Still, if, as Derrida claims, there is nothing outside the text, then the image of the native is the textualization of the erasure of native sovereignty in Australia. At a time when native land rights are a major issue in Australian politics, a recognition of the manipulations of white indigenization in literature might be a stimulus to the reinstatement of the indigenous.

NOTES

1. This paper provides a sketch of a theoretical approach used in various other studies (Goldie) and thus examples are kept to a minimum. The comments refer specifically to Australian literature but the majority of the assertions are applicable to a number of analogous literatures, most obviously Canadian, in both English and French, and American but also New Zealand and various South American. To look beyond the 'Indian' context, South African literature also 'fits', with J. M. Coetzee's *Waiting for the Barbarians* a perfect example of the valorization of the semiotic field of the indigene. For a general comparison, the ideological framework of Robert F. Berkhofer's *The White Man's Indian: Images of the American Indian from Columbus to the Present* is different from the present study but the conclusions are similar.
2. Dates in the text refer to first publication. For some early texts, these are only approximate.

WORKS CITED.

'Alpha Crucis' [Robert Dudley Sidney Powys Herbert]. 'Trucanini's Dirge.' *The Song of the Stars: and Other Poems.* London: Cassell, Petten, Galpin, (1882). 142-144.

Bakhtin, Mikhail. *The Dialogic Imagination: Four Essays.* Trans. Caryl Emerson and Michael Holquist. Ed. Michael Holquist. Austin: University of Texas, 1981.

Benterrak, Krim, Stephen Muecke and Paddy Roe. *Reading the Country: an Introduction to Nomadology.* Fremantle: Fremantle Arts Centre Press, 1984.

Berger, John. *Ways of Seeing.* London: BBC, 1972.

Berkhofer, Robert F. *The White Man's Indian: Images of the American Indian from Columbus to the Present.* New York: Vintage, 1979.

Broome, Charles. 'The Blood of Marlee: A Romance of North Australian Wilds.' *The Steering Wheel and Society and Home* June 1939: 50-52; July 1939: 48-49; August 1939: 49-51; Sept. 1939: 47-49; Jan. 1940: 52-52; Feb. 1940: 54-55; April 1940: 50-51; and May 1940: 48-50.

Coetzee, J.M. *Waiting for the Barbarians.* 1980. Harmondsworth, Middlesex: Penguin, 1982.

Dark, Eleanor. *No Barrier.* 1953. London: Collins, 1960.

____________ . *Storm of Time.* Sydney: Collins, 1948

____________ . *The Timeless Land.* 1941. London: Collins, 1943.

De Boos, Charles. *Fifty Years Ago.* N.p.: n.p., 1867.

Derrida, Jacques. *Of Grammatology.* Trans. Gayatri Chakravorty Spivak. Baltimore: Johns Hopkins, 1976.

Drewe, Robert. *The Savage Crows.* Sydney: Collins, 1976.

Elliot, Brian, ed. *The Jindyworobaks.* St. Lucia: University of Queensland Press, 1979.

Eyre, Edward John. *Journals of Expeditions of Discovery into Central Australia, and Overland from Adelaide to King George's Sound. In the Years 1840-41: Sent by the Colonists of South Australia. With the Sanction and Support of the Government: including an Account of the Manners and Customs of the Aborigines and the State of their Relations with Europeans.* 2 vols. London: T. & W. Boone, 1845.

Fabian, Johannes. *Time and the Other: How Anthropology Makes Its Object.* New York: Columbia University, 1983

Fanon, Frantz. *Black Skin White Masks.* Trans. Charles Lam Markmann. 1952. St. Albans, Herts: Paladin, 1970.

Foucault, Michel. *Power/Knowledge: Selected Interviews and Other Writings 1972-1977.* Trans. Colin Gordon et al. Ed. Colin Gordon. New York: Pantheon Books, 1980.

Gilman, Sander. *Difference and Pathology: Stereotypes of Sexuality, Race and Madness.* Ithaca: Cornell University Press, 1985.

Goldie, Terry. 'The Aboriginal Connection: A Study of *Tecumseh* by Charles Mair and "The Glen of Arrawatta" by Henry Kendall.' *World Literature Written in English* 21 (1982): 287-297.

___________. 'An Aboriginal Present: Canadian and Australian Literature in the Twenties.' *World Literature Written in English* 23 (1984): 88- 96.

___________. 'Contemporary Views of an Aboriginal Past: Rudy Wiebe and Patrick White.' *World Literature Written in English* 23 (1984): 429- 439.

___________. 'Emancipating the Equal Aborigine: J.B. O'Reilly and A.J. Vogan.' *Span* (New Zealand) 20 (1985): 47-66.

___________. *Fear and Temptation: The Image of the Indigene in Canadian, Australian and New Zealand Literature.* To be published by McGill-Queen's in 1989.

___________. 'Indigenous Stages: The Indigene in Canadian, New Zealand and Australian Drama.' *Australasian Drama Studies* 9 (1986): 5-20.

___________. 'The Necessity of Nobility: Indigenous Peoples in Canadian and Australian Literature.' *The Journal of Commonwealth Literature* 20 (1985): 131-147.

___________. 'Signs of the Themes: the Value of a Politically Grounded Semiotics.' *Future Indicative: Literary Theory and Canadian Literature.* Ed. John Moss. Ottawa: University of Ottawa, 1987. 85-94.

Gunn, Mrs. Aeneas. *We of the Never-Never.* 1908. London: Hutchinson, 1954.

Healy, J.J. *Literature and the Aborigine in Australia 1770-1975.* St. Lucia: University of Queensland Press, 1978.

Herbert, Xavier. *Poor Fellow My Country.* 1975. Sydney: Pan, 1977.

Hodgman, Helen. *Blue Skies.* London: Duckworth, 1976.

Hogan, James Francis. *The Lost Explorer: An Australian Story.* Sydney: Edwards, Dunlop, [1890].

Ingamells, Rex.. *Of Us Now Living: A Novel of Australia.* Melbourne: Hallcraft, 1952.

___________. *Selected Poems.* Melbourne: Georgian House, 1944

JanMohammed, Abdul R. 'The Economy of Manichean Allegory: The Function of Racial Difference in Colonialist Literature.' *Critical Inquiry* 12.1 (1985): 59-87.

Kendall, Henry. *The Poetical Works of Henry Kendall.* Ed. T.T. Reed. Adelaide: Libraries Board of South Australia, 1966.

___________. *Leaves From Australian Forests.* 1869. Adelaide: Rigby, 1975.

Keneally, Thomas. *Bullie's House.* Sydney: Currency, 1981.

___________. *The Chant of Jimmie Blacksmith.* 1972. Ringwood, Victoria: Penguin, 1973.

Macherey, Pierre. *A Theory of Literary Production.* Trans. Geoffrey Wall. London: Routledge & Kegan Paul, 1978.

Maris, Hyllus and Sonia Borg. *Women of the Sun*. Sydney: Currency, 1983.

Mathew, John. *Australian Echoes Including The Corroboree and Other Poems*. Melbourne: Melville and Mullen, 1902.

McCrae, George Gordon. *The Story of Balla-deadro*. Melbourne: H.T. Dwight, 1867.

McGarrity, John. *Once a Jolly Blackman*. Melbourne: Wren, 1973.

Mudie, Ian, *Corroboree to the Sun*. Melbourne: Hawthorn, 1940.

Murray, Les. *The Boys Who Stole The Funeral: A Novel Sequence*. Sydney: Angus & Robertson, 1980.

Ong, Walter J. *Orality and Literacy: The Technologizing of the Word*. London: Methuen, 1982.

O'Reilly, John Boyle. *Moondyne: A Story of Life in West Australia*. 1880. Adelaide: Rigby, 1975.

Palmer, Vance. *The Man Hamilton*. 1928. Adelaide: Rigby, 1960.

Patrick, John. *Inapatua*. Melbourne: Cassell Australia, 1966.

Praed, Mrs. Campbell. *Fugitive Anne*. London: John Long, [1903].

Pratt, Mary Louise. 'Scratches on the Face of the Country; or, What Mr. Barrow Saw in the Land of the Bushmen.' *Critical Inquiry* 12:1 (1985): 119-143.

Prichard, Katharine Susannah. *Coonardoo*. 1929. Sydney: Angus & Robertson, 1975.

____________. 'Happiness.' *Kiss on the Lips and Other Stories*. London: Jonathan Cape, 1932. 107-132.

Richardson, Henry Handel. *The Fortunes of Richard Mahony*. Collected edition. London: Heinemann, 1930.

Rowcroft, Charles. *Brandon the Bushranger*. London: Leisure Library, n.d. First published in 1846 as *The Bushranger of Van Diemen's Land*.

Said, Edward. *Orientalism*. London: Routledge & Kegan Paul, 1978.

Sayce, Conrad. *Comboman: A Tale of Central Australia*. London: Hutchinson, [1934].

Sheppard, Trish. *Children of Blindness*. Sydney: Ure Smith, 1976.

Spivak, Gayatri Chakravorty. Address. University of Queensland, Brisbane, Australia, 1 Aug. 1984.

____________. 'Three Women's Texts and a Critique of Imperialism.' *Critical Inquiry* 12.1. (1985): 243-261.

Stephens, James Brunton. *The Poetical Works of Brunton Stephens*. Sydney: Angus & Robertson, 1902.

Stow, Randolph. *To the Islands*. London: Secker & Warburg, 1982.

Stuart, Donald. *The Driven*. Melbourne: Georgian House, 1961.

____________. *Malloonkai*. Melbourne: Georgian House, 1976.

Townsend, Christine. *Travels With Myself*. Sydney: Wild & Wooley, 1976.

White, Patrick. *A Fringe of Leaves*. 1976. New York: Avon, 1978.

____________. *Voss*. 1957. Ringwood, Victoria: Penguin, 1981.

Wilks, William. *The Raid of the Aborigines*. Transactions of the Bibliographical Society of Queensland Second Series 1. Brisbane, 1936.

Wolf, Eric R. *Europe and The People Without History*. Berkeley: University of California Press, 1982.

Yeats, W.B. 'The Second Coming.' *The Collected Works of W.B. Yeats*. London: Macmillan, 1952. 210-211.

SUSAN SHERIDAN

'Wives and mothers like ourselves, poor remnants of a dying race': Aborigines in Colonial Women's Writing

The bicentenary of invasion and settlement, 1988, challenges non-Aboriginal Australians as never before to confront and analyse the racism that pervades hegemonic cultural discourses and practices. Looking back to the noisy decades around the turn of the twentieth century, the crucial formative period of modern Australian cultural nationalism, one is struck by the silence of and about Aboriginal people. White Australians' exclusion of Aboriginals has been, I would argue, crucial to our self-constitution as 'Australian' – an identity, a unity, whose meaning derives from its discursive displacement of the 'other' race, just as its power as a nation state derives from the appropriation of Aboriginal land.[1] In that respect, Australian culture is still colonial.

A colonial culture constitutes itself as an identity, a unity, on the basis of its discursive constructions of racial difference: the excluded 'other' becomes the ground on which the national figure is delineated, the buried foundation on which its structure of power is erected. In an account of the way in which the dominant culture represents to itself its own identity by simultaneously defining and denying the difference of the 'other', what is at issue is not correcting misrepresentations, nor replacing them with authentic ones, but rather recognising the ways in which the meaning of the one derives from its discursive (dis)placing of the other. In the discussion which follows, then, 'Aboriginality' is a term in white discourse and not a reference to historical/social persons.[2]

Late nineteenth-century discourse on race difference is one of the axes on which Australian cultural nationalism has been constructed. The other axis is gender difference: constructions of femininity have been excluded, women as social subjects have been marginalised, in dominant representations of Australianness, and women's cultural production has been buried except when it was compatible with the malestream.[3] For this very reason women's representations of Aboriginal people are significant, for they manifest not only the ambivalence characteristic of all colonial discourse but also, contradictorily, some recognition of women's shared position with these other Others. In particular, Aboriginal women as represented in their writing are occasions of momentary affirmations of the potential affinity of women in a culture that is also patriarchal.

The question is not, of course, whether white women writers were racist but, rather, whether and how their racism has differed from white men's.[4] Inevitably they draw on the 'available discourses'[5] of evolution and racial purity, which construct Aboriginals as radically 'other'; yet the marginal position assigned to women as cultural agents means that they will deploy these discourses differently from white men. They construct race difference and relate it to gender difference in specific ways, which on examination reveal the ambiguities of their position as members of the dominant power – but not quite; similarly, the ambiguity of their position as women, shared with Aboriginal women – but not quite.

These ambiguities are strikingly caught in the statement from which this essay's title phrase is taken: Aboriginal women are 'wives and mothers like ourselves' wrote Louisa Lawson in the leading article of her feminist paper, *The Dawn*, in 1897; but they are also 'poor remnants of a dying race'. Because of this, she urges her readers 'to show consideration and kindness ... sympathizing in their troubles, alleviating, as far as possible, their hardships, and honoring their womanhood as we honor our own'.[6] The recognition of likeness, of identity as women across the racial divide, is strikingly unusual for that historical period, but even more striking is the simultaneous invocation of this shared gender *identity* and of racial *difference* in its most extreme form – the commonplace reference to Aborigines as a dying race.

In the context of 1890s public discourse Lawson's statement is unusual in mentioning Aborigines at all. The journalism of that period manifests almost total silence about the Aboriginal inhabitants of the continent. Assertions of white racial identity and purity abound, but they are most commonly articulated through the exclusion of the Chinese, the Kanakas, Afghans and Indians – those peoples who appeared to threaten by their presence as immigrant or indentured workers the achievements of the new labour movement. The 'White Australia' policy which emerged from this period does not seem to have been articulated with reference to the Aborigines.[7] They were simply not perceived as actors on the contemporary scene.

The majority of Aborigines in south eastern Australia were, for white urban writers at this time, out of sight and out of mind, in fringe camps around country towns or on remote reserves. (Lawson refers to 'Bush readers' who would know what she is talking about.) Moreover they were *written* out of sight by the operation of the prevailing evolutionist discourse on race. This discourse constructed Aborigines as a race doomed inevitably to die out after contact with the more highly evolved Europeans, the belief being that they represented the most primitive form of humanity, one which could not survive in contact with the supposedly more evolved and superior white race. This discourse gained force with the spread of popular Darwinism in the late 19th century, although the notion of the dying race had emerged very early in colonial writings.[8] By the late nineteenth century it obviously functions as a displacement of white knowledge that the massacres and disease which accompanied invasion and settlement had had near-genocidal effects. Furthermore, the *biological* definition of race in evolutionist discourse meant that only so-called 'full-bloods' were considered as authentic Aborigines, and others were rendered invisible.[9] The constructing race as a fixed essence that cannot change, but can only live or die, that discourse allows no possibility of a culture of resistance and survival, and thus denies the historical experience of Aboriginals in southern and eastern Australia. That is, the ideological work of racism within nationalist discourse around the turn of the century had silently buried the miscegenation and near-genocide involved in its pioneer past.

Gillian Cowlishaw has argued that this discourse on a racial purity of 'blood' was never displaced in Australian social anthropology, but remains submerged in the concept of 'traditional Aboriginal culture' as the defining characteristic of Aboriginality.[10] She reminds us of the enormous influence which anthropological discourse has had for at least the past century, in the culture at large as well as in government policy on Aboriginal affairs. Certainly, Australian governments have continued to arrogate to themselves the power to determine who is and who is not counted as Aboriginal, a situation which has prevailed until the recent upsurge of political activity by people claiming Aboriginal identity for themselves. And the ideas just outlined are far from dead in current commonsense discourse about race relations in Australia and elsewhere.

In the context of feminist debate, Lawson's statement about Aboriginal women is equally unusual. Feminist activists eager to contest the emerging masculinist definition of national culture and to place their own agenda in the public eye[11] rarely drew attention to class differences among women and certainly not to differences of race and ethnicity.

The young Miles Franklin in her 1909 comic novel about the women's vote, *Some Everyday Folk and Dawn*, allows her characters to refer casually to 'black gins' as a caricature of everything a respectable white woman is not.

Lawson's statement, by involving the ideologically sacred category of motherhood as the principle of unity among women, avoids this whole question of the sexual status colloquially attributed to 'black gins' in racist patriarchal discourse. Australian feminists appear to have been remarkably reticent about sexuality, even on questions of women's sexual vulnerability: prostitution was generally referred to euphemistically, and there was nothing – as far as we know yet – like the British campaign against the Contagious Diseases Acts to push them into taking a more explicit stand. And it would have been in relation to such issues that the popular construction of Aboriginal women as prostitutes might have emerged in public debate.[12] Although many feminists were vehement about men's sexual 'selfishness',[13] there seem to be few overt attacks on the history of their sexual exploitation of Aboriginal women. Two literary references to de facto marriages between an Aboriginal woman and a white man imply criticism of the man but not of the woman: Louisa Lawson's ballad, 'The Squatter's Wife' (who is met on her arrival on the selection by the sight of two huts, one for her and the other for his 'black gin' [sic] and her family), and Catherine Martin's novel, *The Silent Sea* (1892), where the husband sends his Aboriginal woman away and attempts to keep the child she has borne by him.[14] In her reference to 'Wives and mothers like ourselves', however, the common womanhood that Lawson wants to 'honor' is identified with motherhood.

The affirmation and honouring of women's shared identity as mothers may be traced back in Australian women's writing to Eliza Dunlop's poem on the Myall Creek massacre of 1838, 'The Aboriginal Mother', and forward to Catherine Martin's 1923 novel, *The Incredible Journey*. In the poem such an affirmation is implicit in the sentiments attributed to the Aboriginal woman, and Dunlop's strategy in representing her thus has been criticized as merely illustrating a 'European theme' of women's vulnerability; yet this criticism of the poem's 'authenticity' in representing an Aboriginal woman is not so very far removed from those of Dunlop's male contemporaries who chided her for giving an 'entirely false idea of [their idea of] the native character'. Both are somewhat beside the point, given that the poem is quite explicit in its polemical purpose of awakening sympathy for 'a people rendered desperate and revengeful by continued acts of outrage'.[15]

Almost a century later Catherine Martin published her novel, *The Incredible Journey,* with a similar purpose.[16] The wider significance of her story, she argued in her Introduction, is its 'peculiar ethical value', because when 'a wild woman of the lowliest race which has struggled to the rank of humanity' demonstrates such heroic and devoted love, 'it seems a pledge that Nature has some affinity with good as a development of her order' (p. 13). Here again is the classic ambivalence of colonial discourse, the simultaneous affirmation and disavowal of likeness, the construction of racial difference as absolute. As Margaret Allen argues in her Introduction to the new edition, Martin was challenging the contemporary view of Aborigines' lower natures by affirming that the womanly quality of maternal love transcends this racial difference. The evolutionary scale of race is left unquestioned, however. There are perhaps undertones here of a specifically feminist version of evolutionary theory, which contradicted the male view that women were less highly evolved than men by arguing that maternal love was highest on the scale of human feeling, the most altruistic.[17] In this respect, Martin's novel is closer to the late nineteenth-century works we have been considering here, even though it was not published until 1923, when the author was an elderly woman. Nevertheless, the evolutionary discourse on race persisted: it emerges clearly in Prichard's 1929 Introduction to *Coonardoo,* the text often cited as the great breakthrough in white representations of Aboriginality.

The emphasis on motherhood as constitutive of a shared femininity is less evident in women's writing of the earlier period which belongs to the colonial romance genre of exotic adventure in the outback. Far from being seen as actors on the contemporary scene of nation-making, Aborigines as constructed in these texts are doubly distanced from it: they appear in the romance genre favoured by women but scorned by male nationalist writers, and, within that genre, they appear as distant in place and time from the scene of contemporary writing. The setting of these texts is not so much the 'Bush' as it is constructed by male nationalist writers like Henry Lawson,[18] but that other place, the dream-country of writers like Rosa Praed and Jeannie Gunn, the 'Never-Never' land of the far North and West, or in the unspecified outback locations favoured by Barbara Baynton. It is a construction of an imaginary 'frontier' which has specific meanings in women's writing, most notably as an escape from daily domesticity and the straitjackets of middle-class patriarchal social exchange. Much later, Katherine Prichard's fiction set in the Kimberleys would show signs of this inheritance from earlier women's popular romantic writing.

In these remote settings, Aboriginal characters are usually presented as retaining some features of traditional tribal life, although they are already deprived of their traditional lands and living in camps on cattle stations (but not, as so many actually were in the south-east, on missions or in towns). This works to construct them as exotic for the fiction's readership – exotic and sometimes threatening, like the 'wild' or 'Myall' blacks that are a shadowy presence in the more romantic of these texts. That is to say, the Aboriginal characters are represented, with an ambivalence characteristic of colonial discourse, as an 'other' both familiar and menacing, in its difference, to the white subject of that discourse:[19] they are both fierce and childlike in their 'wildness', both barbaric and orderly (in terms of their own culture), both treacherous and loyal servants, and so on. Thus they are pitied for their imminent doom as a 'race', but also feared for the threat of their reprisals for land expropriated, women raped, children taken away and whole groups massacred by white settlers.

This fascination with the exotic gives rise to an interest in traditional mythology which emerges in the recounting of 'dreamtime stories' by white writers. The result is a kind of commodification of the myths – which we see still going on in relation to aboriginal art. Sacred tales are retold in such a way as they can be read as bedtime stories for white children (Kathleen Langloh Parker) or, more offensively, as occasions for derision at their 'primitive superstitions' (such as the references to 'debil-debils' and so on in *The Little Black Princess* by Jeannie Gunn). Traditional stories are exchanged between the Aboriginal women characters in *The Incredible Journey*, which at least grants them a fictional status akin to their original cultural purposes. In making these appropriations, women writers were taking part in a proto-anthropological tradition of observing Aboriginal culture which was already well established by white men, and by and large they shared in its racism as well as its ambivalent respect for cultural difference.

Within this tradition of observation, certain indices of difference earned no deference at all from white writers: these are Aboriginal social practices and laws, rather than myths and rituals, and are of special interest in relation to representations of sexuality and gender order. As Ross Gibson's study of early colonial writings shows, whites often expressed disapproval of the Aboriginals' sexual division of labour and also of arranged marriages between old men and young women, two practices which they regarded as especially barbaric. Their emphasis on the 'natural' degradation of these practices allowed, of course, the implication that the 'civilized' white race never oppressed women in comparable ways. Frequent objections to the power of tradition, as embodied in tribal elders, appear to be an expression of the progressivism with which they justified ideologically the widespread strategy of colonization by depriving the elders of their traditional authority.

The earlier male writers particularly deplored the 'despised and degraded' condition of Aboriginal women, even referring to them as 'slaves'.[20] In later women's texts, this chivalarous white perception of the ill-treatment of black women is used very differently to make the feminist point that all women are badly treated under patriarchal regimes. It is another instance of representing women as unified across cultural difference, like the 'wives and mothers' argument: for example, in Praed's *Policy and Passion* a woman character complains that white women are no better off than lubras, for 'we are sold like them', she says.[21]

The early commentators appear to have been fascinated by Aboriginal courting customs which they saw as 'a romantic ritual of dominance and surrender', entailing 'the seizure by physical violence of any woman whom a warrior desires for a mate'.[22] Gibson also notes that while they are happy to attribute such brutal lust to Aboriginal men, these male writers scarcely mention the indelicate subject of miscegenation. What they focus on instead is the romance of elopement in defiance of tribal law. In most colonial fictions where it is employed, this motif of the 'free marriage' brings disruption and violence in its wake. It is a useful plot device, therefore, which also incidentally functions to underline the alleged instability of Aboriginal tribal life. The writers' target, if specified, is usually the barbarity of Aboriginal custom, in particular its deference to the power of the old men. But the use of this device may also be read as a discursive displacement of the *historical* situation where a different kind of illicit union, that between white man and black woman, frequently caused disruption and violence.

In women's fiction the motif of young Aboriginal lovers eloping to evade tribal-law marriage is also very popular, but its use brings into play different attitudes from those of the male writers. In Rosa Praed's *Lady Bridget in the Never-Never Land*, such an elopement proves to be the testing point of the heroine's marriage, as liberal-minded wife and Black-despising husband have a battle of wills over whether to assist the runaway couple, a young man who works on the station and a 'half-caste' girl married to an older man. One literary critic even reads this motif as central to the narrative, as the occasion of the white couple's marital discord[23] (although there is also 'another man' on the scene to provide the classic opposition between Australian and English lovers). After she has left him, Lady Bridget's distraught station-owner husband is finally forced to wish:

> If only he had yielded to her then about the Blacks! If he had curbed his anger, shown sympathy with the two wild children of Nature who were better than himself, in this at least that they had known how to love and cling to each other in spite of the blows of fate! ... That he should have lost Bridget because of the loves of Wombo and Oola! It was an irony – as if God were laughing at him.[24]

There is a marked contradiction here between the romantic 'wild children of nature' image, and the denigration implied in the final words. The affinity of the black and the white lovers is momentary, and an occasion for irony on the man's part.

In Praed's novel, then, this motif of elopement (which really acquires the status of a fable in colonial fiction) is linked with the romantic critique of arranged marriages as a male exchange of women's bodies. As an aspect of the exotic imaginary frontier, it is incorporated into a Romantic discourse on nature and passion as opposed to social constraints and duties, where the runaway Aboriginal couple function as an image of the white woman's desired freedom.[25] In this respect, it could be argued that the woman novelist, while complicit in covering up the theme of miscegenation in colonial society, is also expressing resistance to the patriarchal denial of her personal and sexual autonomy. It is this patriarchal construction of femininity which also casts Aboriginal men in the role of sexual threat and Aboriginal women in the role of sexual rivals for white women. Insisting on sympathy with the Aboriginal *couple* against the forces of the Law, a woman writer may be read as subverting this aspect of patriarchal ideology. That is, the fable of the runaway marriage in colonial fiction can be *read* differently when women use it.

Rosa Praed's *Fugitive Anne* (1902) presents interesting variations on the theme of escape, and an ambivalent challenge to the construction of the black man as sexual threat. The heroine runs away from her brutal husband with the help of an Aboriginal man, once her childhood playmate, now her servant. Rejoicing in her new-found freedom in a manner reminiscent of North American 'wilderness narratives' but rare for a female protagonist,[26] she writes in her notebook: 'Better death in the wild woods than life in chains' and 'Anne Marley hails Nature, the emancipator!'[27] There is a 'strange affinity' (p. 34) between her and Kombo [sic], as together they become outlaws from both the white community (represented by her pursuing husband) and the local Aboriginal tribes who are Kombo's traditional enemies.

But the tensions of race class and sexual difference in this relationship are exacerbated by the discovery that the settler friends to whom Anne was fleeing have been killed by blacks. This incident recalls the Hornet Bank killings, as described in Praed's memoirs of her youth in outback Queensland, when a neighbouring family was killed by Aborigines in a reprisal raid. In that text there is a noticeable conflict between her horrified reporting of white men's tales of black treachery and violence and her appreciative accounts of childhood experience with Aboriginal women and children.[28] Arguing from this autobiographical material that *Fugitive Anne* is structured by the 'fantasy element of [Praed's] connection with the Aborigines', Healy makes much of Anne's sexual vulnerability and the sexual fear he attributes to Praed;[29] but this reading ignores the novel's freedom fantasy, and ultimately contributes to the patriarchal myth of white women's sexual fear of Aboriginal men, which has so often been used to justify white men's violence against the colonized and the subordination of 'their' women.

What is one to make of Praed's choice of a name, Kombo, which colloquially refers to sexual relations between black women and white men ('going combo')? In the novel, Kombo is principally cast in the role of the good servant, guardian and, indeed, devotee (for Anne is regarded as a kind of goddess, and demonstrates her powers when necessary by bursting into song with the 'Ave Maria' or 'God Save the Queen'!). The major narrative tension is between this role and the text's racial discourse, which repeatedly swings between affirmations of affinity and denigrations of the 'barbaric' Aboriginal. Evolutionist ideas enter the realm of the truly fantastic when Anne and Kombo find themselves in a 'lost civilization' of South American (Mayan) descent, and comparisons are drawn denigrating the more 'primitive' Australian blacks in favour of these 'red men'. It is, significantly, in relation to this more 'civilized' race that the problem of Anne's sexuality is played out: now that there is a suitable European hero on the scene, she becomes jealous of his sexual interest in the Mayan high priestess; but her 'childlike and feminine' expression of this jealousy arouses the hero, who is already turned off by the priestess's lack of 'womanly weakness and its consequent charm' (pp. 373, 363). It is a neatly negotiated vindication of feminine sexuality in the approved late Victorian mode: refined, responsive, more 'evolved'.

Moving away from the genre of outback adventure, we find in Barbara Baynton's *Human Toll* (1907) a strange colonial version of the novel of female development. Here the problematic nature of feminine sexuality is played out in the conflict between the somewhat autistic heroine, Ursula, and her sexually aggressive 'other', Mina. The Aboriginal couple who fill the conventional role of 'good servants' attempt to protect Ursula from Mina's victimization and to help her protect Mina's child from abuse, just as they alone had attempted to protect Ursula as a child. 'There is no colour line in love', comments the narrator.[30] Yet it is their love for the helpless child and their near-helpless mistress that is invoked here: the 'colour line' in sexual love remains a taboo subject in this colonial text.

Katherine Prichard's celebrated broaching of this taboo, in *Coonardoo* (1929), effectively writes the white woman out of the script: Hugh's wife is a stereotyped frivolous and sexually repressive white woman. More to the point, it is his mother who trains Coonardoo as a household servant 'for him', as it were. Her role may be read as contributing to the Aboriginal woman's ultimate destruction as the prized object over which the two white men, Hugh and Geary, fight. The insoluble problem of individual love between black and white is played out in terms of male desire only. Despite her central role in this novel, Coonardoo comes to symbolize the silence and paralysis of will which is the usual fate of the black woman in colonial fiction[31] – her presence in the text is signified by images of shadows, and by her habitual murmur of assent, 'Eeh-mm'.[32]

The Incredible Journey is the only colonial woman's text of this period that I can find in which the Aboriginal woman is central to the narrative and is constructed as a subject in her own right. The story of Iliapa's journey across the desert to reclaim her son, abducted by a ruthless and powerful white man, is structured as a quest in which she undergoes physical and spiritual trials, and in which she is helped or hindered by a variety of other people. Foremost among these is Polde, the woman friend who accompanies her and whose characterisation is a foil to hers. The relationship between them is represented as central and sustaining. As Margaret Allen points out in her Introduction, this novel is extraordinary in placing Aboriginal characters at the centre of the novel and encouraging readers to 'identify' with them – but I think it could be added that the centrality of *women* characters is even more significant in the history of discursive representations of Aborigines.

Their relations with other women are also harmonious and supportive. The squatter's wife and daughters help them on their way with transport, food, and new dresses that they quickly 'run up' on the sewing machine; it is made clear that this relationship is based upon reciprocity, on the wife's gratitude to Iliapa's father for finding her children when they were lost in the bush. The tribal women whom they meet while crossing the desert help them escape from the men of their tribe, who are determined to kill the two travellers in reprisal for their disturbing some male ritual objects – there is a suggestion here of female bonding against male power.

This is one of several incidents in the novel where tribal laws are broken, and which suggest the disruption caused to traditional culture by white invasion and settlement. While it is an accident which makes Iliapa's husband believe that he has broken tribal law, the women involved in similar transgressions of the law act deliberately. In the incident from which the action of the novel springs, Iliapa's aunt sends a message to her designated husband-to-be, purporting to be from the girl's father, breaking the agreement – an action apparently motivated by the aunt's desire to wield power. Polde's interference with the sacred objects is said to be done out of ignorance, because she had not been brought up to believe the things that Iliapa had been taught (p. 92). There is a suggestion here that the women are avenging their exclusion from male power and ritual. Martin seems, on the evidence of this novel, to have respected the strength and centrality of Aboriginal people's beliefs but to have harboured hopes that they would 'modernise' in adaptation to white culture.

The characterisation of Iliapa is worth commenting on in this connection. She is knowledgeable about and respectful of traditional law, but she is also said to have some characteristics like the whites – the capacity to work hard and with concentration in her duties as a housemaid (which Polde definitely lacks, pp. 46-7), and she 'had learned to think of the future', like white people (p. 74). Similarly her husband is said to have almost an 'individual conscience', unlike the tribal sense of right and wrong (p. 30). Yet in the final scenes of the novel, when the man who has abducted her son tries to trick them out of claiming him back, it is Polde who resists him and gathers support from other whites by her loud denunciations – the more 'Aboriginal' of the two women (that is, the less assimilated or adapted) is better able to defend herself against their white enemy. Still, the final card in Polde's triumphant denunciation of the man is to invoke the aid of Queen Victoria who (so she has learned from the station children) is 'the bestest little queen of England and of the Blacks' (p. 78, p. 155). Martin's vision of race reconciliation veers perilously close to the comic, yet the final scene of family reconciliation returns the novel to the heroic mode.

When the present Queen of England opened the new Parliament House in Canberra recently (May 1988), there was a large and vocal demonstration by Aborigines outside the building. Needless to say, they were not appealing for regal protection but stating their political presence. Their shouts could be heard behind the mild and modulated broadcast commentary which, absurdly, refused to acknowledge their presence. When the demarcation line between inside and outside was again broached by a small girl dressed in the colours of the Aboriginal Land rights movement stepping out of the crowd to present a bouquet to the Queen, the air of parody created by this intervention was complete.

In Australia in 1988 Aborigines are very much in evidence as actors on the contemporary scene. From all over the continent they converged on Sydney to march on Invasion Day, January 26 (otherwise known as 'birthday of a nation') – no 'poor remnants of a dying race', but a strong movement of all those who claim kin as Aborigines, based on the Land Rights campaign but sinking its internal differences and spreading wider.

Is Australian culture still colonial, then? There are clear signs at last that the hegemonic culture's certainties about race difference are being challenged. The discourses on Aboriginality now available include, most significantly, that of a political identity as Aboriginal which is claimed by growing numbers, a discourse on survival and independence. The politics of Land Rights appear at last to have forced talks about a treaty on land ownership. Affirmations of this kind make it possible to *see* that assertions of unity by the hegemonic culture, in contrast, are always made at the expense of the excluded 'others' – Aborigines in particular, but other cultural groups, more recently migrated than the Anglo-Celtic majority, as well.

Aboriginal women are now speaking for themselves, and affirming that their primary commitment is to their people's movement. If an appeal to women's unity is at all possible today, it must be made in recognition of this primary commitment. It cannot be, like Louisa Lawson's call to recognise 'wives and mothers like ourselves', based on a limited definition of 'women', but must include all aspects of womanhood, and recognise that 'we' are both like and unlike each other. It must be an appeal for a politics of affinity in particular women's struggles, not a claim to sameness, identity. A recognition of difference is as politically important today as the recognition of likeness was in 1897: difference, that is, as embodying a history that is autonomous yet contingent with our own, as white women. Patriarchal definitions of women's difference as a failure to be the same as men are paralleled by racist definitions of the difference of colonized peoples as a failure to be the same as the colonizers. But it is not the same structure of oppression, not the same experience: Aboriginal women are teaching us this, above all.

Let one of their number have the last word here, at least. Speaking of the Aboriginal movement, Bobbi Sykes uses the female metaphor of pregnancy and birth afresh:

We do not always talk
of our pregnancy
for we are pregnant
with the thrust of freedom;
And our freedom looks to others
As a threat.[33]

NOTES

1. Aboriginal occupation and ownership of the land was not recognised in law, which regarded the land as *terra nullius*, belonging to no-one. See Henry Reynolds, *The Law of the Land* (Ringwood, Victoria: Penguin, 1988).
2. This analysis of the discursive operation of racial difference derives from Edward Said, *Orientalism* (New York: Random House, 1978) and from Homi Bhabha, 'The Other Question', *Screen*, 24, 6 (1983), pp. 18-36), and 'Of Mimicry and Man: the Ambivalence of Colonial Discourse', *October*, no. 28 (Spring 1984), pp. 125-33.
3. Susan Sheridan, '"Temper, Romantic; Bias, Offensively Feminine": Australian Women Writers and Literary Nationalism' in Kirsten Holst Petersen and Anna Rutherford, eds, *A Double Colonization: Colonial and Post-Colonial Women's Writing* (Mundelstrup, Denmark: Dangaroo Press, 1986), pp. 49-58.
4. cf. Susan Gardner, 'A "'Vert to Australianism": Beatrice Grimshaw and the Bicentenary', *Hecate* 13,2 (1987/8), pp. 31-68, p. 51.
5. Stephen Muecke, 'Available Discourses on Aborigines in Peter Botsman, ed, *Theoretical Strategies* (Sydney: Local Consumption Publications, 1982), pp. 98-111.
6. 'A Word for the Blacks', *The Dawn*, November 1, 1987, p. 1.
7. C.D. Rowley, *The Destruction Of Aboriginal Society*, vol. 1 (Canberra: A.N.U. Press, 1970), p. 1; see also Raymond Evans, 'Keeping Australia Clean White' in Verity Burgmann and Jenny Lee, eds, *A Most Valuable Acquisition* (Melbourne: McPhee Gribble/Penguin, 1988), pp. 170-88, p. 172.
8. Various documents cited in Jean Woolmington, *Aborigines in Colonial Society 1788-1850* (North Melbourne: Cassell, 1973) and Ross Gibson, *The Diminishing Paradise: Changing Literary Perceptions of Australia* (Sydney: Angus & Robertson, 1984). Henry Reynolds comments that with 'scientific racism' came the loss of even the Christian belief in the 'brotherhood of man': *Frontier: Aborigines, Settlers and Land* (Sydney: Allen & Unwin, 1987), p. 128-9.
9. Gillian Cowlishaw, 'Australian Aboriginal Studies: the Anthropologists' Accounts' in Marie de Lepervanche and Gillian Bottomley, eds, *The Cultural Construction of Race* (Sydney: Sydney Studies in Society and Culture no 4, 1988), pp. 60-79.
10. ibid., p. 64.
11. Marilyn Lake, 'The Politics of Respectability', *Historical Studies*, 22, 86 (1986), pp. 116-31.

12. See for example Claudia Knapman, *White Women in Fiji 1835-1930* (Sydney: Angus & Robertson, 1986), pp. 170-72.
13. Lake, op.cit., and Judith Allen, 'Rose Scott's Vision: Feminism and Masculinity 1880-1925' in Barbara Caine et al., eds, *Crossing Boundaries: Feminisms and the Critique of Knowledges* (Sydney: Allen & Unwin, 1988), pp. 157-66.
14. Louisa Lawson, *The Lonely Crossing* (privately published, c. 1900); on Martin, see Margaret Allen, 'Catherine Martin, Writer: Her Life and Ideas', *Australian Literary Studies,* 13, 2 (1987), pp. 184-97.
15. As the poet explained it later: see Elizabeth West, 'White women in Colonial Australia', *Refractory Girl* nos. 13/14 (1977), pp. 54-60, p. 58. Dunlop's poem is cited at length in Elizabeth Webby, 'The Aboriginal in Early Australian Literature', *Southerly,* no. 40 (1980), pp. 45-63.
16. First published 1923. Page references in the text are to *The Incredible Journey* (London: Pandora, 1987).
17. This commonplace of late nineteenth-century feminism may have derived its evolutionary credentials from the biologists, Geddes and Thomson, who argued that female energies previously allocated to reproduction would now be placed at the disposal of society, which would gain from the predominance of feminine altruistic feelings over the more primitive masculine egoism; see Jill Conway, 'Stereotypes of Femininity in a Theory of Sexual Evolution' in Martha Vicinus, ed, *Suffer and Be Still: Women in the Victorian Age* (Bloomington: Indiana University Press, 1973), pp. 140-54, p. 145.
18. Lawson told Mary Gilmore that he wouldn't risk ridicule by writing about Blacks, so she reported in a letter to R.H. Croll, 28 December 1946, in *Letters,* selected and edited by W. Wilde (Carlton: Melbourne University Press, 1980), p. 219.
19. Bhabha, 'The Other Question', op.cit.
20. Gibson, op.cit., pp. 187-8; they were, of course frequently enslaved by white men: see Reynolds, *Frontier,* pp. 73-4.
21. Rosa Praed, *Policy and Passion* (London: Bentley, 1881), p. 34.
22. Gibson, op.cit., p. 185.
23. J.J. Healy, *Literature and the Aborigine in Australia* (St Lucia: University of Queensland Press, 1978), pp. 69-70.
24. Rosa Praed, *Lady Bridget in the Never-Never Land* [1915] (London: Pandora, 1987), p. 285.
25. Later women writers construct the Aboriginal woman as symbol of the sexual desire denied to white women in patriarchal culture: see Susan Sheridan, 'Women Writers' in Laurie Hergenhan, ed. *A New Literary History of Australia* (Ringwood: Penguin, 1988).
28. On women in captivity-and wilderness-narratives, see Annette Kolodny, 'Turning the Lens on "The Panther Captivity": a Feminist Exercise in Practical Criticism', *Critical Inquiry,* 8, 2 (1981), pp. 329-345).
27. Rosa Praed, *Fugitive Anne* (London: John Long, 1902), p. 31; page references in text to this edition.
28. Rosa Praed, *My Australian Girlhood* (London: Fisher Unwin, 1902), p. 4 et passim.

29. Healy, op. cit., p. 66-8.

30. Barbara Baynton, *Human Toll* [1907] repr. in Sally Krimmer and Alan Lawson, eds, *The Portable Barbara Baynton* (St Lucia: University of Queensland Press, 1980), p. 217.

31. Abena P.A. Busia, 'Miscegenation as metonymy; sexuality and power in the colonial novel', *Ethnic and Racial Studies*, 9, 3 (1986), pp. 360-72; on the role of the 'native servant' in white women's novels of female autonomy, see Gayatri Spivak, 'Three Women's Texts and a Critique of Imperialism', *Critical Inquiry*, 13, 1 (1986), pp. 243-61, pp. 253-4.

32. Sue Thomas, 'Interracial Encounters in Katherine Susannah Prichard's *Coonardoo*', *World Literature Written in English*, 27, 2 (1987), pp. 234-44, p. 242.

33. From 'Cycle' in Kevin Gilbert, ed, *Inside Black Australia* (Ringwood: Penguin, 1988), p. 38.

Sally Morgan

A Fundamental Question of Identity

AN INTERVIEW WITH SALLY MORGAN

INTRODUCTION

My Place[1] is an extraordinary, moving family autobiography in which the author, Sally Morgan, describes her attempt to trace her family origins. She tells of her childhood, drawing warm, humorous and engaging images of her mother and grandmother in particular, and describes her dawning realisation, in her teen years, that her family was different and that she knew very little about their history.

So she set out to gather some information. Initially she met strong resistance from her family, which only strengthened her curiosity and resolve, and as she began to discover the facts, ever so slowly, her anger was roused at the enormity of the injustices buried in the history of this country. 'It could all have been done differently', Sally points out 'Aboriginal people didn't have to be treated that way'.

In 1982 Sally Morgan travelled back to her grandmother's birthplace. What had started out as a tentative search turned into an overwhelming spiritual and emotional pilgrimage as Sally and her family were confronted with their own suppressed history and fundamental questions about their identity.

Sally Morgan's whole family (and her husband, Paul) was gradually drawn into her search for truth, and finally her grandmother and mother were able to tell their own stories, which are incorporated into *My Place*, but not without enormous pain for all concerned. Sally says at one point in the book:

> I wanted to cry. I hated myself when I got like that. I never cried, and yet since all this had been going on, I'd wanted to cry often ... it was absurd. There was so much about myself that I didn't understand.

For Sally's grandmother, talk of the past was especially painful. Sally's mother, however, eventually became very involved in the writing of *My*

Place. In fact, Sally talks about it as 'our book'. It's a true family autobiography.

Sally Morgan is also establishing a reputation as an artist. She has works in numerous collections, including the Dobell Foundation and the Australian National Gallery in Canberra.

Nancy Keesing has said of the book: '*My Place* is as compelling and as impossible to put down as a detective story, but unlike that genre, it is deeply informed with life and truth'.

What follows is a record of several conversations that Mary Wright has had with Sally Morgan and Sally's mother Gladys.

Your book tells us that you started to write it when you began to question your origins.

S: Yes, that's true. My first motivation was anger – I get very angry at injustice, and I thought, 'Somebody should put this down, people should know about these things'.

So it wasn't so much to simply explore your family history and discover where you came from, although that was linked to it, but more to provide a record?

S: Yes, because we had been deprived of that crucial knowledge as children, and I didn't want my own children to be deprived. I felt that it was a record for them and if no-one else read it, it kind of didn't matter. Remember how you came round one night, Mum, and I said I'm going to write a book and you laughed?

G: Well, you're always going to do something. I just treated it as a joke at first.

S: I always have big ideas, but I never deliver. But then when I did....

G: She was like a terrier.

S: I wouldn't normally be like that except that it was really important to me.

Gladys, it was hard for you when Sally was writing the book wasn't it?

G: I think the problem was that as a child I'd been made to feel so ashamed.

S: It was very hard. We would either be getting on, or we wouldn't be talking to each other. She'd say, 'I've had it, that's it, no more, Sally, no more. You want to keep bringing up the past'. And I'd get angry with her because I'd think she was covering up something. See, Mum hadn't talked about her background much, and when she did finally start talking it was very upsetting for her. She had a lot of emotions that she hadn't worked through.

G: I think it was really important to me, and I didn't realise it at first. I got rid of such a lot of things I had buried there.

Yes, there was a real sense of pull and tug for you. Part of you wanted to help Sally, and part of you just couldn't face it.

S: That's exactly how it was. Whereas with my grandmother it was just like a brick wall. So I was really lucky I think that before she died she told me *anything*.

Because there are still some things she didn't tell you.

S: Oh, that's right, and I think, 'Oh, why didn't you tell me everything', but really, considering her life, I think I was very lucky to get what I did. I think it was probably only that my grandmother was diagnosed as being terminally ill that started making her think that perhaps she could say something. Also, I started reading her extracts from the stories my Uncle Arthur had given me, but not telling her who it was about, just that it was a man I knew. She thought it was fantastic, and she would laugh and cry, and when I told her it was her own brother's story, she got very jealous, and then she'd say, 'Well, I've got a better story than that', and I'd say, 'Well, you're no good because you won't talk. For all we know you might have a silly story'. Eventually she came round, and then it became important to her to tell. I think it became important to her because she wanted to feel she had achieved something outside her family setting. Once she decided to tell her story, she became more persistent than me. It gave her a sense that she had a value as a human being; she had something to say that other people might find meaningful.

You started to write the book while you were still asking questions; you were still chasing facts, the process of which was later written into the book.

S: Yes, it was totally incomplete, and of course I was having trouble getting information. Mum and Nan and my brothers and sisters found it very upsetting, and they'd say 'Just leave it alone'. And I'd think, 'Should I? Should I leave it alone?', and I would think 'Oh, it's not worth it'; and then I'd think 'Yes, it *is* worth it', so it was a real kind of mixed-up thing.

There were points when I was reading it when I'd think, 'I'd have given up by now if I were Sally', and then you'd say 'I felt I had to have one more go at Nan', and you'd go back and tackle her about something in her past. And I'd take a deep breath and think 'Can I stand it?' because of the pain I knew you were chipping away at.

S: Yes, it was terrible. We used to cry a lot. By the time Mum got involved, she was crying all the time, I was crying all the time; Paul'd come home and there'd be no dinner, and he'd say, 'Fish and chips again tonight?' and I'd say, 'Yeah', and he'd say, 'Had a bad day?' and I'd say 'Yes', and cry some more.

In the book you describe how as a kid, you really didn't question your mother's and grandmother's lives. You didn't have a sense of their lives beyond your house in Manning.

S: No, nothing at all. Total ignorance – and innocence I guess. I think my sister did, but she didn't talk to me about it. She was much more socially mature than me, and so she was always more aware of things like that.

So there weren't any stories about what you mother or grandmother had done in their youths?

S: Well, we knew Nan had worked for a particular family, but we didn't have a context. We just thought, 'Everyone has a job, that must have been her job'. We didn't understand the social circumstances of her life. As we got older and started to see the effects of her life – she was quite bitter, and afraid of authority, for example – we began to wonder why she was like that.

It wasn't until you were at school and other kids started to ask you where you were from that you questioned your origins.

S: That's right, and even then I didn't realise why they asked me. I thought I was like everyone else, and everyone else thought I wasn't! When I asked Mum she was shocked at first, and when I explained the kids at school were asking, she said, 'Tell them you're Indian', and I thought that sounded really exotic. the kids could accept that – they just didn't want me pretending I was Australian when I wasn't!

That little white lie...

S: Yes! I first started to question seriously what my origins were when I came home from school and found my grandmother crying, which was extremely unusual for her, because she tended to suppress that sort of emotion. I asked her what was wrong, and she said, 'I'm crying because you children want a white grandmother, and I'm black'. I looked at her and realised she was black, and all these years I'd thought she was white! Oh dear!

How do you both feel, now that the book is a reality?

S: Nervous. Embarrassed.

Embarrassed?

G: I feel sick. I feel like my whole life's paraded before everybody.

S: Actually, I don't feel embarrassed so much – what do I feel? I'm worried that all of a sudden people will think, 'This woman's an expert on Aboriginal affairs', and they'll ask me questions and expect me to have an answer, when I don't, I'm just an ordinary person.

G: What I've always hated is people feeling sorry for me, and I would hate that to happen, because when I think of it, I've really had a fantastic life. I've got so many memories. I've managed just lately to be able to talk about where I was brought up; up until now I haven't been able to, so it's good.

S: A lot of good's come out of the bad.

Nancy Keesing likens the book to a detective story. It seemed to throw up more questions than it answered.

S: Yes, there are still lots of things unanswered, I think we really only touched the tip of my grandmother's life. I think she probably had a quite dreadful life, but we can only guess, just by the effects it had on her. And there were broader questions of racism and Government policy ... there was a real snob thing in those days, there were the upper, middle and lower classes, and then there were the natives. But I tried to be generous to the family who controlled my grandmother's life.

Yes, you can see that in the book, but they hang themselves, anyway.

S: They do, don't they?

And to give them their due, they probably thought they were doing the right thing by your grandmother.

S: Oh, yes, but I don't think my grandmother ever felt grateful to them! And since I've written this, I've met so many older Aboriginal people who've just had terrible lives. A lot of them won't talk about it. They're frightened that if they tell the truth they'll incite young Aboriginal people to violence, you see.

In 1982 you made a trip back north to your grandmother's birthplace. That was obviously crucial.

S: Yes, now we go up every year. I don't think we realised how important it was until we actually did it. I knew I wanted to go up North, but I didn't know why – it was just an instinct. We thought everyone would be dead, and no-one would remember our family because it was too long ago. We felt stupid going up to strange people and saying, 'Did you know my grandmother?' We just went up on spec, and we were all uptight and nervous.

Gladys, you weren't sure whether you wanted to go, were you?

G: No well, I just wanted to take a metal detector up there (she laughs).

S: I think Mum felt to start off with, like me, that it was a waste of time and money and potentially it was, we could have gone up there and found nothing. But it all worked out, though, didn't it. We kept bumping into people.

Who then said you must see so and so...

S: Yes, and we really found out much more than we expected to. And now each year when we go back we find out more, don't we?

G: Yes, because they think about it and they wait for us to come back so they can tell us something else they've remembered. It's a funny feeling – I suppose it's like when people go into monasteries or to health farms to get renewed. Well I find that when I go up there, I get spiritually renewed. It's a belonging, and you just feel part of everything that's there.

The land – physically, the land?

G: Yes, everything, the people, the land...

S: We always get very emotional – Paul always complains and says, 'Oh, these aren't holidays'. (She laughs).

Paul was obviously very supportive.

S: Yes, I think he used to get as upset as we did, sometimes.

G: He did, didn't he? He'd get really sad.

S: No, he was fantastic. I probably couldn't have done it without him, because it was so emotionally draining that most guys would have just found it too much.

G: No, he was fantastic. Poor Paul, with all these women!

Speaking of women, it really seems that the women in you family...

S: are domineering?

They figure more, and they figure more in terms of caring about your project.

S: My brothers found it too hard to cope with. it wasn't that they weren't supportive, but they just couldn't cope with the emotion.

G: It's a bit of an Aboriginal trait, because when you look at any family, there's always the mother and grandmother there.

S: It's a matriarchal society, and also, from what we can see going back, all the women in our family have been strong characters in different ways. I mean, I know I'm domineering! And Mum is in her way, too. That's probably why we conflict sometimes. People complain about me and say 'Oh, you're such a strong person, Sally', but I mean, look what I grew up with!

Some of the warmest bits of the book for me were stories of Gladys interacting with her mother ... two very strong figures interacting. And you grandmother comes through as being a wonderful character.

S: She was a very strong person.

G: (laughter) She *was* strong.

S: (laughs, too) She was great. She had the most weird sense of humour but she'd been really badly damaged, and I'd love to have seen what she would have been like if she hadn't had those experiences, I think she would have been quite a girl, don't you?

G: Yes, because I mean the book doesn't tell half of it.

S: She could mimic people, and she had an extremely sarcastic sense of humour. She'd mimic Mum, and make her so angry sometimes, but she'd also make you laugh.

G: She always had the ability to make me laugh when I was angry, and I used to get so upset with myself for letting her do it.

S: It's amazing, really, that she retained so much of her humour; perhaps it helped her to survive.

But do you think that's a feature of Aboriginal people, to retain that humour? I mean, to me My Place *is humorous in the same way that, say* The Dreamers *or* No Sugar *are humorous, that in the direst of situations Aboriginal people can laugh, and laugh at the position they find themselves...*

S: Oh, yes.

Which, I think, might have caused problems for non-Aboriginal people who saw The Dreamers, *who didn't want to laugh because they were afraid of being racist; they couldn't appreciate that Aboriginal humour is really unique?*

S: Yes, I can understand that ... when we go up north they'll tell the most horrifying stories, and then they'll crack a joke. One of our grandfathers up north tells a story about how when he was a kid he was sold. The station owner sold him to the butcher for ten shillings because he was strong – and then he'll burst out laughing and say, 'But that's all I was worth then'. It's funny to him that someone paid ten shillings for him, but underneath there's the pain.

G: I was just thinking the other day about the time I was going to do my will, and Nanna was furious because I never left her anything.

S: And we tried to explain to her that she'd be dead before Mum, but it wasn't the point, the point was that Mum should have left her something.

G: I had to end up leaving her something to shut her up. She was really hurt, crying and carrying on, saying 'To think, my own daughter...'

As I say, she comes across as a wonderful, wonderful person.

S: That's good, because Mum read through the book the other night, and she was worried that my grandmother had come across as being too bitter.

For me she was more ironic and afraid, and remarkably non-bitter for her experiences.

G: I think I felt that now she's died, I think of all the good times; I think about things and I laugh ... so when I read the book I was surprised. I hadn't read it for a couple of years.

Why did you take the book to Fremantle Arts Centre Press?

S: Ken Kelso knew I was writing it, and he suggested I take it down, so I took about half a dozen chapters, and Ray Coffey really loved it, and from then on, every time I finished a section I'd send it down, and we ended up with a whacking great manuscript that was miles too long...

G: And you had all the photos, too...

Yes, I was going to ask about the photos. There was a conscious decision made, wasn't there, not to include photos, because it would then assume the mantle of some kind of social historical reference, when really it wasn't, it was an extension of the Aboriginal story-telling tradition?

S: Yes, I'd prefer it was read like that.

Can we talk about your painting? You drew as a kid.

S: Yes, I used to draw a lot, and then I gave it up after a negative experience with my art teacher, and Mum had always wanted us to grow up to do something really super, like be a doctor, and I think in those days Mum was realistic enough to see that to earn a living as an artist you'd have to be exceptionally good.

G: No it wasn't that, I was worried about you going to Paris, you wanted to go.

S: That's right, I did ... at that stage she didn't want any of us to grow up, you see! She's over that now, she's prefer it if I went somewhere else.

G: I feel like sending her somewhere, sometimes!

S: And then on one of my trips up North I went out to visit an old relative of ours who lives out on the edge of the desert. he's the local artist, and he showed me some of his drawings, and I thought 'Well, mine can't be so bad', because a lot of his stuff was similar to what I did, so I thought that if he could do his, I could do mine! So I came back and started again. But I really had a mental block about it, I really had to force myself to put something on paper. And then I bought a packet of those magic textas, you can change the colours, it was fun, and then Paul said, 'How unprofessional, you should be painting, not doing magic texta drawings, so he bought me some paints ... borrowed some money from you, didn't he? So Mum financed my first painting. That was only last November.

Six months ago!

Yes, six months ago I started painting.

And you had some work in the Birukmarri Gallery in Fremantle?

S: Yes, and I sold all of that, and then some people in Sydney asked me to put some work in an exhibition, and the Dobell Foundation bought some of that, and now I've got a Sydney commission.

Were you drawing on your Aboriginality, albeit unconsciously, as a child for your art? How was your work different?

S: It was very flat. I couldn't draw a three-dimensional picture if I tried. I never felt the need to put in any horizon lines; I've always used really lairy colours; I've always liked patterns; I've always drawn animals, with little borders, and those things I saw in my Uncle Solomon's drawings. So I think I was probably drawing on it, but was totally unaware of it.

The painting on the cover of the book was done especially for the book, wasn't it?

S: Yes, it was originally a drawing. And so in sic months the response to my work has been really overwhelming. I've got lots of orders and not enough time.

And you're working on another book at the moment?

S: Yes, I'm doing a biography on one of my grandfathers, with a grant from the Bicentennial Authority. And then I'd like to do two anthologies, one on stories about people being taken away, and another one on citizenship – the whole irony of the first Australians having to apply for Citizenship.

G: But then they saw the humour in that, too. There are so many funny stories.

S: They used to call it a dog licence.

G: And they weren't allowed to talk to anyone who was black.

S: I tend to get that material from my work around the Pilbara, but it would be good to get stories from the south-west and the goldfields. People were taken away from all over the place.

G: I think the thing is though that the people up north are related to us, and they'll talk. But if we went down south or to the Kimberleys...

S: Probably they wouldn't trust us. They wouldn't know how we fitted into the system. They've got to trust you before they'll tell you a story – especially when you're asking them for something that's painful. Which is fair enough.

I've collected stories from two old ladies I know; they know it's for a book, and they were quite happy to tell, but they're two extremely sad stories, one is absolutely horrific, but they wanted...

G: They wanted it known. Because they've got old now.

S: They want people to know what happened to them. But two isn't enough!

So you enjoy writing?

S: Yes, it's really hard work. I enjoy painting much more. Writing involves striving for words which is difficult, and it needs research in the Battye Library, and it means being really involved with people, which can be so heartbreaking.

G: It's like when we went down to the school to talk.

S: Oh it's really embarrassing. We went to give a talk at a girls' school, and we were sitting out the front – they had to give us chairs because we both had diarrhoea, because we were so nervous, so I said, 'You'll have to give us chairs because we won't be able to stand up, we're too weak', and I went first, and started to tell some history and some stories, and it was very sad, and Mum got all upset, so when it came to her turn, she started telling about a sad memory from her childhood and she burst into tears and just sobbed in front of all these teenagers, and all the girls were crying ... we've never given a talk since (laughter).

Do you see a relationship between your art and your writing?

S: There's a connection in that in both of them I use dreams a lot as part of the creative process. There's a spiritual side to my writing that I find I can't get away from, and that's true of my art. I'm also interested in not just writing oral histories, but painting oral histories, doing the same thing in a different form.

Like the cover of the book. You're both very spiritual, aren't you?

S: Yeah, I guess...

G: We have dreams all the time. I've had that all my life. I said to Sally, 'We won't put all those things in, people will just think we're a bit weird'.

S: Nan had dreams, too, but she wasn't as open about it, Arthur was more open.

Is there a relationship between the spirituality of your heritage, if you like, and your Christian beliefs?

S: I think one can enhance the other. I have many relations who wouldn't have the same beliefs as me, and would probably disagree with my religious beliefs, but they still have that Aboriginal spirituality, which I just think comes as part of that culture and as part of that inheritance. Having that in you tends to make you sensitive to other forms of spirituality, whether it comes in Christian terms or any other. You understand other people's religious beliefs quite easily. I think Nan had always been made to feel that anything that was Aboriginal was bad, and ...

G: That's the reason she wasn't allowed to use her own language. It was so wrong ... yes, she had lots of visions and things, but it was just kept in the family. To us it's very natural. I hope it's never lost, because you feel like you're at one with everything.

It was extraordinary that your grandmother didn't use her language, yet she remembered it.

S: Yes, I was totally shocked when I heard her talking. She was actually fluent; I suspect that she might have used it in her head.

But if that's the case, what an extraordinary double life.

S: Yeah, that's right. Makes you think that she was really quite a bright lady.

G: Oh, she was. She could put it over me all the time! (laughter).

Gladys, speaking of double lives, you were concerned about how your family was perceived, weren't you? There was a facade...

S: Mum always wanted to do well socially, didn't you? To do things the right way? Because Nan was very proper.

G: I think the whole thing was that as a kid I was in a very formal atmosphere, and some of that carried over. I was always worried people would find out I was an Aboriginal.

S: I think she thought they'd look down on her. Whereas now everyone in Australia will know. (laughter)

G: I was very scared of authority. I was always scared I might have the children taken away. That would have destroyed me.

So that law (that children fathered by white men couldn't be looked after by their Aboriginal mothers) still operated? In suburban Perth of the sixties?

G: They'd only need some small thing. I was always frightened to bring any attention to us. I always kept a low profile. If the kids had gone, they probably would all have been taken to separate places.

S: And my grandmother would have just died.

G: Oh, well, yes, she would have died. She'd just have had a broken heart.

S: I've met people who were taken away in the sixties. It wasn't enforced as rigorously as it used to be, but it was still in place, and it still frightened people.

So all that reinforced your need for the facade.

S: Yes, to live a lie, to be something you weren't, just to survive.

The book incorporates your mother's, grandmother's and Uncle Arthur's stories; you got them on tape and transcribed them. Have you still got the tapes?

S: Yes, I've got the tapes. It took hours to transcribe them.

So the stories are word for word?

S: Virtually. See, when we did the tapes we had no system, so I had bits all over the place. I never asked Mum any questions, she just talked as she remembered. So cutting and pasting, I had bits here and there, and then it was retyped as it made sense. And for me, I started off at several different points in time and wrote what I could remember, and then researched at different times, and later it all started to come together. Originally I started to write about different themes, but I found that it was difficult to get the chronology. That's probably why it took me so long – it took me six years to write and to research. See, the original manuscript was much longer – it was actually three times the length. There were stories that kind of went off on tangents. It was very easy to go off on another funny story (laughter) – we chucked a few of those out.

So when you were telling your story, Gladys, or when you were typing it up, Sally, was there a temptation to politicise them a bit? I mean, did you have to be careful, not to project your anger into them?

S: In Mum's case, because she's so articulate, virtually what is written is what she said, word for word. She wrote her own story, and I just put it together. But with my grandmother, sometimes I would ask her a question, and older Aboriginal people will answer you, but not always verbally. So they'll you look at you, and you know what that means. that was really hard for me, because I knew what she was telling me, and she wanted me to know, but it hadn't been spoken. So I had to decide, do I include this or do I leave it out. And there were a couple of really crucial things; I'd asked her if she'd been pregnant before. That was a terrible thing, it was agony for her...

G: It was a shame...

S: And she couldn't talk about it, but her look gave me an answer. Initially I left it out, because I didn't know how to handle it, and later on as we researched more and found more out, I realised I had to write it in, because it *was* information she had given me. So I wrote it in very simply.

So you had to be careful to put the words that represented the look, and overcome the temptation to actually put your words into her mouth?

S: I think there was a danger there to get up on my high horse, but I think what I learned when I was writing it was that you don't have to be explicit to say something. It's better to just put something simply and let it tell its own story. I think it has more impact. And also if you're going to bash people over the head they don't always listen. You've got to get to people's hearts, make them feel about something ... if people could *just* see Aboriginal people as a people with the same human emotions, the same feelings; as just ordinary people.

1. Sally Morgan, *My Place* (Fremantle Arts Centre Press, Fremantle, 1986).

EXTRACTS FROM *MY PLACE* BY SALLY MORGAN.

My Place traces the author's family history through three generations. It is a slow and very painful recovery of a past, full of humiliation and hurt, caused by white Australians' treatment of Aborigines. The personal histories of the writer, her mother, her grandmother and her grandmother's older brother overlap and weave together, creating a picture of struggle and suffering, culminating in the grandmother's withholding of part of her story, because it is just too painful. But the book also celebrates not only the family's survival but also the survival of the Aboriginal way of life and Aboriginal values in spite of separation and near slave conditions.

The following extracts contain highlights from each of the four life stories, told in the book.

From SALLY MORGAN'S STORY

In April that year, my youngest sister, Helen, was born. I found myself taking an interest in her because at least she had the good sense not to be born on my birthday. There were five of us now; I wondered how many more kids Mum was gong to try and squeeze into the house. Someone at school had told me that babies were found under cabbage leaves. I was glad we never grew cabbages.

Each year, our house seemed to get smaller. In my room, we had two single beds lashed together with a bit of rope and a big, double kapok mattress plonked on top. Jill, Billy and I slept in there, sometimes David too, and, more often than not, Nan as well. I loved that mattress. Whenever I lay on it, I imagined I was sinking into a bed of feathers, just like a fairy princess.

The kids at school were amazed to hear that I shared a bed with my brother and sister. I never told them about the times we'd squeezed five in that bed. All my class-mates had their own beds, some of them even had their own rooms. I considered them disadvantaged. I couldn't explain the happy feeling of warm security I felt when we all snuggled in together.

Also, I found some of their attitudes to their brothers and sisters hard to understand. They didn't seem to really like one another, and you never caught them together at school. We were just the opposite. Billy, Jill and I always spoke in the playground and we often walked home together, too. We felt our family was the most important thing in the world. One of the girls in my class said, accusingly, one day, 'Aah, you lot stick like glue'. You're right, I thought, we do.

The kids at school had also begun asking us what country we came from. This puzzled me because, up until then, I'd thought we were the same as them. If we insisted that we came from Australia, they'd reply, 'Yeah, but what about ya parents, bet they didn't come from Australia'.

One day, I tackled Mum about it as she washed the dishes.

'What do you mean, "Where do we come from?"'

'I mean, what country. The kids at school want to know what country we come from. They reckon we're not Aussies. Are we Aussies, Mum?'

Mum was silent. Nan grunted in a cross sort of way, then got up from the table and walked outside.

'Come on, Mum, what are we?'

'What do the kids at school say?'

'Anything. Italian, Greek, Indian.'

'Tell them you're Indian.'

I got really excited, then. 'Are we really? Indian!' It sounded so exotic. 'When did we come here?' I added.

'A long time ago', Mum replied. 'Now, no more questions. you just tell them you're Indian.'

It was good to finally have an answer and it satisfied our playmates. They could quite believe we were Indian, they just didn't want us pretending we were Aussies when we weren't.

Towards the end of the school year, I arrived home early one day to find Nan sitting at the kitchen table, crying. I froze in the doorway, I'd never seen her cry before.

'Nan ... what's wrong?'

'Nothin'!'

'Then what are you crying for?'

She lifted up her arm and thumped her clenched fist hard on the kitchen 'You bloody kids don't want me, you want a bloody white grandmother. I'm black. Do you hear, black, black, black!' With that, Nan pushed back her chair and hurried out to her room. I continued to stand in the doorway, I could feel the strap of my heavy schoolbag cutting into my shoulder, but I was too stunned to remove it.

For the first time in my fifteen years, I was conscious of Nan's colouring. She was right, she wasn't white. Well, I thought logically, if she wasn't white,then neither were we. What did that make us, what did that make me? I had never thought of myself as being black before.

That night, as Jill and I were lying quietly on our beds, looking at a poster of John, Paul, George and Ringo, I said, 'Jill ... did you know Nan was black?'

'Course, I did.'

'I didn't, I just found out.'

'I know you didn't. You're really dumb, sometimes. God, you reckon I'm gullible, some things you just don't see.'

'Oh ...'

'You know we're not Indian, don't you?' Jill mumbled.

'Mum said we're Indian.'

'Look at Nan, does she look Indian?'

'I've never really thought about how she looks. Maybe she comes from some Indian tribe we don't know about.'

'Ha! That'll be the day! You know what we are, don't you?'

'No, what?'

It took a few minutes before I summoned up enough courage to say, 'What's a Boong?'

'A Boong. You know, Aboriginal. God, of all things, we're Aboriginal!'

'Oh.' I suddenly understood. There was a great deal of social stigma attached to being Aboriginal at our school.

'I can't believe you've never heard the word Boong', she muttered in disgust. 'Haven't you ever listened to the kids at school? If they want to run you down, they say, "Aah, ya just a Boong". Honestly, Sally, you live the whole of your life in a daze!'

Jill was right, I did live in a world of my own. She was much more attuned to our social environment. It was important for her to be accepted at school, because she enjoyed being there. All I wanted to do was stay home.

'You know, Jill', I said after a while, 'if we are Boongs, and I don't know if we are or not, but if we are, there's nothing we can do about it, so we might as well just accept it'.

'Accept it? Can you tell me one good thing about being an Abo?'

'Well, I don't know much about them', I answered. 'They like animals, don't they? We like animals.'

'A lot of people like animals, Sally. Haven't you heard of the RSPCA?'

'Of course I have! But don't Abos feel close to the earth and all that stuff?'

'God, I don't know. All I know is none of my friends like them. You know, I've been trying to convince Lee for two years that we're Indian.' Lee was Jill's best friend and her opinions were very important. Lee loved Nan, so I didn't see that it mattered.

'You know Susan?' Jill said, interrupting my thoughts. 'Her mother said she doesn't want her mixing with you because you're a bad influence. She reckons all Abos are a bad influence.'

'Aaah, I don't care about Susan, never liked her much anyway.'

'You still don't understand, do you', Jill groaned in disbelief. 'It's a terrible thing to be Aboriginal. Nobody wants to know you, not just Susan. You can be Indian, Dutch, Italian, anything, but not Aboriginal! I suppose it's all right for someone like you, you don't care what people think. You don't need anyone, but I do!' Jill pulled her rugs over her head and pretended she'd gone to sleep. I think she was crying, but I had too much new information to think about to try and comfort her. Besides, what could I say?

Nan's outburst over her colouring and Jill's assertion that we were Aboriginal heralded a new phase in my relationship with my mother. I began to pester her incessantly about our background. Mum was a hard nut to crack and consistently denied Jill's assertion. She even told me that Nan had come out on a boat from India in the early days. In fact, she was so convincing I began to wonder if Jill was right after all.

When I wasn't pestering Mum, I was busy pestering Nan. To my surprise, I discovered that Nan had a real short fuse when it came to talking about the past. Whenever I attempted to question her, she either lost her temper and began to accuse me of all sorts of things, or she locked herself in her room and wouldn't emerge until it was time for Mum to come home from work. It was a conspiracy.

One night, Mum came into my room and sat on the end of my bed. She had her This Is Serious look on her face. With an unusual amount of firmness in her voice, she said quietly, 'Sally, I want to talk to you'.

I lowered my *Archie* comic. 'What is it?'

'I think you know, don't act dumb with me. You're not to bother Nan any more. She's not as young as she used to be and your questions are making her sick. She never knows when you're going to try and trick her. There's no point in digging up the past, some things are better left buried. Do you understand what I'm saying? You're to leave her alone.'

'Okay Mum', I replied glibly, 'but on one condition'.

'What's that?'

'You answer one question for me?'

'What is it?' Poor Mum, she was a trusting soul.

'Are we Aboriginal?'

Mum snorted in anger and stormed out. Jill chuckled from her bed. 'I don't know why you keep it up. Why keep pestering them? I think it's better not to know for sure, that way you don't have to face up to it.'

'I keep pestering them because I want to know the truth, and I want to hear it from Mum's own lips.'

'It's a lost cause, they'll never tell you.'

'I'll crack 'em one day.'

Jill shrugged good-naturedly and went back to reading her *True Romance* magazine.

I settled back onto my mattress and began to think about the past. Were we Aboriginal? I sighed and closed my eyes. A mental picture flashed vividly before me. I was a little girl again, and Nan and I were squatting in the sand near the back steps.

'This is a track, Sally. See how they go.' I watched, entranced, as she made the pattern of a kangaroo. 'Now, this is a goanna and here are emu tracks. You see, they all different. You got to know all of them if you want to catch tucker.'

'That's real good, Nan.'

'You want me to draw you a picture, Sal?' she said as she picked up a stick.

'Okay.'

'These are men, you see, three men. They are very quiet, they're hunting. Here are kangaroos, they're listening, waiting. They'll take off if they know you're coming.' Nan wiped the sand picture out with her hand. 'It's your turn now', she said, 'you draw something'. I grasped the stick eagerly.

'This is Jill and this is me. We're going down the swamp.' I drew some trees and bushes.

I opened my eyes, and, just as suddenly, the picture vanished. Had I remembered something important? I didn't know. That was the trouble, I knew nothing about Aboriginal people. I was clutching at straws.

FROM ARTHUR CORUNNA'S STORY

(c. 1893 - c. 1950)

My name is Arthur Corunna. I can't tell you how old I am exactly, because I don't know. A few years ago, I wrote to Alice Drake-Brockman, my father's second wife, and asked her if she knew my age. She said that I could have been born around 1893-1894. Later, her daughter Judy wrote to me and said I could have been born before that. So I guess I have to settle for around there somewhere. Anyway, I'm old, and proud of it.

My mother's name was Annie Padewani and my father was Alfred Howden Drake-Brockman, the white station-owner. We called him Good-da-goonya. He live on Corunna Downs nine years before marrying his first wife, Eleanor Boddington. She had been a governess in the area. While on the station, he shared my aboriginal father's two wives, Annie and Ginnie.

Ginnie, or Binddiding as we called her, was a big built woman. She was older, argumentative. She bossed my mother around. I used to cry for my mother when she was in a fight. I'd run round and grab her skirts and try and protect her from Ginnie. Ginnie only had one child by Howden, and that was my half-brother, Albert.

My mother was small and pretty. She was very young when she had me. I was her first child. Then she had Lily by my Aboriginal father. Later, there was Daisy. She is my only sister who shares with me the same parents. I was a good deal older than her when they took me away to the mission, she was only a babe in arms, then. My mother was pregnant with other children, but she lost them.

On the station, I wasn't called Arthur. I had my Aboriginal name, Jilly-yung, which meant silly young kid. When I was a child, I copied everything everyone said. Repeated it like a ninety-nine parrot. The people would say, 'Silly young kid! Jilly-yung!'

I loved my mother, she was my favourite. My mother was always good to me. When others were against me, she stood by me. She used to tell me a story about a big snake. A snake especially for me, with pretty snake's eggs. 'One day', she said, 'you will be able to go and get these eggs'. I belonged to the snake, and I was anxious to see the pretty snake's eggs, but they took me away to the mission, and that finished that. It was a great mystery. If I had've stayed there, I would have gone through the Law, then I would've known. I didn't want to go through the Law. I was scared.

When we went on holidays, we called it going pink-eye, my Aboriginal father carried me on his shoulders when I was tired. I remember one time, it was at night and very dark, we were going through a gorge, when the feather foots, ginnawandas, began to whistle. I was scared. The whistling means they want you to talk. They began lighting fires all along the gorge. After we called out our names, my family was allowed through.

One day, I took a tomato from the vegetable garden. I'd been watching it for days. Watching it grow big and round and red. Then, I picked it and Dudley saw me. He was Howden Drake- Brockman's brother and we called him Irrabindi. He gave orders for my Aboriginal father to beat me. Maybe he had his eye on that tomato, too.

I was beaten with a stirrup strap. I spun round and round, crying and crying. I was only a kid in a shirt in those days. My Aboriginal father never hit me unless an order was given. Then, he had to do it, boss's orders. He was good to me otherwise, so I never kept any bad feelings against him.

Dudley Drake-Brockman wasn't like Howden. They were brothers, but they were different. Dudley was a short little man. He couldn't ride. He was cruel and didn't like blackfellas. My people used to say about Dudley ngulloo-moolo, which means make him sick. We didn't want him there. In the end, he got sick and died.

I used to play with Pixie, Dudley's son. We used to fight, too, but I never beat him. I was afraid of his father. My mother used to say to me, 'Jilly-yung, never beat Pixie in a fight. When he wants to fight, you walk away.' She was a wise woman.

Howden was a good-looking man, well liked. He could ride all the horses there, even the buck jumpers. Old Nibro told me that. He used to help him break them. There was one big, black horse he named Corunna. He would always ride him when he went out baiting dingoes.

I remember Howden used to dance on his own in the dining-room. He'd be doin' this foxtrot, kicking his leg around with no partner. I used to watch. There was a big dining-room then, and a great, huge fan that we had to pull to cool people off who were eating there. They gave us a handful of raisins for doing that.

From GLADYS CORUNNA'S STORY

(c. 1931-1983)

'There's been so much sadness in my life', Mum said, 'I don't think I can take any more'.

'You want to talk about it?'

'You mean for that book?'

'Yes.'

'Well ...', she hesitated for a moment. Then, with sudden determination, she said, 'Why shouldn't I? If I stay silent like Nanna, it's like saying everything's all right. People should know what it's been like for someone like me.'

I smiled at her.

'Perhaps my sister will read it.'

I have no memory of being taken from my mother and placed in Parkerville Children's Home, but all my life, I've carried a mental picture of a little fat kid about three or four years old. She's sitting on the verandah of Babyland Nursery, her nose is running and she's crying. I think that was me when they first took me to Parkerville.

Parkerville was a beautiful place run by Church of England nuns. Set in the hills of the Darling Ranges, it was surrounded by bush and small streams. In the spring, there were wildflowers of every colour and hundreds of varieties of birds. Each morning, I awoke to hear the kookaburras laughing and the maggies warbling. That was the side of Parkerville I loved.

That was my home from 1931 when I was three years old. I was only able to go back to my mother at Ivanhoe three times a year, for the holidays.

I think Alice Drake-Brockman thought she was doing a good thing sending me to Parkerville. Sometimes, she'd come up and bring Judy, June and Dick with her for a picnic. That was always in the spring, when the wildflowers were out. Dick and I got on well, we were very close. He treated me like his sister.

I loved it when they all came up, because the other kids were so envious. There was a lot of status in knowing someone who had a car. I thought I'd burst for joy when I saw the black Chev creep up the hill and drive slowly down the road, to halt at George Turner. All the other kids would crowd up close, hoping I'd take one of them with me. I'd jump down from the wooden fence we sat on while we waited and hoped for visitors and I'd walk slowly towards the car. I felt very shy, but I was also conscious of the envy of the others still sitting on the fence behind me. It was a feeling of importance that would last me the whole of the following week. I always promised the other kids that next time, I might take one of them. It made me king until the following Sunday, when someone might get a visitor who brought a box of cakes. Even so, cakes weren't as important as a car ride, because it was very hard to make a cake last a full week

I often prayed for God to give me a family. I used to pretend I had a mother and a father and brothers and sisters. I pretended I lived in a big flash house like Ivanhoe and I went to St Hilda's Girls' School like Judy and June.

It was very important to me to have a father then. Whenever I asked Mum about my father, she'd just say, 'You don't want to know about him, he died when you were very small, but he loved you very much'. She sensed I needed to belong, but she didn't know about all the teasing I used to get because I didn't have a father, nor the comments that I used to hear about bad girls having babies. I knew it was connected to me, but I was too young to understand.

I had a large scar on my chest where my mother said my father had dropped his cigar ash. I tried to picture him nursing me, with a large cigar in his mouth. I always imagined him looking like a film star, like one of the pictures the big girls had.

The scar made me feel I must have had a real father, after all. I'd look at it and feel quite pleased. It wasn't until I was older that I realised it was an initiation scar. My mother had given it to me for protection.

In the May holidays, I usually went to Ivanhoe. Willie would drive me down to Perth and I'd be met by Alice.

I was always pleased to see my mother and really excited that I was going to be with her for two whole weeks. She'd give me a hug and then take me into the kitchen for a glass of milk and a piece of cake.

I loved Ivanhoe and I really loved Judy, she was so beautiful and she always made a fuss of me. She liked to dress me up, but I'd cry when she insisted on putting big satin bows in my hair. I didn't want to look like Shirley Temple.

I remember one holiday at Ivanhoe when I was very upset. I was in the kitchen with my mother. She had her usual white apron on and was bustling around, when Alice came in with June. I couldn't take my eyes off June. She had the most beautiful doll in her arms. It had golden hair and blue eyes and was dressed in satin and lace. I was so envious, I wished it was mine. It reminded me of a princess.

June said to me, 'You've got a doll, too. Mummy's got it.' Then from behind her back, Alice pulled out a black topsy doll dressed like a servant. It had a red checked dress on a white apron, just like Mum's. It had what they used to call a slave cap on its head. It was really just a handkerchief knotted at each corner. My mother always wore one on washing days, because the laundry got very damp with all the steam and it stopped some of it trickling down her face.

At Christmas, I also went to Ivanhoe. We'd all sleep out on the balcony at the rear of the house, we had a lovely view over the Swan River from there.

At the top of the house was a large attic which June was allowed to use as a playhouse, it was a lovely room. There were seats under the windows and dolls and a dolls' house. There were teddies and other toys and a china tea-set. We'd play tea parties and practise holding out our little fingers like grown-ups did. June's dolls were lovely, they were china and dressed in satin and lace.

It was strange, really, at the Home, nobody owned a doll. There were a few broken ones kept in the cupboard, but when you asked to play with them, you had to play in the dining-room until you'd finished. You were never allowed to take one to bed.

I was lucky, because I had a rag doll my mother had given me called Sally Jane. I loved her very much. She was kept at Ivanhoe for me and Mum let me take her to bed every night.

On Christmas morning, we'd wake up early and check the pillowslips we'd hung on the ends of our beds the night before. Alice always gave me a new dress, with hair ribbons to match. Mother always made me doll's clothes and I would dress Sally Jane in one of her new dresses. We were very happy together, Judy, June, Dick and I. It was like having a family.

Every year after each of the holidays, I found it harder and harder to leave my mother and return to Parkerville. I couldn't understand why I couldn't live at Ivanhoe and go to school with Judy and June. You see, I hadn't really worked out how things were when your mother was a servant. I knew the family liked me, so I couldn't understand why they didn't want me living there.

But after Mum had been at Morgans' about two years, Alice asked her if she would come back to Ivanhoe to work. I wanted her to stay at Morgans', because it was easier for her, but I think Mum still felt a loyalty to the family. It was easy for people to make her feel sorry for them. She was too kind-hearted.

Alice's mother had come to live with them and she was very difficult to look after. I think that's why they wanted Mum back. She had to accept a cut in wages and no annual holidays, but she went anyway. She told me that it was to be permanent and she'd never be leaving there again.

I went to Ivanhoe for Christmas that year, I was about fourteen by then. Judy, June and Dick suddenly seemed a lot older than me. It wasn't the same as our carefree childhood days. Even though we had all loved each other as children, something had changed. We weren't children any more, Judy, June and Dick had begun to get more like their mother. They treated Mum like a servant, now, she wasn't their beloved nanny any more.

June had a friend who was a bit of a snob and this girl was always putting me in my place because I was only the maid's daughter. I'd go and sit in Mum's room and cry. I was suddenly very unsure of my place in the world.

I still ate with the family in the dining-room, but I felt like an outsider, especially when Alice would ring a little brass bell and my mother would come in and wait on us.

I suddenly realised that there hadn't been one Christmas dinner when Mum had eaten her meal with us. She'd had hers alone in the kitchen all these years. I never wanted to be in the dining-room again after that, I wanted to be in the kitchen with my mother.

FROM DAISY CORUNNA'S STORY

(1900-1983)

My name is Daisy Corunna, I'm Arthur's sister. My Aboriginal name is Talahue. I can't tell you when I was born, but I feel old. My mother had me on Corunna Downs Station, just out of Marble Bar. She said I was born under a big, old gum tree and the midwife was called Diana. Course, that must have been her whitefella name. All the natives had whitefella and tribal names. I don't know what her tribal name was. When I was comin' into the world, a big mob of kids stood round waitin' for to get a look at me. I bet they got a fright.

On the station, I went under the name Daisy Brockman. It wasn't till I was older that I took the name Corunna. Now, some people say my father wasn't Howden Drake-Brockman, they say he was this man from Malta. What can I say? I never heard 'bout this man from Malta before. I think that's a big joke.

Aah, you see, that's the trouble with us blackfellas, we don't know who we belong to, no one'll own up. I got to be careful what I say. You can't put no lies in a book.

Course, I had another father, he wasn't my real father like, but he looked after us just the same. Chinaman was his name. He was very tall and strong. The people respected him. they were scared of him.

He was Arthur's Aboriginal father, too. He was a powerful man.

The big house on Corunna was built by the natives. They all worked together, building this and building that. If it wasn't for the natives, nothing would get done. They made the station, Drake-Brockmans didn't do it on their own.

At the back of the homestead was a big, deep hole with whitewash in it. It was thick and greasy, you could cut it with a knife. Us kids used to mix the whitewash with water and make it like a paint. Then we'd put it all over us and play corroborees. Every Saturday afternoon, we played corroboree. We mixed the red sand with water and painted that on, too. By the time we finished, you didn't know what colour we were.

I 'member the kitchen on Corunna. There was a tiny little window where the blackfellas had to line up for tucker. My mother never liked doin' that. We got a bit of tea, flour and meat, that was all. They always rang a bell when they was ready for us to come. Why do white people like ringin' bells so much?

Every morning, they woke us up with a bell. It was only 'bout five o'clock, could have been earlier. We all slept down in the camp, a good way from the main house. Every morning, someone would light a lamp, walk down into the gully and ring a bell. When I was very little, I used to get frightened. I thought it was the devil-devil come to get me.

There was a tennis court on Corunna. Can you 'magine that? I think they thought they were royalty, puttin' in a tennis court. That's an Englishman's game. They painted it with whitewash, but it didn't stay white for long, I can tell you. I had a go at hitting the ball, once. I gave up after that, it was a silly game.

When I got older, my jobs on Corunna changed. They started me working at the main house, sweeping the verandahs, emptying the toilets, scrubbing the tables and pots and pans and the floor. In those days, you scrubbed everything. In the mornings, I had to clean the hurricane lamps, then help in the kitchen.

There were always poisonous snakes hiding in the dark corners of the kitchen. You couldn't see them, but you could hear them. Sssss, ssssss, ssssss, they went. Just like that. We cornered them and killed them with sticks. There were a lot of snakes on Corunna.

Once I was working up the main house, I wasn't allowed down in the camp. If I had've known that, I'd have stayed where I was. I couldn't sleep with my mother now and I wasn't allowed to play with all my old friends.

That was the worst thing about working at the main house, not seeing my mother every day. I knew she missed me. She would walk up from the camp and call, 'Daisy, Daisy', just like that. I couldn't talk to her, I had too much work to do. It was hard for me, then. I had to sneak away just to see my own family and friends. They were camp natives, I was a house native.

Now, I had to sleep on the homestead verandah. Some nights, it was real cold, one blanket was too thin. On nights like that, the natives used to bring wool from the shearing shed and lay that beneath them.

I didn't mind sleeping on the verandah in summer because I slept near the old cooler. It was as big as a fireplace, they kept butter and milk in it. I'd wait till everyone was asleep, then I'd sneak into the cooler and pinch some butter. I loved it, but I was never allowed to have any.

Aah, but they were good old days, then. I never seen days like that ever gain. When they took me from the station, I never seen days like that ever again.

They told my mother I was goin' to get educated. They told all the people I was goin' to school. I thought it'd be good, goin' to school. I thought I'd be somebody real important. My mother wanted me to learn to read and write like white people. Then she wanted me to come back and teach her. There was a lot of the older people interested in learnin' how to read and write, then.

Why did they tell my mother that lie? Why do white people tell so many lies? I got nothin' out of their promises. My mother wouldn't have let me go just to work. God will make them pay for their lies. He's got people like that under the whip. They should have told my mother the truth. She thought I was coming back.

When I left, I was cryin', all the people were cryin', my mother was cryin' and beatin' her head. Lily was cryin'. I called, 'Mum, Mum, Mum!'. She said, 'Don't forget me, Talahue!'.

They all thought I was coming back. I thought I'd only be gone a little while. I could hear their wailing for miles and miles. 'Talahue! Talahue!'

They were singin' out my name, over and over. I couldn't stop cryin'. I kept callin', 'Mum! Mum!'

I must have been 'bout fourteen or fifteen when they took me from Corunna. First day in Perth, I had to tidy the garden, pick up leaves and sweep the verandahs. Later on, I used an old scythe to cut the grass. All the time, I kept wonderin' when they were goin' to send me to school. I saw some white kids goin' to school, but not me. I never asked them why they didn't send me, I was too 'shamed.

Funny how I was the only half-caste they took with them from Corunna. Drake-Brockmans left the others and took me. Maybe Howden took me 'cause I was his daughter, I don't know. I kept thinkin' of my poor old mother and how she thought I was gettin' educated. I wanted to tell her what had happened. I wanted to tell her all I was doin' was workin'. I wasn't gettin' no education. How could I tell her, I couldn't write. And I had no one to write for me.

We moved into Ivanhoe, a big house on the banks of the Swan River in Claremont. I was lookin' after children again, there was Jack and Betty, Judy, June and Dick. I was supposed to be their nanny. You know, like they have in England. I had to play with them, dress them, feed them and put them to bed at night. I had other chores to do as well. I never blamed the children, it wasn't their fault I had to work so hard. I felt sorry for them.

At night, I used to lie in bed and think 'bout my people. I could see their campfire and their faces. I could see my mother's face and Lily's. I really missed them. I cried myself to sleep every night. Sometimes, in my dreams, I'd hear them wailing, 'Talahue! Talahue!', and I'd wake up, calling 'Mum! Mum!' You see, I needed my people, they made me feel important. I belonged to them. I thought 'bout the animals, too. The kangaroos and birds. And, of course, there was Lily, I wondered if she had a new boyfriend. I missed her, I missed all of them.

Alice kept tellin' me, 'We're family now, Daisy'.

Thing is, they wasn't my family. Oh, I knew the children loved me, but they wasn't my family. They were white, they'd grow up and go to school one day. I was black, I was a servant. How can they be your family?

I did all the work at Ivanhoe. The cleaning, the washing, the ironing. There wasn't nothing I didn't do. From when I got up in the morning till when I went to sleep at night, I worked. That's all I did really, work and sleep.

By jingoes, washing was hard work in those days. The old laundry was about twenty yards from the house and the troughs were always filled with dirty washing. They'd throw everything down from the balcony onto the grass, I'd collect it up, take it to the laundry and wash it. Sometimes, I thought I'd never finish stokin' up that copper, washin' this and washin' that. Course, everything was starched in those days. Sheets, pillowcases, serviettes, tablecloths, they was all starched. I even had to iron the sheets. Isn't that silly, you only goin' to lay on them.

The house had to be spotless. I scrubbed, dusted and polished. There was the floors, the staircase, the ballroom. It all had to be done.

Soon, I was the cook, too. Mind you, I was a good cook. I didn't cook no rubbish. Aah, white people, they got some funny tastes. Fussy, fussy, aaah, they fussy. I 'member I had to serve the toast on a silver tray. I had to crush the edges of each triangle with a knife. Course, you never left the crusts on sandwiches, that was bad manners. Funny, isn't it? I mean, it's all bread, after all.

I had my dinner in the kitchen. I never ate with the family. When they rang the bell, I knew they wanted me. After dinner, I'd clear up, wash up, dry up and put it all away. Then, next morning, it's start all over again. You see, it's no use them sayin' I was one of the family, 'cause I wasn't. I was their servant.

I 'member they used to have real fancy morning and afternoon teas. The family would sit on the lawn under a bit, shady umbrella. I'd bring out the food and serve them. You know, I saw a picture like that on television. It was in England, they were all sittin' outside in their fancy clothes with servants waitin' on them. I thought, well fancy that, that's what I used to do. They must have that silly business in quite a few countries.

I 'member the beautiful cups and saucers. They were very fine, you thought they'd break with you just lookin' at them. Ooh, I loved them. Some of them were so fine, they were like a seashell, you could see through them. I only ever had a tin mug. I promised myself one day I would have a nice cup and saucer. That's why, whenever my grandchildren said, 'What do you want for your birthday?', I always told them a cup and saucer.

In those days, the Drake-Brockmans were real upper class. They had money and people listened to them. Aah, the parties they had. I never seen such parties. The ladies' dresses were pretty and fancy. I always thought of my mother when I saw their dresses. How she would have loved one.

I never like Perth much, then. I was too scared. I was shy, too. I couldn't talk to strangers. People looked at you funny 'cause you were black. I kept my eyes down. Maybe some of those white people thought the cat got my tongue, I don't know. I'm not sayin' they was all bad. Some of them was nice. You get nice people anywhere. Trouble is, you get the other ones as well. 'Cause you're black, they treat you like dirt. You see, in those days, we was owned, like a cow or a horse I even heard some people say we not the same as whites. That's not true, we all God's children.

Course, when the white people wanted something, they didn't pretend you wasn't there, they 'spected you to come runnin' quick smart. That's all I did sometimes, run in and out. Someone was always ringin' that damn bell.

I'm 'shamed of myself, now. I feel 'shamed for some of the things I done. I wanted to be white, you see. I'd lie in bed at night and think if God could make me white, it'd be the best thing. Then I could get on in the world, make somethin' of myself. Fancy, me thinkin' that. What was wrong with my own people?

In those days, it was considered a privilege for a white man to want you, but if you had children, you weren't allowed to keep them. You was only allowed to keep the black ones. They took the white ones off you 'cause you weren't considered fit to raise a child with white blood.

I tell you, it made a wedge between the people. Some of the black men felt real low, and some of the native girls with a bit of white in them wouldn't look at a black man. There I was, suck in the middle. Too black for the whites and too white for the blacks.

When Gladdie was 'bout three years old, they took her from me. I'd been 'spectin' it. Alice told me Gladdie needed an education, so they put her in Parkerville Children's Home. What could I do? I was too frightened to say anythin'. I wanted to keep her with me, she was all I had, but they didn't want her there. Alice said she cost too much to feed, said I was ungrateful.

She was wantin' me to give up my own flesh and blood and still be grateful. Aren't black people allowed to have feelin's?

I cried and cried when Alice took her away. Gladdie was too young to understand, she thought she was comin' back. She thought it was a picnic she was goin' on. I ran down to the wild bamboo near the river and I hid and cried and cried an cried. How can a mother lose a child like that? How could she do that to me? I thought of my poor old mother then, they took her Arthur from her, and then they took me. She was broken-hearted, God bless her.

I felt, for Mum's sake, I should make one last effort to find out about her sister. So a few nights later, when Nan and I were on our own, I said, 'There's something I want to ask you. I know you won't like it, but I have to ask. It's up to you whether you tell me anything or not.'

Nan grunted. 'Ooh, those questions, eh? Well, ask away.'

'Okay. Has Mum got a sister somewhere?'

She looked away quickly. there was silence, then, after a few seconds, a long, deep sigh.

When she finally turned to face me, her cheeks were wet. 'Don't you understand, yet', she said softly, 'there are some things I just can't talk 'bout'. Her hand touched her chest in that characteristic gesture that meant her heart was hurting. It wasn't her flesh and blood heart. It was the heart of her spirit. With that, she heaved herself up and went out to her room.

One night later that week, Nan called me out to her room.

'What on earth are you doing?' I laughed when I found her with both arms raised in the air and her head completely covered by the men's singlet she was wearing.

'I'm stuck', she muttered, 'get me out'. I pulled the singlet off and helped her undress. It had become a difficult task for her, lately. Her arthritis was worse and cataracts now almost completely obscured her vision.

'Can you give me a rub?' she asked. 'The Vaseline's over there.' I picked up the jar, dobbed a big, greasy lump of it onto her back and began to rub. Nan loved Vaseline. Good for keeping your body cool and moist, she always told me. She had a lot of theories like that. I continued to massage her in silence for a few minutes.

'Ooh, that's good, Sally', she murmured after a while. As I continued to rub, she let out a deep sigh and then said slowly, 'You know, Sal ... all my life, I been treated rotten, real rotten. Nobody's cared if I've looked pretty. I been treated like a beast. Just like a beast of the field. And now, here I am ... old. Just a dirty old blackfella.'

I don't know how long it was before I answered her. My heart felt cut in half. I could actually see a beast in a field. A work animal, nothing more.

'You're not to talk about yourself like that', I finally replied in a controlled voice. 'You're my grandmother and I won't have you talk like that. The whole family loves you. We'd do anything for you.'

There was no reply. How hollow my words sounded. How empty and limited. Would anything I said ever help? I hoped that she sensed how deeply I felt. Words were unnecessary for that.

My Place

SALLY MORGAN

Wandering Girl

INTRODUCTION

Wandering Girl[1] by Glenyse Ward is one of the first books to be published by the newly established Aboriginal press Magabala Books. It is an autobiographical account, featuring so many of the aspects which have become part and parcel of Aboriginal lives as late as into the 60s: Forcible removal from home, growing up on a Mission Station, being sent out to work as a servant. Glenyse Ward describes the loneliness and injustices of such a life, but she also celebrates the human warmth she met amongst friends and the will to survive which finally led to her escape.

The principle behind the selection of the extracts from *Wandering Girl* is to highlight the importance of self-affirmation in Aboriginal writing. In an article called 'New Directions in South African Literature'[2] the South African writer and critic Njabulo Ndebele discusses the importance of writing beyond protest in the literature of a colonized people. He sees the first step in such writing as stating what he calls 'the moral position'. 'To know' becomes to know how badly you are treated, and the statement of this in the form of creative writing becomes the goal. It lays bare to the world the glaring injustices and cruelties, and it believes in the persuasiveness of the morally superior standpoint. This is the essence of much protest writing, and it is an important and necessary step, but is also has its limitations. It can create a 'rhetoric of moral embitterment' in the colonized people, and it pre-supposes a colonizer with a conscience willing to be disturbed by a confrontation with his own evil. It is in essence, a liberal, rather than a radical genre, despite its often violent nature, and it – sometimes unwittingly – gives a lot of space and thought to the 'other', the whites and how they might think or feel.

A further step in the evolution of the literature of an oppressed people, Ndebele suggests, is to dislodge the whites from the centre of the scene of imagination and celebrate – or lament – black lives in their interaction with one another. These extracts do just that. They are a celebration of survival.

They create a counter-image to the misused, oppressed black servant, cowering at the edge of white family photographs. This one, at least in these passages, holds centre stage, whether in the shower, in the dining room or at the piano. The whites are, however, not totally absent. They patrol the minds of the two servants with their very real threats of punishment, reminding us how pervasive their control of the lives and imagination of the oppressed people is.

These extracts can also be read in another light. They are the nightmare of the oppressor. In his book *The Wretched of the Earth*[3] Franz Fanon describes the colonized people, his people, as 'an envious people'. They want to live in the colonizer's house, sleep in his bed etc., and this is the worst fear of the colonizer. Acting out the fantasy of the reversal is putting a utopia into reality – if only for a limited space of time – and it is clearly more subversive than protests or complaints. It celebrates affirmative action and creates an insubordinate role model.

The extracts also point out the difficulties of total liberation. Even in a temporary utopia the Aboriginal servant sings 'Do you Ken John Peel?'. Cultural liberation is obviously much harder than political liberation. However, the celebration of survival in these extracts and their implied vision of a world after liberation are important steps taking 'protest' into the realm of self-affirmation. Moving on to write the book takes this vision squarely into reality, and the present volume bears witness not only to survival, but to cultural liberation.

NOTES

1. Glenyse Ward, *Wandering Girl* (Magabala Books, Broome, 1988).
2. Njabulo Ndebele 'Beyond "Protest": New Directions in South African Literature' in *Criticism and Ideology* ed. Kirsten Holst Petersen, Scandinavian Institute of African Studies, Uppsala, 1988, pp. 205-17.
3. Frantz Fanon *The Wretched of the Earth*, Grove Press, New York, 1968.

Kirsten Holst Petersen

I was all alone again. Off I went to the cleaning cupboard. Out with the tin of Bon Ami and the scrubbing brush – to go and do the job I had saved up. I used to hate scrubbing her shower recess because every line between the tiles had to be scoured and polished!

Quietly, I entered the bedroom, which I must say was absolutely beautiful, decorated out with pale pink wallpaper in flower patterns. The curtains were a deep pink colour that blended in with her lovely fluffy white carpet.

I never minded cleaning down her dressing table, as I used to love picking up her figure ornaments and her bird shaped ones, and just gazing at them. They looked so real with the reds, greens and blues splashed over them.

And smelling all the different shaped bottles of perfume! Some were so strong I just about passed out with the whiff of them.

I put the Bon Ami down on the floor of her shower recess. This was one morning that I wasn't going to scrub those tiles. I would get myself cleaned up instead. I trotted off to her linen cupboard and picked out her best fluffy pink towels, with the aroma of lavender through them, went back to her room and laid the towels out on her big brass bed, waiting for me there.

Then I slipped my clothes off, selected one of her fine soaps and stepped into the recess. It was my best shower since being at the farm, oh it was a far cry from the dog house dribble I usually stood under.

That soap smelt really sweet as I rubbed it all over me, then opened up her shampoo and emptied half the bottle on my head. There were soap suds everywhere. I got so carried away.

After my shower I pranced out on her fluffy white carpet, not noticing the wet footprints I was making. At the dressing table I just about tipped over one of her bottles and splashed perfume all over me. Then I decided to sprinkle on some powder!

I finished getting dressed and looked around – I'd given myself a double cleaning job. There were splashes and powder all over the place. The beautiful bedroom looked like a whirlwind hit it. I didn't mind. I was smelling so nice, it made me feel so good. And when she came home I would be smelling like vinegar again, for I had plenty of work to do.

Alone for the day, I could ask my old friend to come up for lunch. It was too late for morning tea. Reaching the orchard, I cupped my hands over my mouth and sang out his name a couple of times. I heard him answering back, 'Down here, lassie,' so I wandered down the land nearest to the river, and spotted him picking pears and oranges.

'Hi,' I said to him as if I had known him for years. He stood up and asked me how I was feeling. I told him I was on my own, as everybody had gone to town. I told him that she wanted more fruit to be picked and bottled.

He offered to help me straight away. I thanked him and asked eagerly if he would like to come up to the house and have dinner? He said he could. I told him that I'd go and get things ready. He said he'd be there at twelve o'clock and would bring the buckets of fruit up with him on the old tractor and trailer.

I felt so happy within myself that I skipped all the way back to the house. Even the mess those boys had left behind didn't dampen my spirits as I went about cleaning the kitchen and getting this particular dinner ready.

I set the table with her finest crockery, which she only used for very important guests – I felt that her workers were just as important and after all, it was a special occasion, old Bill was a friend of mine. I was buoyant now that I had someone I could talk to and laugh with about things. It was a far cry from walking around gloomy all day.

I laid the cold meats and salad on the table as I heard the tractor stop outside. Then I went to help Bill bring in the fruit. We put it on the sink, and I directed Bill out to the old wash house to wash his hands as I went back into the kitchen to make the tea.

Bill came in and I told him to go through to the dining room. He sat down and sang out to me, 'Hey lassie, have you got the King and Queen coming for dinner?' He gave out one of his boisterous chuckles which echoed all through the house. I took the pot of tea in to find Bill already helping himself, so I took my place at the table.

I copied her fashion, and spread the serviette across my lap. I didn't want my scraps to fall on my good clothes. I laughed out aloud. What a joke! Bill must have seen the funny side too, as we both went into fits of laughter.

Was it possible that a slave girl in second hand clothes and an old handyman could sit up to a table laid with the best of crockery eating a meal fit for a queen?

He sensed that I was deep in thought and said, 'What's up, lassie?' I looked up and said that I didn't want to rush my cup of tea, then explained to him about the jobs she had lined up for me.

His wrinkled old hands still clasped around the cup, his melancholy eyes gazed up at me as he said. 'Shosh lassie, while you are getting the fruit ready, I'll go out to the shed and chop the wood and stack the woodboxes for you.'

I thanked him and said it was very kind of him. Bill said he'd have another cup of tea, so I hopped up gladly and went to make a fresh pot. When I returned I sat down and poured his cup, then asked him if he liked music?

A big smile spread across his face. He leaned his frame into the back of his chair and said, 'I sure do.' He let out a bit of a chuckle and I noticed a sparkle in his watery eyes.

'Oh, it's been a long time since I sat around the old piano. When I was a little boy back home mother used to play in the comfort of our lounge, with an open fire spreading warmth from the hearth to every corner of the room. We used to feel so cosy as we sang to our heart's delight – but that was a long time ago, lassie!'

We both had tender memories of childhood but I never asked him where his home was or where he was from. I guessed in time he'd let me know. He sat there with a faraway look in his eyes. I interrupted his thoughts, when I asked him, if he knew songs like. 'Do You Ken John Peel' and 'Waltzing Matilda?'

We both sat back and laughed, then stood up from the table. Bill said he'd go and get the wood chopping done, I said I'd go and get the fruit done – then we could sit back for the rest of the afternoon and entertain ourselves at the piano.

Now that we both had finished drinking our tea we cleaned up our mess and went into the visitors' room. I lifted off the pure white linen cloth she had draped over the antique chairs and drew them up to the piano. Bill sat there, rubbing his two old bony hands together as his weary eyes scanned every corner. 'My, lassie, isn't this a grand room?'

'Yes Bill,' I sighed, wishing my bedroom was as beautiful as this; but I knew this could never be.

As I ran my fingers over the piano keys, I felt real glad that I had some company. It was so much more fun! Before when I used to come in here on my own, when she went into town, I had never felt as glad as this.

It was more human having someone to answer you back, than you answering only yourself back. I found I was getting into that habit since I'd been working for this boss.

Bill startled me out of my thoughts, when he began clearing his throat. He asked if I knew a song called, 'Little Brown Jug?' He started to hum the tune to see if I could recognize it.

'Oh, of course I know the song, Bill.' And I started to play it straight away, not waiting for Bill to sing. When I played one verse, I looked at him to see if he was ready to sing. I kept right on playing.

He had his mouth wide open in lockjaw fashion, but no sound was coming out. I just let it rip!

The old man looked so astonished. He peered up to the ceiling with his hands outstretched and cried out, 'Where's it gone?'

I could not stop myself from laughing at him and apologizing at the same time. In the end the old man was cracking up himself and wiping the tears from his eyes. I think that both of us were suffering with a bad case of nerves.

After we had a few more songs and laughs, our nerves settled down and our voices began to come loud and clear. Then I said to Bill, 'I'll play you one of my favourite songs, one I learnt in the mission. It goes, 'I love to go a'wandering, along the mountain track...'

After I finished, Bill gave me a clap. I felt very honoured, stood up and curtsied to my one-man audience as I accepted his appreciation, then laughed as I could see the funny side of it all. If the boss knew that we had turned her V.I.P. room into a concert hall while she was in town on business - I shuddered to think what would happen...

We spent the rest of the afternoon use singing and enjoying ourselves. Bill had a couple of goes on the piano. I must say he didn't do too bad. Then I asked him what the time was? He said it was four o'clock! I said, 'Gee, doesn't time fly when you are having fun.'

GRAEME TURNER

Breaking the Frame: The Representation of Aborigines in Australian Film

It is hard to deny that Australia has a racist past, and is only now coming to terms with a racist present. Even the bicentennial celebrations in January 1988 failed to confront the guilt of the past, attempting to observe a tactful silence on the Aboriginal's role in Australia's achievements as a nation. This silence is bound to be broken, however. The Bicentennial year will see the re-enactment of the arrival of the First Fleet, but it will also see the continuation of Justice Muirhead's royal commission into the alarming number of black Australians who have died in police custody in the last few years, and the completion of Justice Einfeld's report on the 1987 race riots on the Queensland/N.S.W. border. In at least one capital city, stencilled messages saying, 'Celebrate 88, kill an Abo', have appeared on pavements and walls. Given such events, and given the relationship between the ideologies of a culture and its representations of itself in film, it is hardly surprising that racism still structures the representation of Aborigines in Australian film.

As Eric Michaels has pointed out, 'the dominant filmic and documentary conventions (not to mention the ethics) applied to imaging Aborigines [in Australian films] are rarely more recent than the 1950s'.[1] There is a small academic industry dealing with this, suggesting typologies, outlining the functions served by the categories which define the representations of Aboriginals, and proposing a history of the ideologies and institutions which produce the categories.[2] Many of these articles have been useful and I will rehearse some of their arguments later in this discussion. But there are a number of problems inherent in white Australian academics attempting to step outside their ideological frame and interrogate white Australia's construction of the Aboriginal. These problems are theoretical - that is, one has to explain what one is doing - and political - that is, it can be seen as an act of intellectual tourism, inspecting the very set of relations which provides white academics with their privilege and power.

In practice, the political contradiction tends to be accepted and borne; it is the theoretical issue which is seen as the simple one. Most discussions of the representation of Aborigines in Australian films argue that they patronize the Aboriginal as a confused primitive; or represent them as limited and constrained by their race (or their 'blood') in ways not experienced by whites; or see them as a disappearing, anachronistic species for whom we should accept responsibility and feel sympathy. Criticisms of such constructions usually make the very proper point that such a body of images or understandings of the Aboriginal proposes a white view of the Aboriginal as definitive. Since the culture's idea of reality is produced by and reproduced in its representations, such definitions become the way in which Aboriginality is understood. If the definitions are racist, they will naturalize racist assumptions.

There is little that is contentious about this. However, the next step is. Customarily, critiques of the representation of Aborigines metamorphose into programmes of intervention in the representational and ideological process, aimed at interrogating and overturning the dominant constructions. They move into a corrective mode, proposing alternative constructions in place of the racist ones. Behind such a programme there is a degree of theoretical slippage in the understanding of representation; in the search for a less racist set of images, representation is effectively defined as the work of accurately capturing, rather than ideologically constituting, the real. This means that the questions asked of the racist versions are not asked of their revision: whose version is being proposed, and in whose interests will it work? In the new version, it is implied, representation has been divorced from ideology.

Those of us who find existing conventions unacceptable would, of course, like Aborigines to be represented in ways that were more 'accurate' – that is, more closely accorded with a non-racist construction of their culture. Even if this can be achieved, however, it is worth asking if white Australians are the ones who should be responsible; there is an implicit paternalism in the call for a white reconstruction of a black reality. What whites recognize as a non-racist image of the Aboriginal may not be recognized as such by Aboriginals. Whites falsely assume that because they can detect the racist agenda underlying so many of their films they are also in possession of the knowledge of what would be a more acceptable agenda to the Aborigine.

The intractability and the importance of such issues was brought home to me by an article on Australian film by the Aboriginal author, Colin Johnson.[3] Johnson begins his discussion with Chauvel's *Jedda* (1955), and although he initially describes it as a 'sort of Tarzan in black face' he goes on to explain that there is an Aboriginal way of viewing this film which contradicts conventional white assumptions of its inherent, if inevitable, racism. Johnson suggests the film has an Aboriginal reading, focussing on 'the stealing of women, the social problem of wrongway relationships, and ... the fear/attraction of Mission-educated Aboriginal women when confronted by their Aboriginality in the form of an Aboriginal male ... in full control of his being'.[4] Johnson sees Tudawali's Marbuk (the male lead in *Jedda*) as 'the only dignified Aboriginal male lead that has been allowed to exist in films made by white directors in Australia'. He supports this judgement in the following remarks: 'I followed up [my interest in *Jedda*] by asking other Aboriginal people whether they found the film more attractive than recent films. Those who viewed the film said that they did, and it was precisely the depiction of the Aboriginal male on which they commented.'[5] Johnson goes on to compare the treatment of Marbuk in *Jedda* with that of Jimmie in *The Chant of Jimmie Blacksmith,* and the Aboriginal community generally in Beresford's *The Fringe Dwellers.* The result of the comparison is to challenge the accepted wisdom of white film critics who see both films as sensitive and accurate portrayals of Aboriginality.

Whatever one may think of, say, Beresford's achievement in *The Fringe Dwellers,* one can see Johnson's point. Robert Tudawali's Marbuk is tremendously powerful in *Jedda.* Tudawali is a star, and carries immense conviction on the screen; it is hard to think of any Australian actor, white or black, who signifies sexual power as comprehensively. It is significant that the challenge Marbuk issues to white society is never actually met. Marbuk dies, as Johnson puts it, 'because he has offended tribal law rather than because of anything the white man has shot at him'.[6] However, my point in reviewing this argument is not to propose a new Aboriginal reading of *Jedda* but rather to emphasize how easily (even inevitably) white critics can reproduce paternalistic assumptions about just what is a favourable, acceptable, or accurate representation of Aboriginal culture. As Johnson's argument makes abundantly clear, it is not a matter of simply inverting conventional narrative structures and centring the Aboriginal as the hero.

One practical point emerges from this. If we are interested in films which challenge rather than simply reproduce existing racist ideologies, we must realize how important it is for black Australians to have access to the media of representation, and to the means of distributing their own representations. But a second point also demands attention: Attacking the conventions of representation is only attacking the very last link in a chain of cultural production. Most interest in the representation of Aborigines in film has focussed on the film texts, to the exclusion of the material connections between texts and their determinants in institutions, government policy and discourse. Such connections require examinations if we are to address the problem of changing the products of our cultural system. The genuine usefulness of Moore and Muecke's article is of this kind, and I want to use it as the means of moving this discussion forward.

Moore and Muecke connect racist representations of Aboriginals with orientations in Australian cultural policy, or, as they put it, 'the way in which representations emerge from the use of filmic codes and techniques as they are articulated within social institutions and policies'. 'What sorts of film-making techniques,' they ask, were 'deployed in the service of the government policy of assimilation, or multi-culturalisms?'[7] They argue that a set of specific categories organized and structured all discursive formations of Aboriginality:

> The first [of these categories] ... is the paternalistic *assimilationist* formation; a number of films were made during the fifties and sixties which were part of this formation. This was followed by a liberal *multi-cultural* formation, and this is with us to the present day. The third formation relates to a linking of Aboriginal groups and individuals with leftist *independent* film-making groups. The films resulting are significantly seen as being produced within an ideology of 'self-determination' (the government's phrase) or 'community control' (the Aborigines' phrase).[8]

They outline an agenda for Australian cultural policy in the 1950s which frames the Aboriginal 'problem' largely in terms of Aboriginals' potential for integration into the white community. *Jedda* is specifically about integration, but offers little hope for its achievement. Moore and Muecke also list a number of government films, such as those made by the W.A. Department of Native Welfare, which were aimed at inculcating white middle-class values into their black charges. Australia's first Aboriginal university graduate and the current head of the Department of Aboriginal Affairs, Charles Perkins, was a particular favourite of film-makers in the sixties, being the subject of two films which depicted him as a model for his people, to whom 'the course of his life' was presumed to be 'as miraculous as a tribal myth'.[9] Australian-produced feature films, of course, were rare in this period but in those which were produced the Aboriginal was used in much the same way Tarzan films used the African.

The advent of the cultural pluralism of the early 1970s might appear to have opened up new opportunities for blacks, but Moore and Muecke argue that multi-culturalism also provided an alibi for later governments who preferred to leave the Aborigines to their own devices; the transfer of responsibility to Aboriginal communities often meant a cut in funding, and a reluctance to take on the Aboriginals' cause in states-rights disputes such as that at Noonkanbah in W.A. in 1979. Nevertheless, the representations of Aborigines in the first decade of the film industry revival, from 1971-1980, were markedly more positive, more knowledgeable, and more tolerant. The value of Aboriginal culture had certainly become more widely accepted but it was also more marketable as Australiana. With recognition came incorporation as such films as *The Last Wave* exploited Aboriginality as a cinematic exotic. Moore and Muecke also make the point that 'multi-cultural' films such as *Storm Boy, The Last Wave, Manganinnie* or *The Chant of Jimmie Blacksmith,* still offered a Romantic, patronizing view of the Aboriginal, constructing them as 'unitary in relation to some essential (and unknowable) principle such as the "spirituality of the dreaming" or "the closeness to nature" which ultimately engenders all action'.[10] This may seem a churlish rejection of a considerable liberalization of white attitudes, but Moore and Muecke's final criticisms of multi-culturalism are telling:

> ...with multi-culturalism a certain 'positivisation' of Aboriginal culture occurs. This positive process of recognition allows for the acceptance of Aboriginal art, dance, language, etc. whilst simultaneously screening out aspects like extended family forms, aspects of Aboriginal law, 'undesirable' social habits, 'unhealthy' environments and economic independence, within a rigid social harmony. In this sense, the notion of 'common humanity' should be seen as a ruse. Multi-culturalism, an admirable doctrine on paper, in effect allows for specific frameworks of recognition and acceptance. It, in effect, makes for new constructions of Aboriginal culture which should not be uncritically accepted as the result of progress or humanitarian leanings.[11]

One should not underestimate the recuperative powers of ideology.

Indeed, as Moore and Muecke move on to more contemporary developments they, too, reveal their comprehensive implication in the ideological system - albeit as proponents of resistance to dominant structures and meanings. In the last section of their study, they are no longer able to maintain the lofty objectivity of the historical survey. Their discussion of contemporary independent films is severely doctrinaire, with the film-makers' good intentions all too predictably juxtaposed against their unforeseen but reactionary consequences. Moore and Muecke's search for a value-free representation or, rather, for a seamless union between a film and their own ideological formations, dominates their last few pages and leads them to criticize films which, while never entirely breaking out of their ideological frame, seem to me to have negotiated significant modifications in dominant views of the Aboriginal. *Lousy Little Sixpence,* for one, retrieved a hitherto submerged history of Aboriginals' treatment (that of welfare agencies' systematic abduction of Aboriginals' children between the 1930s and 1950s) and situated it within a demonology of white racism for black *and* white Australians.

What Moore and Muecke's piece lacks is a degree of generosity in their assessment of the efforts of white and black film-makers to break out of an ideologically regulated representational system. It is supremely difficult to interrogate the system of meaning one uses, *as* one uses it, and still be understood by an audience. The 'failure' Moore and Muecke attribute to the makers of *Lousy Little Sixpence* should not be seen as a personal failure. It simply demonstrates the pervasiveness of ideology, infiltrating films made with the most impeccable of political intentions. As we shall see, the problem is not an isolated one; the history of Australian films is full of productions which have had good intentions but which are inevitably and hopelessly trapped within the very discourses they use.

Jedda, made in 1955, was itself a particularly daring and liberal film for its time. From a contemporary perspective, however, its naivety and Romanticism are only too clear (we tend not to see the assumptions underlying our own period's films so clearly). The characters are defined through their race, and unapologetically so. Any confusion Jedda feels as she is torn between white society and 'her own kind', is depicted as a riot in the blood, a triumph of nature over culture. In one scene, Jedda is playing some western classical music on the homestead piano. Outside, the tribal, sexually threatening, black male - Marbuk - is singing a song which completes deep emotional connections in the young girl. The camera portrays her confusion by cross-cutting between her increasingly exercised face and a painted bark shield hanging on the wall immediately in her view. As her agitation increases, the shield visibly vibrates, the manipulation of focus mimicking the dilation of her vision as she fights to retain her hold on white rationality. This is comic for audiences now; the scene's assumptions are so dated and the filmic techniques used to represent them so melodramatic. But it is representative of the definition of racial difference in our films - then and now - as genetic rather than cultural.

There are standard strategies for differentiating between white and black in Australian cinema.[12] There is, for instance, the invocation of a kind of biological imperative which links 'black' blood and 'black' behaviour. Within such discourses the black is animal-like, helpless before the call of the wild - as is Jedda - and is thus seen to be in some way finally biologically determined. This is related to the next discursive strategy: that of collapsing distinctions between the Aboriginal and nature. Aborigines have been, and continue to be seen as metonyms for an Australian landscape; like kangaroos and Ayers Rock, they are among the natural attributes of the continent. This is dehumanizing, and has served to legitimate white settlers' treatment of the Aborigines as pests well into the twentieth century. It is also a way of displacing the social, cultural and political problems. To see the Aboriginal as a dying species rather than a subordinated culture is to explain their condition as the result of the inevitable operation of natural forces rather than as the product of a specific history. Finally, the most obvious sign of difference is the deployment of blackness itself. A sign of evil, of the primitive and the unknown for western cultures, blackness is mobilized in Chauvel's depiction of Marbuk as a symbol for the instinctive and unconscious recesses of Jedda's personality. Similar symbolic deployments of blackness occur in more recent and (one would have thought) more enlightened Australian films in the service of similar thematic and ideological ends.

The development of white understandings of the particular character of Aboriginal spirituality (that is, we know more than Chauvel did when he made *Jedda*) has not produced the radical reconsiderations one might have expected. Indeed, to be seen as the possessors of an ancient but passé mysticism is not necessarily to the Aboriginals' advantage since it renders them even more unfit for white society, places them at an even greater remove from white rationality. The sense of a culture lost, of an irretrievable epistemology, is all too often invoked as an alibi for restricting white interest in the Aboriginal to the sentimental regret for the passing of their tribal culture. So Eric Michaels' remark, quoted at the beginning of this discussion, that little has changed in Australian film since the 1950s, is perhaps not surprising; it does deserve some extension and demonstration, however, by a survey of some of the 'enlightened' films of the revival.

Walkabout, for instance, was made in 1971 by the English director, Nicholas Roeg. While it was in many respects both intelligent and perceptive, Roeg's film effortlessly recycled conventional views of the Australian landscape and of Aboriginality. The two were intertwined, as frill-necked lizards competed with David Gulipilil in the signification of strangeness, otherness, the Antipodes. Gulipilil's Aborigine acts as the guide for two lost children, mediating between them and the harsh landscape. He also attempts to construct a closer relationship than this with the girl, who (understandably, in the film's eyes) responds with fear and alarm. The rejected Aboriginal hangs himself but the children survive to later indulge in nostalgic daydreams of the lost opportunity of a Romantic idyll in Nature with the noble savage. As in so many films depicting the clash of cultures, the whites survive the ordeal but the black does not.

While Fred Schepisi's *The Chant of Jimmie Blacksmith* (1978) is far more conscious of its assumptions than either *Jedda* or *Walkabout,* there are similarities between the films which do not flatter the more recent production. Jimmie has moments of confusion and frustration produced by the racial cocktail brewing in his veins. When Jimmie, Mort, and the captive schoolteacher reach the desecrated sacred site in the mountains, Jimmie is confused and weakened by his conflicting loyalties and responsibilities. Like Jedda, he is rendered immobile by his biology. As is the case with *Walkabout,* the merging of the black man with nature is a deliberate effect of the film's cinematography,[13] let alone the ideology of the narrative. Schepisi has talked about his deliberate blending of the Aborigine with the landscape, making him indistinguishable from it in order to establish the difference between the Aboriginal submersion in the land and the whites' occupation of the land. Well-meaning though this is, its consequence is the naturalization of the Aboriginal's marginal and subordinated place within white culture, the recycling of racist alibis for their failure to assimilate, and the sentimentalization of their culture. More importantly, for the film as a whole, it obscures the fact that there is nothing 'natural' about Jimmie's condition or the lack of any 'natural' place for him in the social contexts the film provides. In *The Chant of Jimmie Blacksmith,* Jimmie is composed entirely contradictorily, as both social problem and biological battleground; as a product of white history and of the social relations of his race; as a victim of white prejudice and of his own confused blood.

It should be noted that Schepisi's film does genuinely try to renovate racist constructions of Aboriginality, and his intentions deserve respect. Nevertheless, he made no contact with Aboriginal groups to advise him on the project, and accepted a sensationalist advertising campaign that trivialized the main thrust of his film. (The bloody axe-head logo for the film was possibly responsible for what Colin Johnson said was his lingering impression, that of 'beserk boongs hacking to death white ladies').[14]

No such alibi could be offered for Peter Weir's *The Last Wave* (1977), which unashamedly exploits a white mythology of blackness. In a film which continually infers rather than depicts the supernatural, the uncanny, and the mystical, the lingering close-up on the black face is a central strategy for sustaining the threat of disruption. Here all the old assumptions about the difference of the black race are mobilized as motivational agents for a supernatural thriller. Weir's detribalized Aborigines may be living in the city, but they retain a race memory from centuries ago. Their memories are, as it were, in their blood - even the diluted blood of the white lawyer, David, who shares a fraction of their ancestry. Biological determinism at its most uncomplicated provides the narrative justification for the Aborigines' premonition of a tidal wave destroying Sydney; for David's sharing of that premonition; and even for the capacity to register and recognize such a premonition. The whole farrago of supernatural goings-on is given a specific material location: a lost underworld of darkness, ritual, and contagion in the sewers emptying onto Bondi beach. Admittedly, the film has a limited interest in or need for realistic plot-lines or a liberal politics, but its unthinking recycling of Darwinian racial myths is implicitly reactionary.

In many Australian films, the structure of the plot holds the clue to the apportionment of power to Aboriginal culture and its representatives. As Johnson points out, Marbuk is not a victim of the white man, but of his own law, and thus retains a degree of independence not found in (say) Jimmie Blacksmith. One structural factor which Kevin Brown has noted[15] is the number of films depicting a conflict between the black and white worlds which employ a go-between. The rigidity of the racial opposition is established in the need for a character to mediate it. In many cases, the go-between is white: David in *The Last Wave,* the reporter in *Tudawali,* young Mike in *Storm Boy.* In most cases where the go-between is black - *Walkabout, Jimmie Blacksmith, Jedda* - the result of their attempt to cross the opposition is death. Even a film as aware of its constituent politics as Steve Jodrell's recent *Tudawali* still implied that while whites can cross the divide between the cultures, the Aborigines can't. There are important exceptions to this - *Backroads, Wrong Side of the Road* - but the place of the Aboriginal within the structure of the narrative is all too often an index of the limits of his or her personal and social power.

As Jodrell's *Tudawali* reminds us, it is difficult for commercially distributed films to break out of the frame, to resist the simple reproduction of stereotyped characters and existing power relations. Brown's paper on this topic[16] juxtaposed two revealing pieces of research on the practices of casting Aboriginals for Australian films. He recounted the problems the Chauvels experienced in casting Marbuk; they wanted a tribal Aboriginal, deeply black in colour, a perfect icon of the race but one which even then had almost disappeared. The result of the Chauvels' search for the 'right' look inevitably reproduced the existing stereotype rather than suggested some need for its modification. Brown also recounted a description of Schepisi's search for Jimmie Blacksmith - where the same discourse of finding the 'right' look was used. Far from criticizing these two producers, the point was made that the industry authorized such searches as necessities; the film-makers could admit no alternative to the attempt to find the 'right look' - that is, one that entirely meshed with the expectations, even the prejudices, of the projected audience. One is forced to conclude that film's structural relation to its culture, its ability to both produce and reproduce its ideologies but not to substantially change them, makes it unlikely that large-scale renovations in Australian constructions of Aboriginality will originate in a feature film.

The system of racial difference the culture has set up is one which sees white and black as mutually exclusive categories; one is what the other is not. Unless this determining structural relation is exploded it reproduces itself endlessly, no matter how often we shift it onto new terrain. If we *are* to find a way of reconstructing the representation of the Aboriginal race in film, it will be through supporting the efforts of Aboriginals to make their *own* films and to present them to white audiences. Ned Landers' *Wrong Side of the Road* offers an example of what such a film might be like, as it sets out to dissolve differences, to largely dispense with white signifiers of Aboriginality, while still dealing with the subordination of Aboriginal culture.

It is likely that white Australians will have to become more familiar with Aboriginal representations of their world. As Tracey Moffatt has protested in *Filmnews,* Aboriginal film-makers are more active and successful than the white film community may be prepared to admit:

> I'm sick of being told I'm part of a race of people who are continually on the verge of emerging.
>
> For christsakes we're here baby! To mention a few: CAAMA, Murri Image, Madalaine McGrady, Byron Syron, Michael Riley and myself. I've made one film and two videos this year, successful both here and internationally. With my phone ringing hot; SBS, ABC, Film Australia as well as numerous Abor iginal organizations and communities.[17]

Tracey Moffatt's *Nice Coloured Girls* is only one recent example of a well respected if not yet widely screened film about Aboriginals which subverts conventional white coding of Aboriginality. The granting of a television licence to an Aboriginal collective in the Northern Territory also offers hope of an alternative set of meanings and practices emanating from the Aboriginal community. However, this collective, Imparja, is also a sobering reminder of how difficult this reorientation will be: how asymmetrical the power relations are at all levels and in all locations. As a result of pressure from the Northern Territory government (ostensibly worried about discrimination in favour of Aborigines, and the possibility their TV programming would not allow enough for white interests!) Imparja has had to accept a greater degree of commercial sponsorship than originally intended. It is now an informal member of the Nine network, buying its programmes and syndicating much of its advertising through this network. As a result of this and other compromises forced upon them, Imparja still only employs two Aboriginal workers, and programmes only an hour a week of specialist Aboriginal programmes. Its first day of broadcasting offered a chilling reminder of the major media owners' facility for incorporation: opening with a specialist Aboriginal programme, Imparja soon settled down into a diet of sitcoms and cricket.

Nevertheless, the key question is no longer how do whites represent Aboriginals in Australian film, but how are Aboriginals going to do it. Aboriginal film-makers now face the dilemma of constituting an image of themselves - virtually from whole cloth - that will renovate existing images and still be comprehensible. It is still too early to tell just what Aboriginal film-makers will do with the medium, exactly what kinds of intervention will emerge over the next five years, and how these will be incorporated into white iconographies of race. The past has shown how impossible it is for whites to make a film which is independent of the ideological frame; the future will see if the Aboriginals can break free in their use of the medium.

Perhaps the fact that such a question can now urgently be posed indicates that things have changed. As Eric Michaels puts it:

> Aborigines and Aboriginality have always been subject to appropriation by European Australians, so that we consider the production of Aboriginal images for mass consumption as a right, if not a responsibility, of a nation consumed with the manufacture of its own mythology. None of this should prove to be novel considerations for Australian film scholars, engaged as we are in a self-conscious exploration of the received post-modernist debate and its application to the national situation. In that discourse we learn of the power of inscription, the disappearance of the signified, as it collapses into the signifier. What may be news is who Australia now regards as having the rights to make this appropriation.[18]

Less hopefully, Michaels goes on to suggest that whoever ends up dominating the discourses of Aboriginality in film, television, and in the media generally - the 'exotic' avant-garde film producers, the local Aboriginal television communities, or the Aboriginal 'experts' (politically or academically authorized) - 'they will write the new Aboriginal history'.[1]49 This worries Michaels - and should also worry others - as an entirely new set of possibilities are ushered in, all far removed from, and potentially destructive of, the traditional basis of Aboriginal life. Paradoxically, now that Aboriginals are gaining some control over the production, and perhaps soon the dissemination, of their own images they face even greater risks, because there is more at stake than when whites had appropriated this responsibility for themselves.

NOTES

1. Eric Michaels, 'Aboriginal Content: Who's Got It – Who Needs It?', *Art and Text,* 24, 1986, p. 74.
2. See Catriona Moore and Stephen Muecke, 'Racism and the Representation of Aborigines in Film', *Australian Journal of Cultural Studies,* 2:1, 1984, pp. 36-53.
3. Colin Johnson, 'Chauvel and the Aboriginal Male in Australian Film', *Continuum,* 1:1, 1987, pp. 47-57.
4. Ibid., p. 48.
5. Ibid., p. 48.
6. Ibid., p. 48.
7. Moore and Muecke, p. 36.
8. Ibid., pp. 36-37.
9. Ibid., p. 41.
10. Ibid., p. 42.
11. Ibid., p. 46.
12. Kevin Brown, 'Fiction, Documentary and the Aboriginal Look: *The Last Wave* and the Representation of Aborigines in Australian Feature Films', paper presented to the History and Film Conference, Brisbane, December 1987.
13. See the interview with Schepisi in Sue Matthews' *35 MM Dreams* (Melbourne: Penguin, 1984), pp. 23-66.
14. Ibid., p. 50.
15. 'Fiction, Documentary and the Aboriginal Look'.
16. Ibid.
17. Filmnews, 17:11, 1987, p. 2.
18. Eric Michaels, op. cit., p. 73.
19. Ibid.

FILMS REFERRED TO:

Chant of Jimmie Blacksmith, The (1978) dir. Fred Schepisi
Fringe Dwellers, The (1986) dir. Bruce Beresford
Jedda (1955) dir. Charles Chauvel
Last Wave, The (1977) dir. Peter Weir
Lousy Little Sixpence, dir. Gerry Bostock and Alex Morgan
Manganinnie (1981) dir. John Honey
Nice Coloured Girls (1987) dir. Tracey Moffatt
Storm Boy (1976) dir. Henri Safran
Tudawali (1987) dir. Stephen Jodrell
Walkabout (1971) dir. Nicholas Roeg
Wrong Side of the Road (1985) dir. Ned Landers

Tracey Moffatt Photo: Reece Scannell

Changing Images

AN INTERVIEW WITH TRACEY MOFFATT

INTRODUCTION

Tracey Moffatt is one of Australia's most exciting young experimental film makers. She made her debut with *Nice Coloured Girls* which won the prize for the Most Innovative Film at the 1988 Festival of Australian Film and Video, *Frames*. She also won the *Frames* Best New Australian Video Award with a five minute Aboriginal and Islander dance video called *Watch Out*. Tracey Moffat believes that black women have either been overlooked or misrepresented in films made by white people. Her aim is to change this image, she is determined to show that there are strong black women, survivors. Not only does she want to change the images. She wants to present the new images in a different way. 'I really wanted to avoid the clichés and didacticism of earlier films about my people. The last thing I wanted was the usual groans, "Here we go again, another predictable docomentary about Aborigines"'. She has achieved both aims in her film *Nice Coloured Girls* where three young Aboriginal girls go out in the Cross, find a Captain (Sugar Daddy) and roll him.

The film however is not just a simple reversal of Aboriginal women's roles from victims to survivors. Using experimental film techniques the film relates the life of these modern urban Aboriginal women to the lives of the Aboriginal women living in Australia at the time of the white invasion. Tracey Moffatt's concerns go beyond this Australian issue to the broader issue of male/female white/black relationships. *Nice Coloured Girls* is a very important work of art when considering the whole issue of Imperialism, Capitalism, Patriarchy and Racism.

Apart from being an independent film and video maker she is also a photographer. Her work is represented in many places including the Australian National Gallery and the National Gallery of Victoria. Her latest series of photographs *Some Lads* was featured in the NADOC 86 exhibition of Aboriginal and Islander Photographers. This series like *Nice Coloured Girls* is a reaction to traditional images of Aborigines by white Australians. Tracey Moffatt says.

> The concept behind this series of studio portraits of black male dancers came about in reaction to images of black Australian people I was continually seeing presented around me by photographers in books, magazines and galleries. These images tended to always fit into the realist documentary mode usually reserved for the 'ethnographic subject'.
>
> Such examples of this style of representation of indigenous groups exist in all European-colonised countries e.g. North America, Brazil, etc. This 'record them now before they die out' mentality has never been exclusive to Australia.
>
> *Some Lads* takes the utmost example of such a preoccupation – being the mid-nineteenth century scientific studio studies of Aborigines by the early pioneer photographers – but changes the intentions. Here I use a studio situation, the lighting flat, and a similar blank backdrop. The voyeuristic quality remains, heralding the use of the black frame (edge of negative), the window-like frame within the frame. Here I encourage my subjects to enjoy the staring camera (in contrast to the uncomfortable glaring in the earlier century photographs), to intentionally pose and show off. In an attempt to dispense with the seriousness and preciousness, it captures a lyricism and rarely assigned bold sensuality.

This interview took place at Tracy Moffatt's Sydney home on August 3rd, 1988.

Anna Rutherford

INTERVIEW

Hanif Kureishi, the director of My Beautiful Laundrette, *received a lot of criticism from the Pakistani community in England because he portrayed a certain section of that community not only as out and cut capitalists ('fat cats' as Salman Rushdie called them) but as racists as well. You must have suffered a similar reaction from certain members of the Aboriginal community who objected to your portrayal of Aboriginal women in* Nice Coloured Girls.

Yes. I'm an Aboriginal film maker and from certain members of the Aboriginal scene you are pressured into always having to present a positive view of Aboriginal life which I find really annoying. It's very one-sided. I'm interested in saying things about black Australia but I'm interested in saying them in a different way filmically. The film, *The Fringedwellers* is a very Hollywood version of Aboriginal life. There's an attempt to show Aboriginals as human beings with human emotions which is all very nice but it was just a very glossy view I thought, which annoyed a lot of Aboriginal people. For example there was no mention of Land Rights throughout the film. That

Photograph from 'Some Lads' series.
Australian National Gallery, Canberra.

Shooting on location, *Nice Coloured Girls*

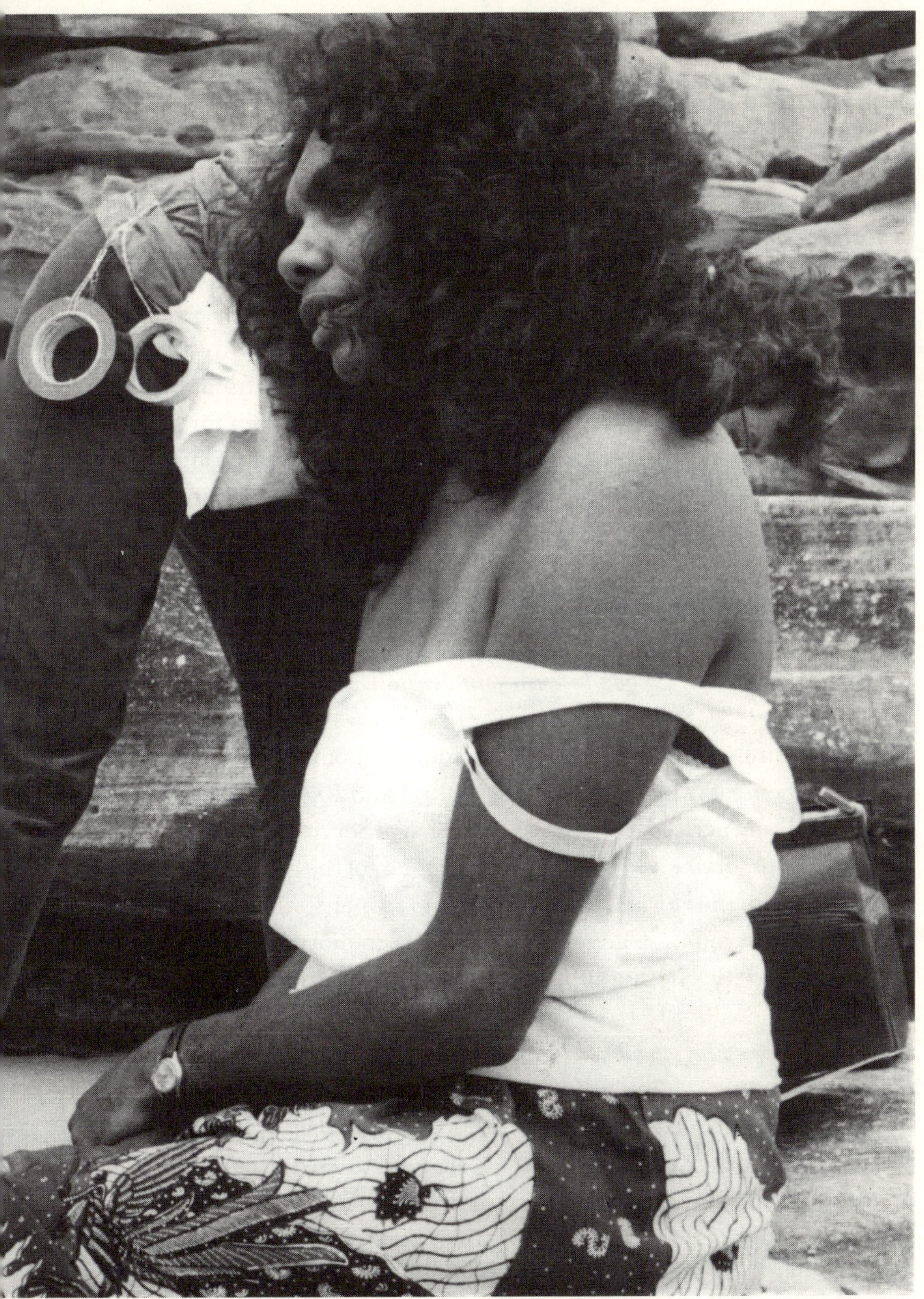

Tracey Moffatt and actress Rosemary Meagher.

doesn't mean that I think that just because you're making a film about Aboriginal people you have to talk about Land Rights but Bruce Beresford, the white director, was wanting to make a film about contemporary Aboriginal society. He hadn't been in Australia for ten years, then came back thinking he could make a film about Black Australia not realising that a lot has changed in ten years. Blacks have become more political. That is one criticism I have of his film.

My film, *Nice Coloured Girls*, concerns three Aboriginal girls who go out in the night in Kings Cross, Sydney, pick up a 'Captain' which is an Aboriginal term for a sugar daddy, have a good night and in the end roll him which is a very real thing, it happens. I used to do it, I used to do it with my sisters. I have been criticized by older Aboriginal women for presenting Aboriginal women like that. But I say to them, 'We're not little angels'. Look at the reactions of the Italian community to *The Godfather* when it was first released. And now fifteen years later no one blinks an eyelid. I think it will be the same with my film. In five years time people will wonder what all the fuss was about.

Do you think there is a big gap between your generation and the older generation?

Yes, but I think I'm yet another generation. I'm not the generation that set up the tent embassy in 1972 and fought the Land Rights battle. I didn't set up the Medical Services, I didn't set up the Legal Services. I've always known there is a legal service and a medical service; I'm of the generation who have benefitted from the work of Kath Walker and so many others like her. We're a different generation, a generation that feels comfortable in talking about Aboriginal society whether it be through film or writing or art.

Can you say something about your background?

I came from Brisbane. My people grew up on an Aboriginal mission outside of Brisbane called Cherbourg. I was fostered out to a white family along with my brother and two sisters. It wasn't however the situation that happened to so many Aboriginal mothers having their children taken away from them. It wasn't like that. It wasn't against my mother's will. My mother knew my foster mother. We grew up with this white family but still had a lot to do with our black relatives; thank God for that. So I have a lot of black relations and a lot of white relations. I went to art school and studied film when I was nineteen. Afterwards I went to Europe and travelled around - that's when I went to Denmark back in 1979. So I come from an art school background, not a film background, I studied film but not in a formal way.

In 1982 I moved to Sydney and became involved in the independent film making scene here which has been very supportive of Aboriginal people as far as film goes. Lots of films came out in the seventies that were produced by left wing independent white film makers here in Sydney, like *My Survival as an Aboriginal*, *Lousy Little Sixpence*, *Wrong Side of the Road*. Very important films and very good films but I didn't feel the need to copy that style of film even though I was influenced by it. I didn't feel I had to set out to make films about the struggle for Land Rights, mining on Aboriginal land, issues dealing with racism which people automatically think that that's what you're going to do because you're a black film maker.

I'm really interested in experimental film making. I know a lot of Aboriginal people would think that that was being esoteric and not dealing with the really important things, like the appalling health problems of so many in the Aboriginal community, or deaths in custody, that sort of thing. And I do work in that area as well. I have been invited to go to Perth in November in order to make a film for some Aboriginal women. It is going to be about some Western Australian Aboriginal women who want to talk about deaths in custody. I'm willing to do that sort of film but I don't think it needs to be done in a straightforward documentary way so I'll be doing something different for them, for instance like the video you just saw (*Watch Out*). The other women who worked on that series produced five minute pieces about Australian women using archival footage to talk about the history of Australian women. But I thought a lot could be said in another way. There's just a dance sequence intercut with family photographs of the girl who choreographed the piece and who appears in the video as the lead dancer. Statements need to be made, but what I'm trying to do is say them in a more interesting way. I don't believe in having to talk down to Aboriginal people. I don't want to make my films simplistic, assuming that people can't understand them unless they are simple. Take the writing of Colin Johnson for instance. He writes for any audience. He is not choosing his audience and neither am I. I think it is very patronising to assume that people are not going to understand your work.

Apart from being a film maker you are also a photographer.

Yes. In between films I work as a freelance photographer. I do a lot of work with the Aboriginal Island Dance Theatre who have recently toured in Germany. It's the only Aboriginal Black Dance School in Australia. The school teaches traditional Aboriginal dance, they have traditional tutors who come down from the North as well as Islander people. You have to be Aboriginal or Islander to get into the school. They also teach jazz ballet, Afro-jazz, tap dance.

You've just done a video on AIDS.

Yes. I was asked by the Aboriginal Medical Service to put together something that Aboriginal people would find interesting to watch, not a straight health video style sort of thing. And so I made *Spread the Word*. We don't go into the history of AIDS or what it is, it is about how to not get it which is the most important thing. It has done very well and I think it is going to be screened on Channel Four in London. There was a conference on AIDS recently over there and all the Australians brought over their commercials and the only thing they were interested in looking at over there was this film we had produced for the Aboriginal community. Not only urban based Aboriginals but also Aboriginal communities living in traditional situations in Arnhem Land have liked it and related to it so I think I have been able to cater for most Aboriginal people. It was important to make this film for Aboriginal people because they are sick of looking at white people. We were giving out the same information – use condoms, don't share needles if you do use drugs – but it was brown people saying it and therefore I think you are going to get Aboriginal people's attention. We also used Aboriginal humour in the video to get the message across, little 'in' jokes and Aboriginal English which is different to English English or white Australian English.

Do you think that the films you have made and plan on making will have an impact on the white community as well as the Aboriginal community.

Yes, I think so. *Nice Coloured Girls* has been screened in many festivals around the world. I have been invited to the Edinburgh Film Festival because they are having a retrospective of Australian independent film making and I have been invited to give a talk along with two of Australia's top film theorists. I think my work is receiving attention and awards not just because it is dealing with Aborigines or because I am an Aborigine but because I am experimenting with different film forms which is what I want to do. *Nice Coloured Girls* has been in a lot of festivals. I went to Italy with it last year and it has recently been on in New York in a showing of films run by the Collective for Living Cinema under the title 'Sexism, Colonialism, Misinterpretation: A Corrective Films Service', a series of films all made by women and which aimed to look at patriarchy, colonialism and capitalism from an oppositional perspective.

In what ways would you describe your work as experimental?

First of all because it is challenging previous styles of representation of Aborigines in film. It's not going for the straight documentary or realist drama. Films that usually deal with black people, both drama and documentary are always realist in their attempt and I'm not concerned with capturing reality, I'm concerned with creating it myself. And that way the film has a very artificial look about it, in the use of sets and installation and that sort of thing. I like to avoid on location shooting. I like the control of the studio rather than taking the camera out. I'm not concerned with verisimulitude, with the camera seeing everything and being there. In saying this I'm not putting down previous films made by white film makers about Aborigines, for example those very good documentaries that I mentioned earlier and also the work of the Institute of Aboriginal Studies which is into ethnographic film making and which is very useful. But I don't think I need to work in that sort of style.

Do you see a better future for Aboriginal people in Australia?

As far as film making and people becoming involved in the arts I'm very positive about that. The Land Rights situation has become better but we've got these liberal[1] governments back in again and they're going to be changing things.

One important area is the schools where it is essential that Aboriginal Studies courses be introduced. I wish I had had Aboriginal Studies courses when I was at school. I grew up in Queensland - no mention of anything Aboriginal in those schools. I also think that white Australian kids would be interested.

Do you think that there is a more positive and open attitude on the part of white Australians to the Aborigines?

Well where I live in Sydney, in Glebe, I'm surrounded by people involved in the arts, film, they are people doing alternative things and because you are surrounded by a lot of good people you begin to think, 'Oh yeah, things are great', but if you take a trip to the country and you're not allowed into the pub because you're black, that's when you realise that things have not changed. You can't go around presuming that things are becoming groovy, that we're a multicultural society and that people are accepting different looking people these days. I go home to Queensland and nothing's changed. It depresses me. But I want to be optimistic.

NOTE

1. In Australia the Liberal party represents the conservative element of the society.

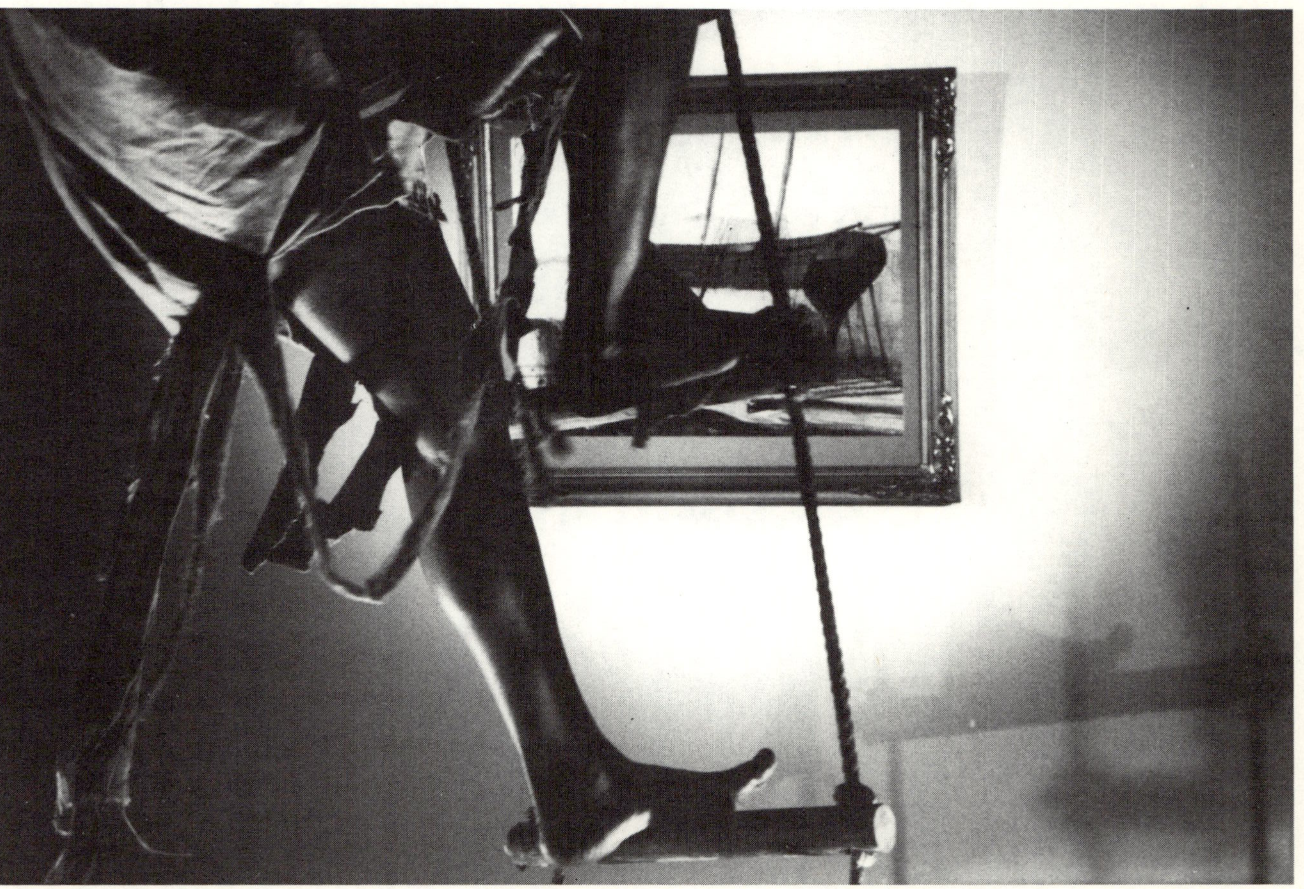

Still: *Nice Coloured Girls*

1. Map of Australian Aboriginal arts and crafts centres c. 1980.

J.V.S. AND M. RUTH MEGAW

The Dreamers Awake: Contemporary Australian Aboriginal Art

A mere twenty years ago most people thought of contemporary Australian Aboriginal arts and crafts as primarily the production of bark paintings and boomerangs, mostly for the tourist trade, or as the European-style watercolour landscapes of the Aranda artists from the Hermannsburg Lutheran Mission east of Alice Springs, of whom the best-known was Albert Namatjira (1902-1959). Collecting Western institutions were generally museums whose interest was primarily in the ethnographic aspects of the art. Since then there have been some remarkable developments in both quantity and range, at a rate which makes any description or analysis likely to be out of date as soon as it is written. In this, Australia's Bicentennial year, Aboriginal art has become one of the prime ways of asserting the continued and distinct identity of Fourth World people where, unlike the Third World, the colonizers never went home.

In 1988 Aboriginal art also includes the acrylic paintings of an increasing number of communities in Central Australia, fine pottery and textiles and the paintings and prints of a range of individual artists, often city-dwellers. At the 1988 Adelaide Festival one of no less than eight exhibitions devoted to contemporary Aboriginal art displayed prints of political protest by both white and Aboriginal artists under the title of *Right Here, Right Now*; without inside knowledge it was impossible to tell which graphics were by whites and which by Aboriginals. In 1979, the Flinders University of South Australia's Art Museum began consciously collecting what, a number of years ago, Nelson Graburn (1976; 1982) first referred to as 'transitional' art, but, with a few honourable exceptions, major art institutions such as the Australian National Gallery, the Art Gallery of South Australia and other State galleries only began buying Aboriginal art, especially that from central Australia, to any significant degree around 1984. Commercial 'fine art' galleries – mostly run by non-Aborigines – have also begun to sell Aboriginal art at ever-increasing prices, and major overseas exhibitions have been held in the

United States and Europe. Aboriginal art has thus, in some forms, become recognized in the white art world as 'High Art'. With these developments have come problems of increasing economic dependence on a white-controlled art market where profits often go to the dealers, not the artists, where the values by which the work is judged may be quite different from those of the artists themselves, and where over-production and competition may in the long run affect prices and thus livelihoods, a problem not unknown to western artists also. In many central Australian communities, the income from art sales is now often the only money coming in from other than governmental sources.

TRANSITIONAL ART

Before the arrival of Europeans, Aboriginal art was part of a complicated network of social relationships, largely ceremonial in character and concerned with connections with land and mythological origins. It was not made for outsiders and, in a precommercial society, it had no monetary value. Much of twentieth-century aboriginal art is 'transitional' in a number of ways. It is the art of people overwhelmed by an alien culture within which they have had to learn to live in order to survive, since the whites have made few adjustments. It has also accepted and used new media of expression; painting in acrylic on board or canvas has joined ground or body painting in the central Australian communities, prints and posters are widely used as are non-traditional colours. The value of the work is now more complex in monetary, aesthetic, social and economic terms and to different categories of people. Finally, many white teachers, missionaries, anthropologists and painters have been influential in the emergence of non-traditional forms of Aboriginal art, as, since the mid-1970s, have the, once again mostly white, art advisors paid for by the Federally funded Aboriginal Arts Board and appointed by aboriginal communities. Whether consciously or unconsciously, they have influenced Aboriginal artistic expression in both form and content (Anderson and Dussart 1988).

Art advisors provide art materials, buy the finished products according to their own criteria of what is technically competent and saleable, and arrange the exhibition and sale of items to the outside world. Many of these people have hoped, sometimes idealistically, sometimes paternalistically, to improve the economic self-sufficiency of Aborigines, and enhance their status in a white man's world, which, however ambiguously, recognises the artist as having some role. Art production provides a form of income which allows Aborigines to remain outside the white world of employment, and thus helps the survival of distinct Aboriginal communities and identity. The system of funding and marketing since the 1970s has also encouraged increasing numbers of communities to take up art production. The combination of government funding and the provision to artists of cash before outside sale, which could otherwise be subject to market vagaries, has meant steady if not spectacular income for some communities, and encouraged emulation by others. The Government has, however, recently suggested that art advisors should not be publicly funded, but paid for by the communities out of their profits. The question of marketing has been more difficult. In recent years successive attempts at setting up Aboriginal-run if publicly-funded bodies for the support of both outback and urban artists and for the marketing of their works have foundered. One such body is Aboriginal Arts Australia, trading as Inada Holdings and funded by the Department of Aboriginal Affairs, with an all-Aboriginal Board. In 1987, 16 communities broke away to form the Association of Northern and Central Aboriginal Artists, with its own *ANCAA* Newsletter. Art advisers are paid for by the Aboriginal Arts Board under the Federal Department of Arts, and they and their artists want more control of marketing for artists. So far the major effect of this breakaway has been greater access to the art of the communities for private galleries and collectors, but ANCAA itself is providing a quite remarkable forum for the exchange of news and views between artists and communities (Isaacs 1987).

For many of the artists themselves, the art provides a link to the Dreamtime past of their ancestors and, even more specifically, shows their connection with the land which many are now demanding back from their white conquerors. This poses a problem for those Aboriginal artists who no longer have distinct tribal or land affiliations, as is often the case in the more densely populated regions of south and eastern Australia. But, whatever the content and continuity of the dreamings, the forms they now take are often commercially motivated, and the production of these forms would almost certainly cease if whites stopped buying them (Anderson and Dussart 1988).

EARLIER DEVELOPMENTS

As in Africa or North America, direct and indirect European influence on aboriginal visual arts has a long history. It is evident in the c. 1860-1901 narrative pen-and-ink drawings of Tommy McRae, an Aborigine of the Upper Murray River, and of his contemporary William Barak who lived at the Aboriginal reserve of Coranderrk near Melbourne. In the centre of Australia in the 1930s Aranda children on the Finke River Lutheran Mission at Hermannsburg were producing drawings in a 'European' manner under the influence of Arthur Much and Frances Derham. In the 1940s lively genre pictures were being executed at the Carrolup Aboriginal School in Western Australia – today an Aboriginal controlled community attempting with white aid to produce its own new forms of art and crafts.

In the 1930s Albert Namatjira developed the foundations of the still continuing Hermannsburg school of Aranda water-colourists under the tutelage of the Victorian artist Rex Battarbee. Some of the current output of such work can be dismissed as tourist *kitsch*, but it too emphasizes the artists' connection with the land. After decades of disdain by white art critics, Namatjira's work has recently been more sympathetically re-assessed (Maughan and Megaw 1986,49-52; Amadio 1986), and a major exhibition on the Hermannsburg artists is planned for 1989.

BARK PAINTING

Though early white explorers report bark paintings in southern Australia, their production is now confined to the north. The pioneering anthropologist Baldwin Spencer and a local land-owner Paddy Cahill commissioned some for the National Museum of Victoria in 1911-12. From the late 1920s regular production for sale was actively sponsored by missionaries in north-eastern Arnhem Land, notably the Reverend Wilbur Chaseling at Yirrkala. The aims were economic self-sufficiency and the reinforcing of Aboriginal identity. Barks are now produced by Tiwi men and women on Bathurst and Melville Islands, in the Kimberley region of Western Australian and above all in Arnhem Land. Bark painting was normally transient before this development and the designs were secret-sacred and in many areas not available to women. The production of barks for sale has encouraged techniques to preserve both bark and pigments. It has also meant that many of the barks for sale to whites used new, non-secret designs in which the artists were willing to indulge the white taste for more representative imagery. This new domain of bark painting exists alongside the continued use of designs for ritual purposes (Berndt, Berndt and Stanton 1982, 51-68). Because of this women are also beginning to paint barks, for example at Yirrkala, using these new domains or portrayals of their everyday life or even Christian iconography as subject matter (Maughan and Megaw 1986, 19-29). Most recently the all-pervading use of acrylic paints has extended even to the 'translation' of bark-painting subjects onto canvas.

TEXTILES, POTTERY SCULPTURE AND BASKETRY

In the north-west desert regions of South Australia dedicated white teachers introduced a whole range of new techniques to the women of the Pitjantjatjara and Yunkuntjatjara communities of the far north-east of South Australia. From 1954, largely under the guidance of Winifred Hilliard at Ernabella, spinning and rug-weaving was introduced but gave way to the less labour-intensive batik printing for fashion fabrics from about 1971 (Hilliard 1985). Anmatyerre/Aliawarra women at Utopia (Green 1981) and Pitjantjatjara and Yunkuntjatjara women at Indulkana also turned to batik. Skills borrowed from Indonesian crafts-workers were used to produce a whole range of swirling foliate designs which have recently been translated by these and a number of other communities into silkscreen or lino prints. Women in the far west of Australia and at Yuendumu in the Centre as well as much further north on Bathurst Island and at Yirrkala have also taken up batik printing. In other parts of Arnhem Land where men traditionally own the clan designs used in bark painting, women have till recently been confined to the weaving of bags, baskets and mats.

While the Tiwi (men and women) of Bathurst and Melville Islands continue to carve and paint their funerary carved *pukumani* poles as part of their own ceremonial life, they are also now producing them for sale as well as other carvings of birds and mythical beings. In a move which Aboriginal art advisor John Mundine sees as a quiet protest for the Bicentennial, he has persuaded the Australian National Gallery to commission an exhibition of

200 *pukumani* poles, which their Aboriginal creators regard as a proper commemoration of 200 years of white occupation. Figures like those on the carvings are being repeated as motifs in the highly successful Bima Wear fabric printing of the Tiwi Designs cooperative. Woodblock and silkscreen printing was begun in 1969 under the supervision of Madeline Clear as a partnership between two young Tiwi, Bede Tungutalum and Giovanni Tipungwuti. The cooperative now employs many other Tiwi on a full-time basis. The use of acrylic and canvas is also beginning, as elsewhere in northern Australia, in an attempt to repeat the success of the contemporary painters of the so-called 'Papunya school' of the Centre.

Other fabric production includes that of Jumbana Designs. This company uses the designs of John Moriarty, originally of the Yanula/Borroloola group, but, like so many other young Aborigines, removed early from his home environment and now a high-level public servant in Adelaide. The most aggressive recent marketing of fabric designs is that of the company formed to promote the designs and prints of Jimmy Pike. Jimmy was born into a nomadic group of Walmadjari in the Great Sandy Desert of Western Australia, but learned to paint in Fremantle gaol, and has achieved recent major recognition as an artist (Lowe 1987).

Some of the fabrics, like some of the craft pottery now produced by various Aboriginal communities, including the Tiwi, have met with considerable white sales resistance for not looking 'Aboriginal' enough. Almost unique in gaining wide recognition and in achieving a freedom of expression in the non-traditional medium of ceramics is the work of Thancoupie (b. 1937) from Weipa on Cape York in northern Queensland, but trained in Sydney. Thancoupie's small-scale pieces and major murals 'symbolise the relationship between the physical and spiritual lives of Aboriginal people' (Thancoupie, quoted in Isaacs 1982, p. 60).

CENTRAL AND WESTERN DESERT PAINTING

The acrylic paintings of the various communities of the Western and Central Desert region represent the most innovative and – again in Western terms – most successful contemporary art movement in Aboriginal Australia. They are based on the traditional iconography of largely curvilinear motifs which are still traditionally employed in ground painting and ritual body-painting, and on sacred objects such as the flat oval stone or wooden *tjuringa* and ground designs, as well as in less 'restricted' forms on shields, spears, carrying dishes and boomerangs and in the illustrating of stories told to children. The translation into the modern, saleable, medium of paint, canvas and artist's board came about in 1971 at the instigation of a young art teacher, Geoff Bardon, then working at the government-established Papunya settlement west of Alice Springs (Bardon 1979; Kimber 1986).

In general such paintings are a formalized mapping of a particular geographical location associated with a specific mythological happening or individual. The word used for the paintings, *tjukurrpa,* denotes at one and the same time 'story' and the Dreamtime. The rights to stories depend on gender, descent, age, initiation and status. Only those with rights in them may reproduce them or, as is sometimes the case, authorize their reproduction by others.

In the early days of the movement many Papunya paintings incorporated clearly recognizable figures and even secret/sacred objects, but with the passing of time there has been an increasing abstraction of motifs, a recodifying which renders impossible precise interpretation by the uninitiated. With the resettlement by the Pintupi in 1981 westwards out of the artificially established centre of Papunya into their old tribal areas centred on Kintore, the overtly complex narrative symbolism of the older artists has given way to a consciously 'conservative' abstraction. With certain artists this has extended to the use of a restricted palette which corresponds to the traditional earth colours of body- and ground painting. Others, especially the newer artists – who now include a significant number of women – continue to exploit the total chromatic freedom allowed by the use of the modern acrylic medium (Brody 1985; Maughan 1986; Maughan and Megaw 1986, 39-49; Maughan 1987).

The success not only in Australia but also on the international art market of the work of such male artists as Clifford Possum Tjapaltjarri (Anmatyerre/Aranda), Charlie Tjaruru Tjungarrayi (Pintupi) (Crocker 1987) or of the younger generation, Michael Nelson Tjakamarra (Warlpiri) (who has worked closely with the Sydney former conceptual artist Tim Johnson – Topliss 1988) has led to an escalation of prices. In 1971 Papunya paintings sold for $A30-40; now they frequently fetch several thousand. The creation of a 'star' system has put strains on communities which are communally-minded and where the paintings are often worked on by several people, though only one may 'own' the story.

Recognition has also encouraged the establishment of other centres of production, for example in the Warlpiri community at Yuendumu west of Papunya where the painting of large-scale canvases has gone hand in hand with the introduction of other ways of maintaining traditional beliefs and values such as programmes made for Aboriginal-controlled satellite television (Michaels 1987). At Yuendumu, it was the women who began painting and they still form seventy per cent of the painters. This may well have been because both the white anthropologists and teachers who encouraged the new art form were themselves women, while at Papunya, Geoffrey Bardon, as a male, found relations with the older men easier in a strictly gender-defined society. Yuendumu painting to date uses a wider range of colours than that from Papunya and Kintore (Anderson 1988), though at the latter most recently one can detect a return to the old 'free' style both by the few surviving older founder members of the movement as well as those new to painting. It has also been suggested that many of the women's stories, particularly those connected with food-gathering or 'bush tucker' are not secret, and therefore some men are also now painting such women's dreamings (Dimmock 1987).

As one of the most recent communities to follow this trend of painting in acrylic on canvas or board, the Warlpiri and Anmatyerre of Mount Allen, the elders of the community took a conscious decision to allow all members, men, women and children to paint, and, from the western viewpoint, some of the technically most accomplished paintings have been by girls as young as twelve, though for Aborigines the stories to which such children are entitled are few. In Western Australia, the Balgo community has turned to acrylic painting for external sale, while other groups have continued to prefer to use ochres on board or canvas, and have themselves developed ways of improving the adhesion of the ochres (Dimmock, 1987,13).

INDIVIDUAL PAINTERS AND PRINT AND POSTER MAKERS

Though many Aborigines object to the use of the term 'urban' – an alternative Aboriginal term, 'Koori', is preferred in the south-east – 'urban' does serve to describe the current residence of many Aboriginal artists outside the communities of Central or Northern Australia. Many of these are working exclusively in non-traditional media. They are more likely to work without community support and to have to deal more directly with white society and the white art world.

Banduk Marika was born in 1954 on Yirrkala Mission in north-east Arnhem Land, but left in her mid-teens and until late 1987, when she became responsible for the new Buku-Larrngay Arts Museum at Yirrkala, spent most of her time in Sydney. She is the daughter of one famous Yolngu bark painter, Mawalan, and sister of another, recently deceased. Banduk concentrates mostly on lino-cuts, but uses images such as the heron which are her traditional property, in a style which recalls that of Yirrkala barks, while insisting on the essentially personal nature of her work. She expressly eschews contemporary or 'political' subject-matter.

Her perceptions of her role as an Aboriginal artist are markedly different for example from those of Trevor Nickolls, (b. 1949 in Port Adelaide and art school trained), and Byron Pickett (b. 1955), originally from the wheatbelt township of Quairading, Western Australia. Trevor Nickolls, who has experimented as much as any other Aboriginal artist in style and subject-matter, in his most recent work consciously uses the dotting technique and restricted symbolism of the traditional art forms of the Centre; works with titles such as *Machine time and Dreamtime* contrast with representations of Manly Point in Sydney Harbour or simple outback landscapes with rocks. His work was also part of the touring Bicentenary Exhibition as was the work of other Aboriginal artists. Nickolls, like many other Aborigines caught between two cultures, regards his work as a personal search for his roots; he has commented, 'I want to be known simply as Trevor Nickolls the painter. I find it restricting to be labelled an Aboriginal painter' (Beier 1985). In this he echoes both those 'traditional' bark painters who introduce themselves to ignorant outsiders as 'artist-fellers' and the striving of Albert Namatjira to find recognition both for his art and his people when he stated his wish 'to paint like a white man'.

Byron Pickett, who in a few years has become one of the most accomplished artists working in screen-printing, regards his work as 'a visual expression of how Aboriginal heritage survives the power of time'. His prints combine photographic images of his own experiences with traditional symbols and written commentary, and are intended to show 'the different worlds of traditional Aborigines and Western culture'.

The commercial success of the 'ethnographic fine arts' has heightened the search for identity by urban-based artists, many of whom have no formal tribal links with the more traditional cultures of the Centre and the 'Top End'. Some have attempted to find their own tribal roots, others have concentrated on the link of Aboriginals and land, while some such as Sally Morgan (b. 1951, living in Perth) or Robert Campbell Jnr (b. 1944, Kempsey, NSW) have used the dotting or hatching techniques of traditional art to tell their own autobiographies or make political statements. There have been conscious borrowings by the 'Koori' artists of Sydney and Melbourne – Gordon Syron, Lin Onus (b. 1948), Jeffrey Samuels, Raymond Meeks (b. 1957) and Fiona Foley (b. 1964); Aboriginal photographers and film makers are also gaining recognition such as Polly Sumner in Adelaide and Tracey Moffatt (b. Brisbane 1960) in Sydney (Johnson 1984; Maughan and Megaw 1986, pp. 63-75; Johnson 1987; Samuels and Watson 1987).

In addition there has been what can be regarded as the cultural appropriation or colonization of Aboriginal imagery by non-Aboriginal artists. This process, which can be traced back to the work of the modernist painter and potter Margaret Preston in the mid 1920s, was continued in the 1940s by the Antipodean school headed by Sidney Nolan and the Boyds and most recently in differing ways by Tim Johnson and Imants Tillers. Such stylistic borrowings parallel the inspiration obtained by the cubists and surrealists from the study of African and North American art. However reconciliatory the intention of such art, it can be seen as a form of cultural appropriation by members of a dominant culture from a subordinated one (Maughan and Megaw 1986, 15-16; Davila 1987).

Finally, the increasing diversity and energy of Aboriginal art in Australia is both exciting and alarming. Exciting, because so many Aborigines are innovative and talented and adaptable artists. Alarming, not for the 'traditionalist' or human zoo approach which deplores any change in Aboriginal society or culture, but because their economic future is increasingly bound up with outside economic forces of the art market, over which, unlike the production of art, the artists have little control. But it is also confirmation of the vitality and adaptability of Aboriginal society.

BIBLIOGRAPHY

Note: the following list includes both references cited in the text and select bibliography of mainly recent publications on contemporary Aboriginal art.

Amadio, N., ed., 1986. *Albert Namatjira: The Life and Work of an Australian Painter* (Melbourne)

ANCAA: Newsletter of the Association of Northern and Central Australian Artists 1, July 1987 – (obtainable from P.O. Box 920, Katherine, N.T. 5780, Australia).

Anderson, C. and Dussart, F. 1988. 'Dreamings in Acrylic: Contemporary Western Desert Art'. In Sutton 1988, Chapter 6.

Bardon, G. 1979. *Aboriginal Art in Australia* (Adelaide)

Beier, U. 1985. *Dreamtime – Machine Time: the Art of Trevor Nickolls* (Bathurst, NSW).

Berndt, R.M. and Berndt, C.H. with Stanton, J.E., 1982 *Aboriginal Art: a Visual Perspective* (Sydney).

Brody, A-M. 1985. *The Face of the Centre: Papunya-Tula Paintings 1971-1984* (exh. cat.). National Gallery of Victoria, Melbourne.

Caruana, W. 1986. *Contemporary Australian Aboriginal Art* (exh. cat.) Australian National Gallery, Canberra ACT.

Crocker, A. 1981. *Mr Sandman Bring Me a Dream* (Sydney)

Crocker, A. 1986. *Charlie Tjaruru Tjungarrayi* (exh. cat.) Regional Art Gallery, Orange.

Davila, J. 1987. 'Aboriginality: a Lugubrious Game?', *Art and Text* 23: 4, pp. 53-7.

Dimmock, S. 1987. 'Tradition and Innovation in Contemporary Aboriginal Art: an Interview with Dr John Stanton', *Praxis M* 17, pp. 12-16.

Edwards, R., ed., 1978. *Aboriginal Art in Australia* (Adelaide).

Graburn, N.H.H., ed., 1976. *Ethnic and Tourist Arts: Cultural Expressions from the Fourth World* (Berkeley, Los Angeles and London).

Graburn, N.H.H. 1982. 'The Dynamics of Change in Tourist Art.', *Cultural Survival Quarterly* 6:4, pp. 7-11.

Green, J., ed., 1981. *Utopia: Women Country and Batik* (exh. cat.) Adelaide Festival Centre Gallery.

Hall, L.-A., ed., 1988. *Right Here, Right Now: Australia 1988.* (exh. cat.) Adelaide Festival, Living Arts Centre.

Hill, M. and McLeod, N. 1984. *From the Ochres of Mungo: Aboriginal Art Today* (West Heidelberg, Vic.)

Hilliard, W.M. 1985. 'Ernabella Batiks', *Craft Australia* (Autumn 1985), pp. 89-93 Isaacs, J. 1982. *Thanocoupie the Potter* (Sydney).

Isaacs, J. 1984. *Australia's Living Heritage: Arts of the Dreaming (Sydney).*

Isaacs, J. 1987. 'An ANCAAA *(sic)* in Stormy Seas', *Australian and International Art Monthly* (September 1987), pp. 20-21.

Johnson, T. and V., eds, 1984. *Koori Art '84* (exh. cat.) Artspace, Sydney.

Johnson, V., ed., 1987. *Australian Art and Aboriginality 1987* (exh. cat.). Portsmouth Festival UK, Aspex Gallery.

Kimber, R.G. (1986) 'Papunya Tula Art: some Recollections August 1971 - October 1972'. In Maughan and Zimmer (eds.) 1986, pp. 43-45.

Lowe, P. 1987. 'Jimmy Pike', *Craft Australia* (Summer 1987/4), pp. 43-5.

Maughan, J. and Zimmer, J., eds., 1986. *Dot and Circle: a Retrospective Survey of the Aboriginal Acrylic Paintings of Central Australia* (exh. cat.) Royal Melbourne Institute of Technology, Melbourne, RMIT Art Gallery.

Maughan, J. and Megaw, J.V.S., eds., 1986. *The Dreamtime Today: a Survey of Contemporary Aboriginal Arts and Crafts* (exh. cat.) Flinders University of South Australia in conjunction with the Royal South Australian Society of Arts, Kintore Gallery, Adelaide.

Michaels, E. 1987. 'Aboriginal Content: Who's Got It – Who Needs It?', *Art and Text* 23: 4, pp. 58-80.

Berndt, R.M. and Berndt, C.M. with Stanton, J.E. 1982. *Aboriginal Art: a Visual Perspective* (Sydney).

Samuels, J. and Watson, C., eds, 1987. *Aboriginal Australian Views in Print and Poster* (exh. cat.) Print Council of Australia, W. Melbourne.

Sutton, P. ed., 1988. *Dreamings: The Art of Aboriginal Australia* (exh. cat.) Asia Society, New York.

Topliss, H., ed., 1988. *Covering the Ground* (exh. cat.) Adelaide Festival, Contemporary Art Foundation.

2. Products of the Hermannsburg 'school'. Above: Ewald Namatjira (Aranda; youngest son of Albert Namatjira) Untitled (272 x 375 mm). Watercolour on artist's board (collection Flinders University Art Museum). Below: Albert Namatjira (Aranda) Landscape on *Woomera* (spear thrower). Earlier than 1944. *Woomera 545 x 140 mm (Private collection).*

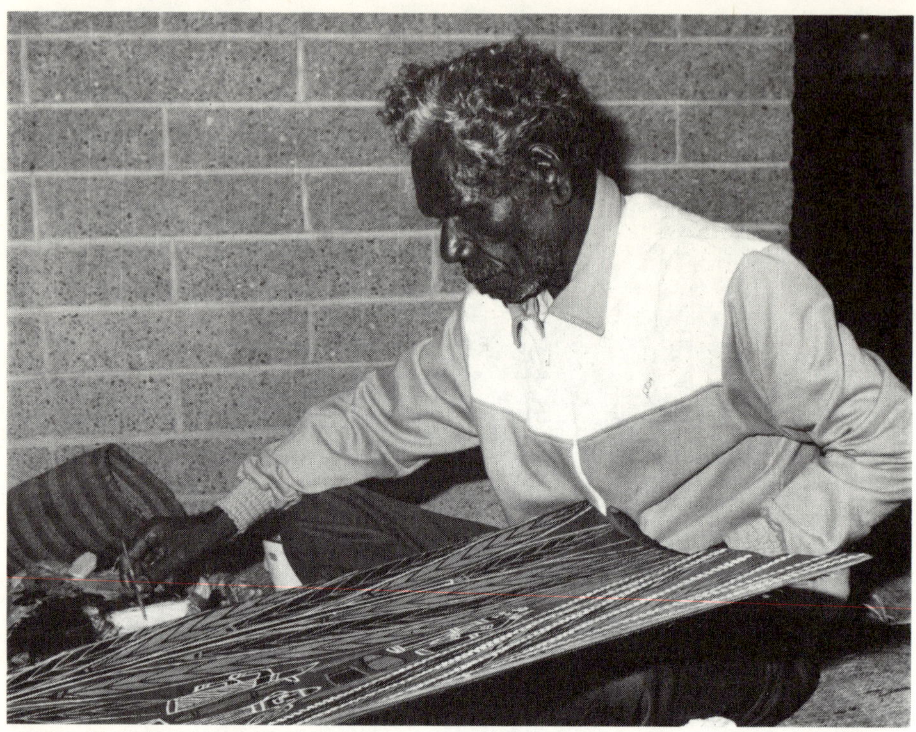

3. David Malangi (Urgiganjdjar language; Ramagining, Northern Territory) during a period as Artist-in-Residence at flinders University of South Australia in 1982 with one of his bark paintings – the design of which was, without authorisation, incorporated in the Australian dollar bill, now no longer in use.

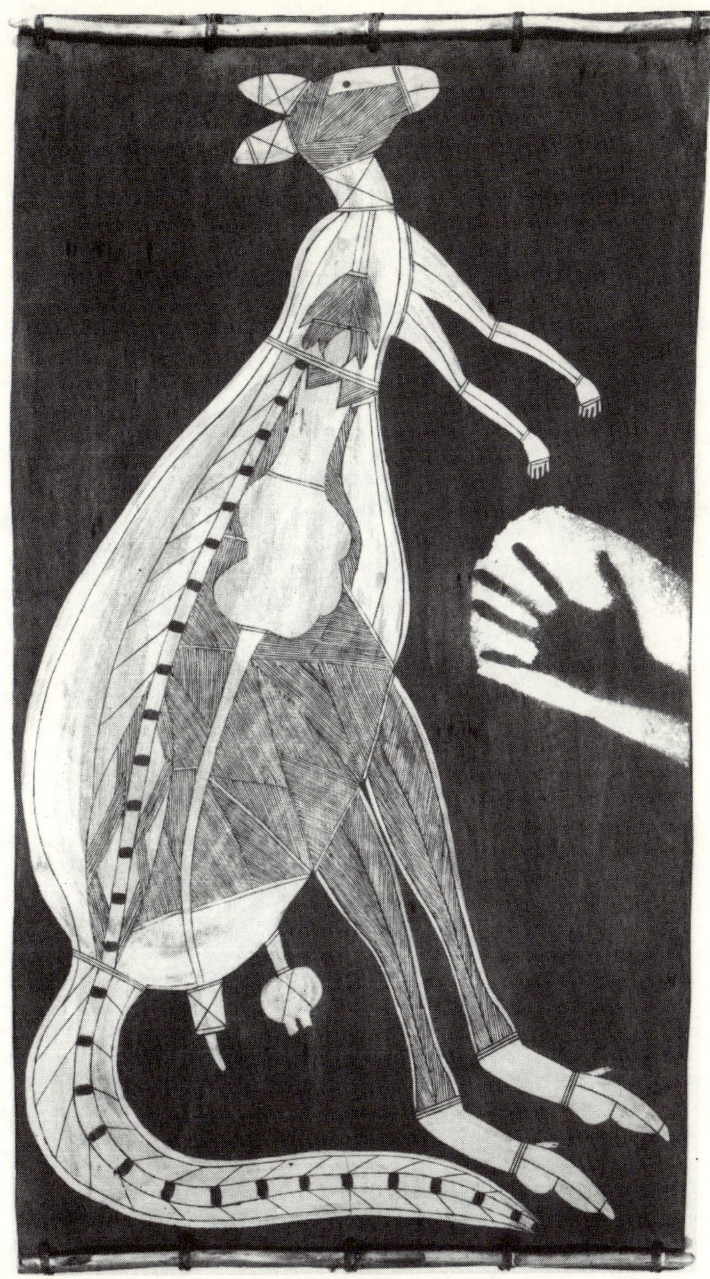

4. Thompson Ulidjirri (Gunwinggu language; Oenpelli, Northern Territory) Kandarik. Pre-1979. Red and white ochres on bark painting in X-ray technique of a male kangaroo. 1000 x 530 mm (collection Flinders University Art Museum).

5. Marrngula Munungurr (Balamumu language; Wandawuy near Yirrkala, Northern Territory). Funeral Ceremony. August 1983. 358 x 810 mm. This is one of a series of paintings of everyday life. To the left are musicians with didjeridu and clap sticks, while at bottom right three women dance the spirit dance (collection Flinders University Art Museum).

6. Work of Pitjantjatjara women working at Ernabella, South Australia. Left: Tjinkuma : Batik on silk 1984. 2340 x 940 mm. Right: Yipati : Untitled silkscreen on paper. Print 250 x 280 mm. (collection Flinders University Art Museum).

7. Bede and Francine Tungutalum (Tiwi language; Bathurst Island, Northern Territory) working on lino-cuts during their period as artists-in-residence at Flinders University in 1980.

8. Above left: Ron Hurley (working in Queensland) Untitled stoneware sculpture 1985. 475 x 340 mm (collection Flinders University Art Museum). Thancoupie (Thanaquith/ Napperanum, working at Weipa, Queensland). Stoneware plate (above right) 350 x 330 mm (Private collection); three stoneware knee pots (below left) and stoneware egg incised with animal shapes (collection Flinders University Art Museum).

9. Kaapa Mbitjana Tjampitjinpa (Anmatjera/Aranda; Papunya, Northern Territory). Acrylic paint on board 1971. 901 x 915 mm. This is believed to be one of the first six of the Papunya paintings to be offered for sale. The design elements include two bull-roarers, two snakes, two ceremonial poles growing out of ground paintings and a series of kangaroo tracks along the bottom (Private collection).

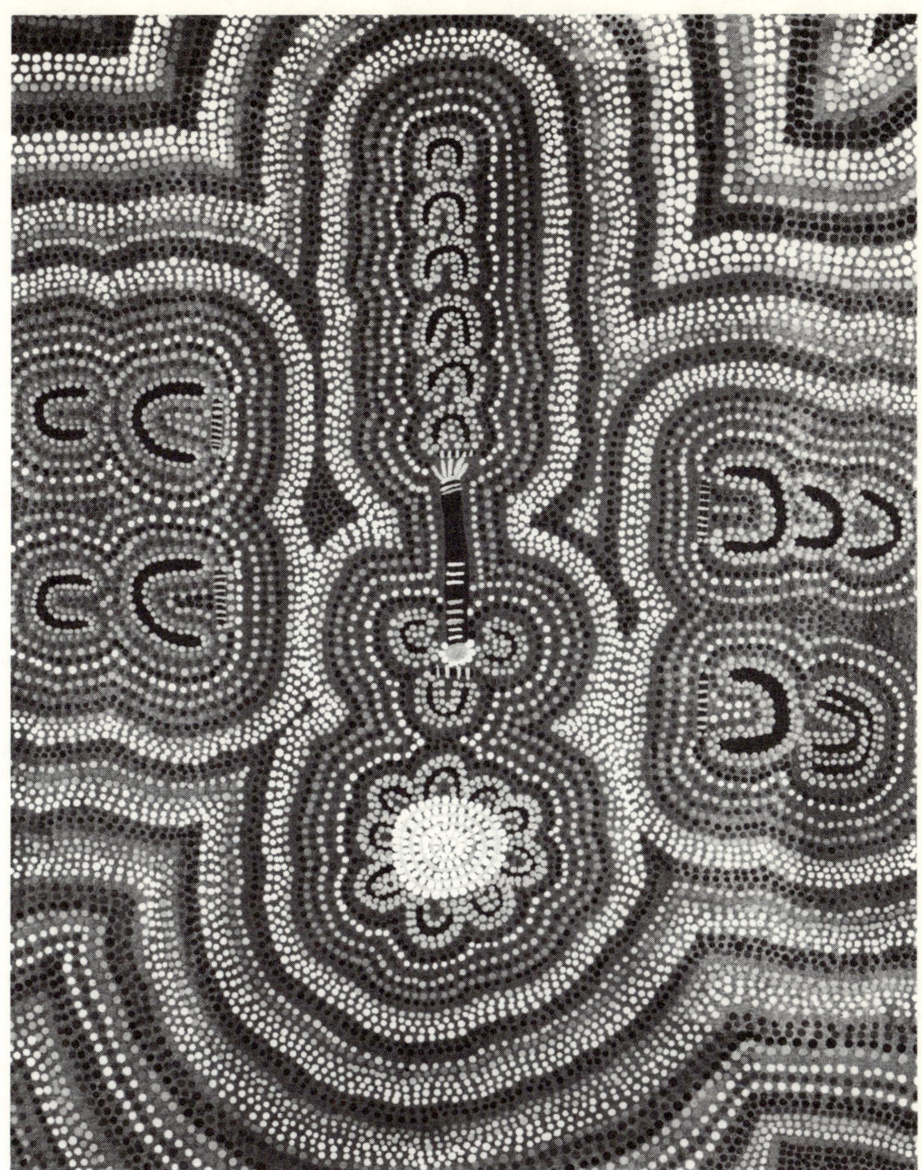

10. Maringka Nangala (Pintupi; Kintore, Northern Territory). Women's Ceremony 1984. Acrylic on canvas 798 x 550 mm. This depicts a women's ceremony forbidden to men. In the centre is a *nulla-nulla* or fighting club. U-shapes represent singing and dancing women. This painting shows the increasing use of dotting in Papunya painting (collection Flinders University Art Museum).

11. An acrylic painting being produced on the ground, as is usual, at papunya West Camp, Northern Territory in 1981. Pintupi artists, left to right, John Tjakamarra, Uta Uta Tjangala, and (foreground) Yala Yala 'Gibbs' Tjungarrayi. Tjangala is the 'owner' of the *pankalanka* (ogre) story depicted here.

12. Trevor Nickolls (b. Port Adelaide; working in Melbourne) Untitled 1982. Acrylic on canvas 510 x 764 mm. This painting shows clear reference to the iconography and dotting technique of Central Desert painting (collection Flinders University Art Museum).

13. Sally Morgan (b. and living in Perth, Western Australia) Citenzenship 1987. Screenprint on paper 570 x 565 mm (collection Flinders Univesity Art Museum).

14 Byron Pickett (b. and working in Western Australia). Cliff's People – Adjamathanha People. Silkscreen on paper 464 x 713 mm, August 1985. The portrait is of Cliff Coulthard, then working in the Aboriginal Heritage Section of the S.A. Department of Environment and Planning, the words by Terry Coulthard (collection Flinders University Art Museum).

NOTE:

The photographs for illustration nos. 3, 7 and 11 are by J.V.S. Megaw; the remainder by the Photographic Service of the Flinders University of South Australia. Copyright in the art works illustrated the individual artists.

Modern Aboriginal Political Art

The following pictures form part of an exhibition of modern Aboriginal posters and screenprints, held at Moesgaard Museum in Denmark. The exhibition has been put together by Ruth and Vincent Megaw from the collection held at the art gallery at Flinders University in South Australia. The Danish exhibition also featured a collection of screenprints by Sally Morgan, kindly lent to us by the artist.

The exhibition, which was part of a bicentennial festival, was deliberately chosen to tell Danes the other side of the story. It aroused much interest and had a good press coverage. One reason why the Danes understood it immediately might be their/our familiarity with the medium. The political poster as both art form and medium for protest is an established tradition. In the sophisticated form of the Aboriginal posters it goes back to the 60s, to the student revolts around Europe – in particular to the Polish cultural protest movement – to the new left films and fringe theatre and to the campaign against nuclear power. The basic iconography of political art is, of course, much older and goes back through the Russian revolution to the pictorial language of the Christian icons. The Aboriginal posters add their own language to the iconography of the raised fist, the slogan and the flag. Aboriginal art forms and modes of expression are incorporated into the modern multi- media form, and the result is striking.

Political survival in the form of land rights, better education etc. is the obvious aim of these prints, but the embedded features of Aboriginal painting styles and motifs speak of the even more essential survival of a culture, which is a prerequisite of political survival.

SALLY MORGAN

Taken Away, Silkscreen on paper

This print was designed for the National Gallery in Canberra. It is from a woman's perspective and illustrates two important things that Aboriginal women have lost since colonisation in 1788, their land and their children. Between 1905 and even until the early 1970's it was the policy to remove children from black mothers who had been fathered by white men. The assumption was that black women were not fit to bring up children with white blood in them. Also, it was seen as a quick form of assimilation. The removed children were brought up by whites in government settlements and missions. They were discouraged strongly from taking any interest in their mothers' culture and in the majority of cases had little contact with their black families, and no contact with the family of the white father because these children were never owned. This policy, more than any other, led to a rapid breakdown of Aboriginal family groups and culture.

NATIONAL ABORIGINES DAY OBSERVANCE COMMITTEE (NADOC)

Race for Life for a Race, 1982. Photolitho poster, 484 x 355 mm. FUAM AUP 153.

In this poster a black male athlete clad in the Aboriginal flag colours is set against the background of an unidentified Pintupi acrylic painting. The reference is to the Commonwealth Games held in Brisbane in 1982, when there were a large number of Aboriginal demonstrations.

NADOC is now established as an Australia-wide week of events held in September of each year.

WESTERN REGIONAL ABORIGINAL LAND COUNCIL

Always Was, Always Will be Aboriginal Land 1985. Photolitho poster 893 x 680 mm. FUAM AUP 130.

This commemoration of the restoration to the Pakantji people of their traditional land at Weinteriga Station is bordered by the black, yellow and red of the Aboriginal flag. It contains a portrait of Jim Whyman, one of the elders of the group, done by an Aboriginal artist Karin Donaldson. In Western Australia there has been no Land Rights legislation.

BYRON PICKETT

(b. Quairading, W. Aus. 1955: lives and works in Tammin, W. Aus.)

Byron Pickett learned screenprinting as a trainee Community Artist in 1984-5 with the Eyre Peninsula Cultural Trust at Port Lincoln and perfected his impeccable technique as South Australia's 150th Jubilee Artist-in-Residence at Flinders University in 1986.

Fellow Australian January 1985. Silkscreen on paper (13/25). Image size 550 x 510. FUAM 2216

This is a self-portrait with a view-finder (or rifle-sight?) centred on the artist's face. The shirt is yellow, the hair black and the skin reddish in tone, giving an approximation to the colours of the Aboriginal flag. On the print is written: 'With pride my children will use the names of our ancestors "Nyoongar" "Njamanji"'. The faint print on the background carries repeated words such as 'Outsider, Fellow Man, Countrymen, Blacks bar, Too Dumb' etc.

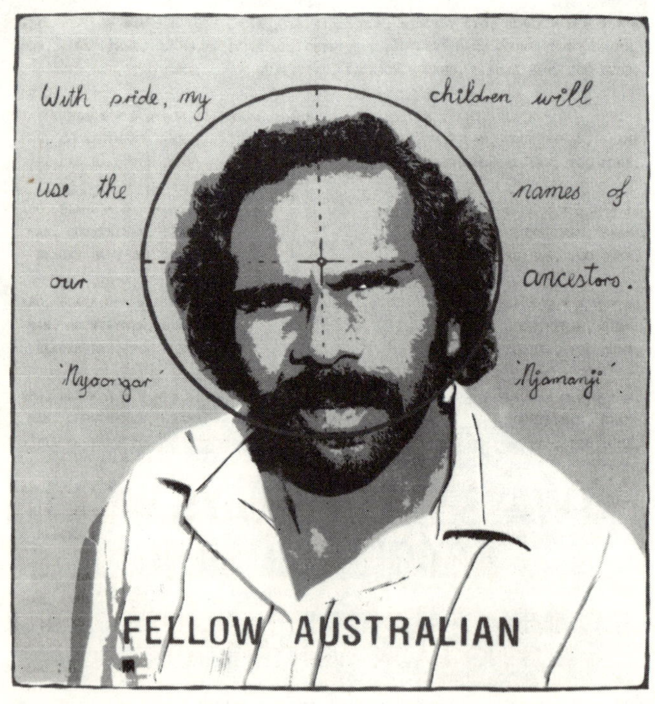

CENTRAL AUSTRALIAN ABORIGINAL MEDIA ASSOCIATION

(for Mutitjulu Community Inc.)

You Are on Aboriginal Land, 1986. Photolitho poster, 725 x 975 mm. FUAM AUP 138

In this striking image based on the Aboriginal flag, the central circle is replaced by the silhouette of Uluru (Ayers Rock), one of the most famous tourist spots in the Northern Territory near Alice Springs and also an Aboriginal sacred site. It was returned to Aboriginal ownership on 26 October, 1985. The Aboriginal translation is in Pitjantjatjara.

SALLY MORGAN

Another Story 1988. Silkscreen on paper. Image size 692 x 325 mm. FUAM 2426

Male and female black stick figures like those of traditional *mimi* spirit figures are outlined in yellow and placed against a reddish background, once again echoing the colours of the desert and of the Aboriginal flag. Above them is a European-style house with verandahs, lawns and a picket fence. The print was a Bicentennial commission from the Australian National Gallery.

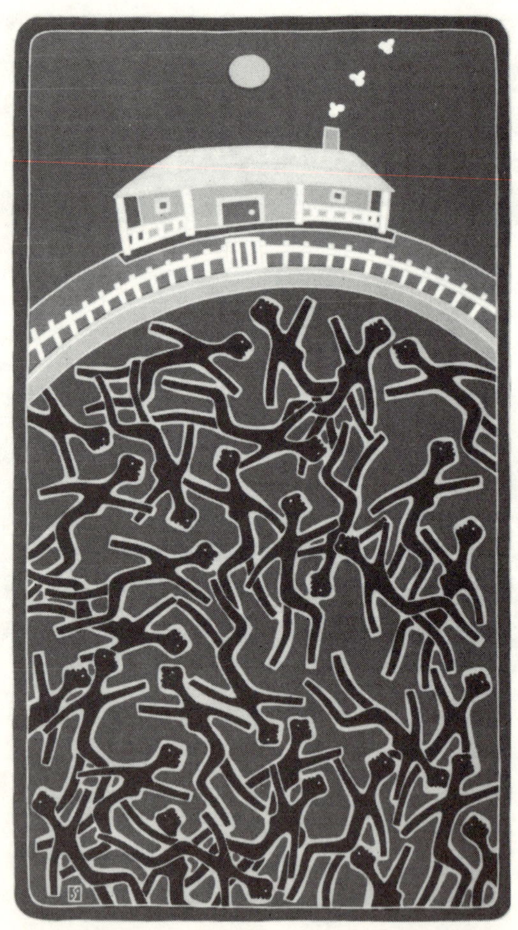

Writing for Children

INTERVIEW WITH PAT TORRES

INTRODUCTION

Pat Torres is based in Broome, Western Australia. Her book the *Story of Crow* was written with her aunt Magdalene Williams, one of the last fluent speakers of Nyul Nyul, the traditional language of the people of Beagle Bay in Western Australia. Pat graduated from university with a BA degree and a Diploma of Education. When she did her degree ten years ago there were only 22 Aboriginal graduates in Australia. Funded by the Australian Bicentennial Authority's National Aboriginal and Torres Strait Islander Program, the stories are published by the first Aboriginal publishing house, Magabala Books, an arm of the Kimberley Aboriginal Law and Culture Centre.

Carolyn Osterhaus

Pat Torres was interviewed by Carolyn Osterhaus in October, 1988.

When and why did you start publishing?

My first two books came out in March this year. The reason why I started to publish was that I thought the stories I was told as a child could be shared by other Aboriginal children and non-Aboriginal children. I found I got a lot of positive information and culture and history out of these stories and I saw the need for other people to appreciate the good things about Aboriginal culture and lifestyle.

Was it a conscious decision to start with writing for children or did it just happen that way?

It was fairly conscious. I started out 10 years ago just basically finding out my own personal background. Along the way came many stories, Dreamtime stories relating to my tribal group. I'm trained as a primary teacher, and I've been involved in Aboriginal education for at least 10 years. I thought I should make some attempt to use all my skills to give information back to the community. By doing that I'm also strengthening my own background.

Do you expect the children's books you are publishing to reach a non-Aboriginal audience as well as an Aboriginal one?

Yes, of course. To me there's a great gap in the materials for children about Aboriginal people, about Aboriginal culture and education. Previous material is really aimed at adult readers.

Having read these books to my own four children, I found it was difficult for them to understand what was happening just by reading the text. I had to explain a lot of the text to them. The words involved a lot of explanation. Because I am trained at primary level, I thought I might be providing a service by preparing books for children both Aboriginal and non-Aboriginal at the early childhood reading level.

I've also been involved in early childhood workshops with the National Aboriginal Education committee which indicated a great lack of relevant material. The curriculum material normally used for Aboriginal studies was inappropriate or irrelevant at times. I wanted to start at the very early reading levels to bridge the gap. I've got an interest in doing books and providing materials for language areas, social studies and science. My ten years of research has resulted in a lot of information and I now need time to develop various education kits.

Are they already being used in schools which Aboriginal children attend?

There are a number of schools using my books and it's increasing every day. For example, the Queensland Department of Education has reviewed my books with the idea of placing them on a list in Aboriginal Studies. In Western Australia, Nulungu College will be using them. Most major school libraries have requested them and they've been advertised in the Aboriginal Education Resources Unit magazine *Djawalidi*. People are writing to Magabala Books quite regularly as they become aware of them. Most major centres know about them.

Is the lack of a common Aboriginal language a problem when it comes to your publications?

My books are bilingual using both English and Aboriginal languages. Wherever the story comes from, I feature the language of that place. I don't find the lack of a common Aboriginal language a problem. The many languages show the richness and complexity of Aboriginal people and their society. I imagine it would be difficult if you wanted to teach one major language in schools. I think people should probably take up the language most relevant to the area they come from, to feature the local language if possible.

In the Kimberleys they teach kids a common orthography. The children use their own language background. I try to help non-Aboriginal readers in understanding how to pronounce words in the books by providing a key, by using the common orthography for that Aboriginal language and by providing a dictionary of all the meanings. I'll do that for every language group that I feature. This may prove difficult in some places because groups in the West Kimberleys have been asked how they would prefer their language written down and this has resulted in a variety of approaches.

One of my major thrusts has been making my material bilingual. I've been trained in linguistics and I have about four Aboriginal languages that I was involved in in my childhood. I know that a lot of people, and my children, are interested in language – it helps to strengthen your identity more if you have your language intact.

Because the Aboriginal language is an oral not a written one, is something lost in writing down the language?

I try to look at it in a realistic sense as much as possible. I would prefer to use the oral tradition but the society we live in today is largely not an Aboriginal system and it's very hard to maintain the traditional ways of handing down the cultural and historical information and expect our children to learn the stories off by heart. So the materials have to be written down. If the old people are gone, your stories are gone too, and to get them down you mostly have to get them down in written form. You do lose a lot in terms of body language and emphasis but at times there are no funds to record the information on tapes with good quality field equipment.

I am concerned that so many languages are under threat and that so many stories will die when the old people go. I also do tapes wherever possible but I had no funds to do tapes of my recent books. In future I will be aiming to provide tapes with my books.

What do you think of Maureen Watson's use of traditional Aboriginal forms to tell modern stories?

I'm very impressed by her. She does maintain the old tradition very strongly through her use of traditional storytelling. I'm a younger woman and I hope that I can follow in her footsteps. But perhaps most of my work will be in a written form because there is a big need for written materials in schools. Maureen is able to visit schools and lecture and do things in an oral way. In Western Australia, but especially the Kimberleys, no one pays you to do your stories. Storytelling is not something people do very regularly in institutions such as those that Maureen Watson has had the opportunity to perform in. We have a different sort of social situation. We are still battling with attitudes, and storytelling programs need to be argued for and justified.

In the past Aboriginal traditional information was handed down in an oral and musical form. Our stories of Dreamtime and the ways people should treat each other were done through stories around campfires and through law and ceremony. Because of the educational process being interrupted we have to look at different ways of passing the information on. Many Aboriginal people don't have a strong land base to practise their traditional ways of passing on knowledge. We have to look at other ways of doing it. Books, music and tapes are all we've got left to do it with.

Why do you do your own illustrations?

There's a lack of Aboriginal people doing designs and I'm trying to develop my own Aboriginal art form based on a style encompassing cave drawings, Mimi art figures and using line drawing techniques. I just sort of picked it up along the way. Noone else was drawing these things in my environment. A lot of my drawings have been shown to me in dreams by my ancestors.

They are the creative energy for my inspiration for illustrating. They've shown me how to draw the figures and have given me the images.

Do you think that the books you publish can and/or will have an effect on the way Aboriginal culture is perceived by whites?

Yes, I do, I go for positive things. A lot of materials previously provided for children in school have showed Aboriginal people in a negative way or living life styles no longer relevant today. Most materials available in schools still show people running around naked in the bush. Nowadays people go hunting but they go hunting with a gun and a Toyota, once again adapting things to fit our needs. Many of these materials still concentrate on pre-contact Aboriginal society and don't show us as we are, namely Aboriginal people living in a contemporary way. Very few Aboriginal people, even people in traditional communities, run around naked in the bush. My books are trying to give a positive portrayal of the Aboriginal people.

Since 1983 I have been working on a reading kit called *Ngaagkiti*. It's a collection of Kimberley oral histories containing about 60 stories and 40 poems which are stories about contemporary experiences of Aboriginal people. It's basically done in English with many Aboriginal words and phrases used in the storytelling. It's going to be produced like a reading card and feature stories, art work, maps locating the areas plus information about the author with multi-disciplinary activities such as comprehension and dictionary meanings. It can be used in a language program, social studies and history programs. My own view is that Aboriginal Studies should be integrated throughout the school curriculum. Most people tend to treat it like a separate unit.

Most of the Aboriginal stories and poems published for children are traditional ones. Are they stories that Aboriginal children will be familiar with or are the books intended to teach them stories they don't know?

What I found in the Kimberleys was that our traditions and culture are still very strong. We still have chances to go to traditional ceremonies, so many of us are familiar with many of the traditional stories. But there are also many who have been removed from their background. These books are giving those children back what they don't know while many have heard these stories or another form of them as they are growing up. We do share many stories throughout Australia and the local group may add on a bit more information as the story travels along. for example, about the kangaroo or the crow. Names may change as the stories move to different areas but once you tell the story the children can often provide their own stories from their groups.

Hadja Press in Melbourne published a book about an Aboriginal girl going to a Land Rights march. Do you have any plans to publish stories of Aborigines in urban environments or are you exclusively interested in traditional stories?

I guess you'd call me a country person. I tend to write from my own background. My stories will basically come from the Kimberleys, and so will be traditional or about the war days, how Aboriginal people were involved in the war.

One story I'd like to do in the future is about a woman, essentially the story of my mother, but I want to do it at a reading level for a child. My mother is a special person, given special spiritual gifts from my Yawuru great-grandfather. As she grew older she became bewildered; perhaps because of not understanding the differences between the two societies she found herself living in. She grew up in a time when black was wrong and Aboriginal women were subject to a lot of hassles. She became confused and tried to make it in the white man's world then realised in later years it was not the path to go. She felt very insecure in that part. My mum has gone back to traditional ways and is much happier in the ways of her life. She's realised her spiritual potential. It was very hard for her and she's thinking about writing her own book. She was a single parent in the days when this was not socially acceptable, however, she managed to achieve many good things in her life. For example, she was the first Aboriginal woman employed as a cocktail waitress. She was good looking and had to face a lot of negative comments from men.

Aboriginal people are very spiritual people. We're able to relate to things on a spiritual level. We are talking for example about the kinds of spiritual gifts possessed by psychics or mediums. Aboriginal society has those kinds of parallels. My mum has special powers to heal, to realise things that are going to happen. It's difficult to explain what I want to say as there are few words in the English language to describe these sensations; you really need to understand European spiritualism to understand what I'm trying to say.

Gurrwayi Gurrwayi, The Rain Bird

Gurrwayi Gurrwayi
It's the Rain bird call,
Don't hurt him or kill him,
Or the rain will always fall.

JOHN JANKE

Crime and Punishment in Australia

**Freedom's just another word for nothing left to lose
nothing ain't worth nothing but it's free.**

The words of Kristofferson's song echoed from the transistor radio and floated through the cells bars of the police lockup at Yarrabah – a small Aboriginal settlement nestled in the tropical green hills across the bay from Cairns in North Queensland. The complex, which includes three cells and a compound is made of concrete, bars and steel mesh, has no shortage of clients; and for the five young men, arrested the night before for drunkenness, freedom is just another word. For them, life on the other side of the cell bars offered little in the way of real freedom. For, as there was no escape from inside the four walls, their world outside presented them with a different set of bars, locks and constraints. Paradoxically, their only key to escapism was alcoholism, and it in turn put them back behind the real bars. In an ironic sequel, the only release from despondency of their cell life, was cell death – perhaps the ultimate freedom.

Black deaths at the Yarrabah jail like many others in the small Aboriginal settlements, and in the towns and cities around Australia, had become a new social phenomenon of the eighties. As the death roll increased and the issue grew, it became permeated with politics and passion. Some Aboriginals wanted revenge, others reform and others recognition of the root causes ... but they all wanted justice.

Since between 1980 and 1987 available evidence indicated that at least 100 Aboriginals had died in the custody of Australian police or prison authorities. It is a year since the Federal Government established a Royal Commission to inquire into the Aboriginal Deaths in custody issue. The Commission, chaired by former Chief Justice of the Northern Territory, Mr Justice Muirhead QC was set up following urgent pleas by Aboriginal organisations and individuals. During the eight months preceding the commencement of he royal Commission in November 1987, sixteen Aboriginals had died in custody or in jails and prisons around Australia. In his opening remarks, Justice Muirhead acknowledged the daunting task which the inquiry presented, but said that it stemmed from a sad and continuing history over the past few years. He said that the rates of these tragedies had accelerated in 1987.

The terms of reference establishing Justice Muirhead's Commission directed him to inquire into deaths in Australia since January 1980, of Aboriginal and Torres Strait Islanders ... while in police custody, in prison or any other place of detention. The Commission would also examine any subsequent actions concerning those deaths, including the conduct of coronial and police inquiries, as well as things which were not done, but ought to have been done. Justice Muirhead is assisted by two counsels – Mr Geoff Eames and Mr Bob Bellear – each has had extensive experience with Aborigines and the law.

In the past year, the Commission of Inquiry has visited most States and the Northern Territory taking evidence from individual Aborigines, organisations, police, jail and court officers, as well as government department officials and medical staff. Many relatives of cell death victims also presented evidence before the Inquiry. At the hearings, Aborigines questioned the ruling of suicide by various coroners, and the Aboriginal Committee to defend Black Rights said that only two of the 106 cell deaths were from natural causes. The committee said that it was aware of cases where death was caused by negligence on the part of jail authorities. In some instances the committee suspected foul play. Most of the deaths had occurred by hanging and in all but three cases involved males. Fifty eight of them had occurred in custody while being held in police lock-ups or watch-houses – while 32 had died in prisons. The most common offence for their being detained was alcohol related, including drunkenness, disorderly conduct and fighting while drunk.

The Australian Institute of Criminology in Canberra – a long time monitor of Aboriginal crime and imprisonment – issued figures which indicated that the Aboriginal prison ratio was worsening. Criminologist with the Institute, Mr David Biles said that Aborigines were over represented in Australia's prisons and jails and the rise was disappointing. According to the Institute's surveys, Aboriginals made up 14.5% of Australia's prison population. This is compared to their 1.3% representation in the overall population. If the statistics were black and white then Justice Muirhead pressed the mathematical point home, when he converted black cell death figures into white deaths. In June this year, at an International Congress on Criminal Law, he told participants that the total amount of black deaths since 1980, on a comparative basis was equivalent to 7400 whites. Mr Biles posed the question that although government authorities spent some $800 million a year on Aboriginal programs, including health, housing and legal aid, the rise in prison ratios for Aboriginals was a cause for concern.

As the inquiry continued, claims and counter claims emerged – with allegations of police brutality and evidence of inconsistency, as well as negligence and lack of understanding by prison authorities. There were also claims of psychotic depression and guilt complexes amongst the prisoners, as well as the obvious nexus between Aboriginals, alcohol, crime and jail – that vicious cycle which seemed to question the very fundaments of Crime and Punishment. Even as the inquiry progressed, news came of yet another Aboriginal death or attempted hangings in various detention centres around the country. With something like 107 deaths being the latest tally, Justice Muirhead's Inquiry was in danger of bogging down and failing to meet the December 1988 deadline given for him to report to the Federal Government.

In April 1988, the Federal Minister for Justice, Senator Tate, announced the appointment of three additional Commissioners: Mr E.F. Johnston QC, Mrs Lewis Wyvill QC and The Hon Hal Wooten QC with the responsibility to conduct investigations in various States. The Commission's time of reporting was also extended with the three new commissioners required to report by June 1989 and playing a co-ordinating role, Justice Muirhead would present his final report by December 1989.

But as the Inquiry continued, among the unfolding series of evidence were rays of hope which offered a chance to improve the situation, if not provide an ultimate solution. In Western Australia, a new Aboriginal visitor scheme to check police lock-up and handling procedures is to be introduced as a first-ever plan to stem cell deaths. Aboriginal visitors will be able to observe, interact with and provide care and companionship for prisoners.

Other proposals contained in a set of draft guidelines, included the requirement for prison officials to account for their actions as part of the process in determining whether death in custody could have been avoided. Another recommendation is that all detention centres be equipped with readily available resuscitation facilities and that staff be fully trained in mouth to mouth resuscitation and cardio-pulmonary massage techniques. Some states were also looking at on-the-spot summons schemes which would obviate the necessity to detain Aboriginals (and others) for minor drink related offences. But again came the question of Crime and Punishment ... when to detain and for what crime? Criminologist David Biles said that the most important principle in deaths in custody was that the very use of custody as a process should be kept to the lowest possible level that is consistent with the safety and well being of the general community. He said that judges and magistrates should be encouraged to impose prison sentences only as a last resort.

The Royal Commission continued ... more towns, more names, more evidence, and as it prepared to enter its most recent stage of hearings – another death, another attempted suicide. Commenting on progress so far, Mr Justice Muirhead said that discussions with Aborigines had given him a clearer perspective as to what are the overview questions, which go to the underlying issues of the deaths. He hoped that a comprehensive advisory structure would be established to allow Aboriginals on a national and regional basis to assist the Commission. Justice Muirhead believed that the Commission's foremost responsibility was to endeavour, by its recommendations, to prevent these terrible deaths in the future. If sufficient progress was not forthcoming Justice Muirhead said that tensions would be increased, and there would be a perpetuation of antagonisms, fears and griefs.

One Hot Night

The train smashes away the hot, still, trembling body of the night and leaves it crumpled upon the hard rocks beside the sleepers. Black and bloody and flecked with light from the dying sun and the prosperous shops or the comfortable middle-class houses or the rushing vehicles on the highway. The train charges noisily onwards, high up on its embankment. It will never reach the stars, but it is too proud for the common, crowded highways. It floats on a lonely uniform course between reality and dreams.

The train rattles and rocks in rhythm to its music. Inside its throbbing belly the black boy who huddles in the very corner is rocked too.

When he got on at Guildford, the three sailors with their painted giggling girl and the old, faded, white couple in their faded best eyed him furtively and coldly.

Just a skinny, scrawny part-Aboriginal boy, with a ragged mop of tangled blue-black hair on top of his hatchet face and a black beard and moustache surrounding it and his thin lips. He holds up his head in pride. His royal black eyes flick scornfully around the carriage for a brief second before he drifts up to the other end and throws himself into the corner to stare out of the window, ignoring the world.

He had a fight with his woman and punched her to the ground. She stared up at him reproachfully with her large sad eyes. Faces going red and orange, then black again in the flickering firelight. People stood silent. Blood ran out of his woman's mouth.

'Don't go to town, Elgin. Ya know the munadj's on the lookout for ya. Specially that big Fathers. Ya wanna go back to jail or what? Ya don't even think of me, unna? I may as well be dead, as much as you care, any rate.'

'Block up, Maydene. I'll do what I wanna do, see? I'm me own boss now.'

'I was better off when you was inside!' the girl cried and he backhanded her across the face and kicked her in the stomach so she gave a queer half-cry.

He knelt down beside her in remorse, and stroked her long black hair back from her bruised face before leaving abruptly. He went away from the communal campfire that held the ever-present circle of shadowy forms close to its warmth or comfort.

People get on the train. People get off. All white. They stare at the dark, sullen youth gazing out the window.

The sailors' girl leaves. Her high-heeled shoes clickety-clack off the platform, then she is swallowed up by the lips of the stealthy night. The Nyoongah's eyes devour her plump white body then, from the corner of his eyes, he spots the three sailors glaring at him. He smiles at them, an evil smile. Spits out the window.

The Indian ticket collector bustles along the corridor. He stares through the youth with arrogant eyes, as if no one is there. He takes the youth's money, though.

Perth station.

Full of noise and colour and dancing lights. Shouting people and shunting trains.

Early yet.

He hunches into his clothes and shuffles outside. He rolls a smoke while the cars roar and rumble around him and people pass him by. So alone in the crowded city.

Over on the other side of the river, the flats stand high and alert, like a tribe of advancing warriors. Lights flicker from balconies and rest on the serene back of the river. Soft music from record players, radios or guitars drifts around the dark shore like a lazily swooping seagull.

Tonight is a night for romance.

Little Caesar Jackell struts importantly down the cool white footpaths. He flits in and out of the shadows like a busy black hummingbird searching for honey.

He disappears.

Silent as a thought, he creeps between the trees and bushes of the garden. Only the whites of his eyes are seen in this world that he knows all too well, if only through the stories of his brothers and cousins.

No one is home.

No dogs.

Big house means big money.

He slinks around to the back and tries a window. Locked. He notices a small louvred window high up on the wall, big enough for him to crawl through.

Quickly and quietly, he drags a box over to the window. He pecks out the glass louvres one by one with agile fingers, like a black crow ripping out the eye of affluence, as it squats, powerless, in its green garden. Then he scurries through the hole he has made, to feed off the living juicy insides.

First he pulls out a packet of smokes from his coat pocket and lights one up to calm his nerves. This is only the second house he has ever broken into, and the first time he has done it alone.

Wait till his eyes become accustomed to the dark, then slip quietly through the house.

He comes to the bedroom. A photograph of an earnest young man glares out at the cheeky thief from among various bottles of perfume on the dressing table.

It can do nothing to him.

He flattens down his bushy hair with a brush and pulls faces in the mirror. The he sets to work.

He finds a small locked metal cashbox with a lucky-sounding jangle inside it, various rings and necklaces in another box and a watch that takes his fancy. In the kitchen, he takes two bottles of beer and a flagon of riesling from the fridge. In another room, he finds more cigarettes, three cigars, and a $10 note. He shoves the biggest cigar into his mouth and grins into another mirror.

On top of a cupboard, his searching fingers feel a hard, cold object.

It is a rifle. A telescopic .303. He searches the drawers of the cupboard until he finds four packets of bullets. This truly is a prize.

He shoves all his loot into a bag he finds, and lowers it out the window. Then the .303, then himself.

Same stars, same people, same lights.

He goes.

Keeps to the back ways as much as he can. No one sees him – or would care if they did.

He reaches the riverside and lights up another cigar. He decides to dump the bag and .303 and come back for them later.

'Takes me, unna?' he brags to the waves that gently slap-lap-lap against the shore. 'Pooooh! Ya one solid man, Caesar Jackell.'

Takes one of the bottles of beer from the bag and wrenches off the top with his white teeth. He pours his cold, golden triumph down his throat. Starlight and city light glint off the bottle. No one is at his celebration party. Only the waves, and the floating rubbish and a few drifting ghostly gulls.

Across the water, the city beckons with crooked fingers and winks from tempting eyes. The buildings dance the dance of the night people, the street people, the nobody people.

His people.

Caesar finishes off the bottle and tries to open the cashbox.

He curses and swears and rips his knuckles open before he smashes the lock with a rock.

Open it eagerly.

Shells.

'Shit!'

Hurl the useless box away, spewing beautifully patterned shells into the air.

He still has the $10.

Drinks the other bottle of beer. Slowly. He relishes the bitterness, and remembers he has robbed a whole house – a big, rich house – all on his own. Last time he was scared as he squatted under a tree chain-smoking, with his eyes darting about nervously, keeping watch for the others. Now he has proven he is as good as they. No, better, because has a .303 and bullets.

He is drunk now.

Pats the barrel then aims it at the curious gulls.

'Bang, bang,' he mutters softly and smiles.

He hides the gun and bag, then stumbles away.

He staggers across the bridge and along the freeway, a small insignificant, drunken moth going to boast and be a big spender for at least one night in his miserable life.

The people pour onto the footpath in a noisy flow. They whirl and eddy, and cling to the sides of cars or heroes in bobbing groups. Inside is a comforting blast of music and synthetic gunfire as the youths become pretend cowboys or soldiers or gangsters or racing-car drivers; all fantasies that are so real for them. Then they squeeze out the door, to become black boys gazed upon in contempt or fear or black girls sitting on the seats, giggling and shouting, eyed over by the white man.

Big Murry James leans into the darkest doorway across the street from Crystal Palace, watching all the Kings and Queens and Princes and Princesses amble in and out.

He is the Court Jester.

He was fostered by a white family and lived with them for fourteen years. Last month, the murmurings of his people stirred in his heart and he wandered home again to Lockridge camp.

Very black, with large round eyes – and a deep voice. A small squashed nose and a low forehead. He hardly ever talks, for it takes a long time for him to work things out. He leaves the thinking to his cleverer cousins and friends while he just gets on with living.

Despite his huge size, he is gentle and kind.

Puff on a cigarette, and dream about the girl he would like to take to bed. The other boys shout and yell their love across the rooftops and drag names from dirty lip to dirty lip, sweetened by knowledgeable laughter. Then they will swoop in and rip a girl off the footpath like an owl pouncing on a squeaking, cowering mouse.

Not Murry. His woman is like a drink kept secure in a bottle so no one but he can partake of her. Her name slides down his throat and warms him whenever he thinks of her.

He sees her now, lost in a crowd of grinning girls gathered around two blonde-haired brothers who came out of Riverbank last week.

Saunter across.

'G'day, Lynette'

'Look 'oo's 'ere! What ya doin'?' she shrieks.

Small and young with a beautiful body, a permanent grin and sparkling dark eyes that have not yet been dulled by brutal sex. She is only fourteen and still a virgin. He is sixteen and shy and not yet used to this dark world that laps around the marble pedestal he has stood upon for so long.

'Nuthin'. Wanna Coke?'

'Get away!' she cries, grinning at him. Then her grin fades to a half-smile, as she looks deeper into him.

'Orright then, if ya like,' she replies.

She understands. She always did from the first, when she caught him staring at her silently across the campfire the first week he drifted in.

He is tall and strong and handsome – in an ugly sort of way. He is quiet and gentle and kind. When he does make love to her, he will not be cruel.

They walk down the street to a coffee lounge.

'Lets go to Beaufort Park, Murry.'

'No. Ole Billy 'Owes died other day. The place is packed with 'Oweses now.'

'Elgin Broppo oughta look out, then. 'Im an' Mantan 'Owes 'ad one big fight, unna?'

'Yeah.'

'Ya got any boya, Murry?'

'Yeah.'

He is proud of the job he has at the panel beater's. He grins down at Lynette then away again at the staring, glaring lights all around him. They rip into his love like fruit fly boring into a delicate, delicious fruit. Get away from the harsh forest of lights. Go to the sea of darkness and shadows and softness and bushes down at Supreme Court Gardens.

'Stick around me, Lynette, an' we'll 'ave a good time.'

'Orright.'

They grin in unison and she moves a little closer to him.

Elgin Broppo slinks into a darkened, rutted lane way near the Beaufort Hotel and peers around the corner at the crowded park. Obscure figures flutter from one circle to another. Furtive mumblings and occasional yells of recognition. The Howeses drink to the death of old Billy.

An ebony trio is squeezed from the park and ambles across the street towards Elgin. He tenses, ready to run, then notices his cousin Jimmy Olsen.

Grins and soft punches as the cousins meet.

'Hey, Elgin, brother. Doan' 'ang round 'ere, budda. Manny 'Owes is drunk as all buggeries.'

'Shootin' off 'ow ya fought 'im dirty, like.'

'Go an' get 'im, Elgin.'

'Doan' talk silly, Larry. Mantan 'ud kill 'im with 'is own mob,' Jimmy growls.

Elgin's sombre eyes gaze thoughtfully over the park. He lifts his lips a little in a suggestion of a smile.

'Another night, yeah.'

'Let's buy a drink, you fellahs.'

'Oo's got the boya?'

'Jimmy busted into a shop, unna? Ya still got monies?'

They troop over to the bottle shop leering out at the dark parked cars.

The proprietor eyes them in an unfriendly way because last night there had been a big brawl in the front bar where the Aborigines drank. But money's money, so he sells them a flagon of Brandevino and half a carton of cans.

Fade away behind the toilets, in the grubby, scuffed sea of dirt. Broken bottles blink their last as they drown in the sea.

The youths drown, too.

Caesar Jackell stumbles into the light-blasted circle outside Crystal Palace. His stage light. His big performance.

'Hey, Donny, I got a gun, ya know.'

'Yeah, an' I got a million dollars.'

'No. True's God. I got a real gun. Bushted thish 'ouse. Easy as pissin', it wash.'

'Look 'ere! Caesar drunk, or what?' a girl shouts happily.

'Yeah, 'e's drunk. Finished.'

'Caesar drunk!'

They gather around him, gabbling and grinning. All blurs and noise. Caesar clutches hold of Donny's sleeve.

'I got a fuckin' gun – and bullets.'

'I'll give ya gun right up ya bony 'ole d'rectly, if ya don't bugger off.'

'I got ten dollars, too, if ya wanna know. I'm fuckin' rich, me.'

They gather closer. Caesar smiles around the group, then swaggers into the poolroom. He nearly trips over his feet and is saved from the disgrace of falling on his face by two girls grabbing him. Everyone howls louder than ever at the joke.

Caesar dances over to the counter. Everyone of importance gathers around, and he is a hero to the drifting night people.

Slaps the $10 note on the counter.

'Fill 'er up, buddy,' he grins.

'Gimme a lend of a dollar, Caesar.'

'Caesar, give me a few bob, please. Go on Caesar, baby.'

'I'm ya people, Caesar.'

Five dollars go.

'I'm keepin' the rest,' he says.

Staggers over to a pinball machine, which blinks at him with the knowledge of an old friend. The people disperse and only two bony, scraggly-haired girls hang around him in the hope of more handouts. He becomes lost in the world of bright lights and bouncing balls and flashing numbers. The only world he wants to know.

Murry and Lynette huddle on the corner with all the white people. They sip their Coke silently.

'Let's go down to Supreme Court Gardens, Lynette.'

She is thoughtful for a moment. Looks up at simple Murry's kind face.

'Yeah, orright.'

They cross over, rubbing against each other in the crowd.

Up the street, with busy people and screeching buses and windows full of white man things.

The gates: and beyond the gates is sweet obscurity that swallows them up.

The Gardens are quiet and cool. The young couple go down past the Court House and through the trees onto the lawn.

No one is there.

They lie under a spreading tree and let the silence and peace blanket them. They finish off their Coke, talking in whispers.

Murry forms the words in his mind and repeats them over and over before rising up above her. She stares up and the whites of her eyes glint in the city light.

'Lynette ... Lynette, ya wanna be my woman?'

'Get away, ya silly bugger.'

'No. Ya know I'm mardong for ya, unna? I just gotta tell ya, that's all.'

She grins uneasily, yet knows that she *does* love him.

Soon, one day, a boy will grab her and suck what he wants from her, then toss her away. She would rather it was this boy than any other.

Murry's large clumsy hands encircle her and she gives an involuntary yelp before his face buries into her own and his lips devour her untainted ones. She struggles for a moment before relaxing. She is fearful of the unknown, yet happy in the comfort that will be her new life.

He peels her jeans down while his heavy fingers fumble around her body. Warm brown skin touches warm brown skin, and a unison of young, gentle, love is born.

The buildings, like stern priests, gaze down. The moon runs in naked freedom across her field, while the stars, clustered like daisies, wait to be put in a chain around her head.

The night – the hot, dusty night – presses down upon the city. Its misshapen head peers over the mountains of tall buildings while its grotesque fingers feel along the streets.

People go home.

Aboriginal children linger in large pulsating groups, sucking as much fun from the night as they can.

Elgin wanders up from Beaufort Park with his cousin Jimmy Olsen. Both are half-drunk and happy.

Caesar Jackell slumps in a dingy doorway, feeling sick. Drags listlessly on a cigarette.

Money, all gone. Friends all gone. He is just like everyone else now. Waiting for the police to come and send him on his way.

'Give us a cigarette,' Elgin mutters and sits beside his little cousin. He grins up at slim, watchful Jimmy.

'What ya reckon, J.O.? Our main man is pissed as a parrot, yeah.'

Ruffles the boy's wiry hair. Caesar turns bleary, dull eyes on Elgin, his hero.

He remembers, and clutches at the straw that is going to save him from drowning.

'I got a gun, Elgin,' he mumbles as he extracts the crumpled cigarettes.

Elgin and Jimmy grin as each takes a cigarette.

'Yeah, I got a gun too. Right 'ere, unna. Big shotgun.' Elgin grins and jabs a finger at his groin.

The older boys laugh.

Caesar sits dazed.

'No, I *'ave* got a gun, ya know. An' jewels, I even got a watch.'

No one listens to him. Jimmy Olsen squints down the street.

''Ere come them 'Owes, budda. Time we was movin'.'

Half-drunk Elgin stares away, with his quiet eyes in some far-off thought of his own.

'You c'n go, Jimmy. I'll wait 'ere. Go later, yeah.'

'Doan' you get in no fight, Elgin, that's all I ask, or else ya 'istory. None of our people around tonight, ya know, 'cept Murry – an' 'e's gone somewhere – an' this silly little prick.'

'Yeah. Well, see ya, J.O. See ya t'morrow, then.'

'Yeah.'

Jimmy disappears.

Just Caesar and Elgin and the city left.

'Ya gunna fight Mantan again, Elgin?'

'Naw. Fightin's stupid. Where's fightin' got ya? In jail, that's where, brother.'

'If ya get me gun, ya can shoot ole Mantan full of 'oles.'

'So ya truly 'ave got a gun.'

'Course. An' jewels an' a necklace an' everything.'

They puff away on another cigarette.

Some Howeses wander by and look the two over with hard Oriental eyes.

'Goin' to be a smash, directly, Caesar. Let's get goin' and find Murry.'

Elgin, the boss, climbs off the seat. Everything is going hazy, but he still walks with a sort of pride. His grubby little page boy swaggers behind him.

Big cousin Elgin who held up a bank and has stolen a dozen cars and beat up two munadj. Big Caesar who broke into a house.

Black boys who idle along. Shy of the bright white lights that expose them for what they really are.

They go up Murray Street.

Past the fire station where the firemen whistle and shout and jeer.

They sit down on the low wall outside the nurses' quarters where girls in short, tight uniforms glide between the iron gates, comfortable in the knowledge of their whiteness and virginity.

No one notices the two Nyoongahs in the shadows under the huge Moreton Bay fig tree that erupts from the footpath in a green volcano. It leads a doomed life, one day to be chopped down by the hands that nurtured it. Just like the people it shelters now.

'Hey boy, 'ow'd you like *'er*?' Caesar grins and spits as a pretty, buxom, young nurse walks past.

'Roasted, with two eggs,' Elgin grins.

Eyes follow her as they would a dream.

'Yeah, just like I was thinkin'.'

Elgin glances at his little cousin and bursts into laughter.

'Listen to 'im talk. Ya couldn't 'ave a moony to save yaself. Don't try foolin' me. I'm almost ya brother, yeah.'

'I done all right with Jenny Doolan.'

'Garn. Y'never touched 'er, even. I was there.'

'Any rate' Caesar sulks, 'I thought we was lookin' for Murry. What we doin' up 'ere?'

'Walkin',' Elgin grunts.

Staggers to his feet. 'Let's get goin'.'

'What we goin' up 'ere for? I wanna get me gun before some jerk finds it, ya know.'

'I'm goin' to say a prayer to turn me white,' Elgin smiles, and his eyes take in the cathedral that looms down upon them, its spire silhouetted against the sky. The Virgin Mary looks out over the city that surrounds it like broken eggshells.

'What ya reckon we steal the cashbox, Elgin?'

'Don't talk silly. 'Ow'd ya know God won't blast ya to bits, eh?'

Caesar laughs loud and young, while Elgin gives a mocking smile.

They leave the cathedral with its awesome shadows and tranquillity up on the hill.

Past the now-silent school. In the daytime (with all its blue heat and flies and dust) green-clad schoolgirls shout in play and hide their self-conscious womanhood behind starched uniforms.

Past the mint, looking like a caged animal behind the iron bars and twisted barbed netting. A snarling white man's animal.

The two descendants of the kings of the old civilisation glance from hooded eyes as a police car swishes past.

Elgin digs his hands deeper in his pockets, and his sharp eyes flick over to the taxi parked beside a block of flats that rear up into the sky. It taunts him with its sleek whiteness. The sleek white owner is upstairs in the flats, fondling his white girlfriend between white sheets.

'Ya can't even pinch a car, Elgin,' Caesar sneers, still sullen from Elgin's gibes about his sexual prowess.

Elgin's eyes flash.

'Couldn't I, ya little jerk? Just you keep watch, budda, an' I'll show ya 'ow one Nyoongah can steal a car.'

The wiry youth crouches beside the taxi and his teeth pull back in a grin. His thin fingers find a crack where the window is wound down and he heaves with all his might. Puts in his hand and unlocks the door.

Caesar stands, tense and afraid, under a tree.

A utility glides past.

Elgin leaps onto the other side of the taxi, while Caesar melts into the tree.

Door open. Silver paper on the fuses.

Two shadows pushing a taxi down the hill. The gentle crunch of tyres on cement. A sudden kick, and the engine bursts into life. Doors slam and Elgin lets out a howl of laughter as he screeches around the corner.

Caesar clutches the door in fright.

Elgin Mortimer Broppo lets all his drunken frustration bubble out in one long whoop of joy.

'*Now* we'll get ya bloody gun an' shoot bloody ole Mantan so full of 'oles 'e'll look like a piece of lace, yeah,' Elgin cries.

Caesar lights a nervous cigarette.

'Not so fast, couz. I wanna live, ya know.'

A faint, persistent thought hammers at Elgin's mind.

Back to jail; back to jail
E.M. Broppo back to jail

The wheel between his thin agile hands whisks the thought away. It bobs with the coloured lights here, then is gone.

Down in the cool peace of the gardens, Murry lies beside Lynette. She smiles serenely at him and he rubs a calloused hand through her hair.

She has become a woman tonight. In the way she dreamed about, down at the dusty camp, when she was small, and read, over and over again, the tattered book on 'Sleeping Beauty'.

Caressed and kissed and loved on this hot night. And her man is still here beside her, tracing patterns in her hair.

'We'd better go soon, Murry. The 'Owes'll be everywhere.'

'They won't bother us,' the giant rumbles.

The girl realises he is still white, in many ways as well as in his manner of making love. She sits up and takes out cigarettes for them both.

'They will if they know ya one of Elgin's people.'

They finish their cigarettes. The incense-like blue smoke drifts around them and the tree squats above them like a buddha. They kiss again, never wanting to leave.

But there are Lynette's father and three brothers to think about – and her uncles and cousins. Just as everything is going well, Murry doesn't want to start a feud of his own.

'Better go.'

They amble up into the lighted city that is becoming dark and empty now.

The buses are all gone.

The Howeses are all there. Too may glowering, hunched Howeses stalking the streets for gentle Murry and feminine Lynette to fight.

They slink back the way they came and down towards the river.

'We'll get a taxi, if there's any goin'. I got the money,' Murry murmurs.

Elgin and Caesar, on their way to get the .303, find them.

The squeal of brakes rips out the guts of the night. The taxi reverses back to gaping Murry and surprised Lynette.

'Shut ya mouth an' open the door, Murry,' rasps little Caesar, eyeing Lynette. He feels more sure of himself now, and happy that – at last – he is going to get his rifle.

Elgin cocks his head over his slight shoulders. Bright eyes twinkle at Murry.

'Where ya been, Murry?'

'Where ya think, Elgin? Down Supreme Court Gardens, unna, Murry?' Caesar says before Murry can answer.

'Ya *wanna* punch in the 'ead, Caesar Jackell, ya big prick?' Lynette snarls.

'Da's true,' returns Caesar, and nudges Elgin. Their teeth gleam as they shudder in silent laughter.

Lynette glowers.

'Ya steal this taxi, Elgin?' Murry mutters as he slides in.

'Nah! 'E bought it, unna?' Caesar cackles.

Elgin smiles a superior smile.

They drive over the bridge. Elgin idles along the riverside slowly.

'Where ya goin', Elgin?' Lynette asks from the back. She is the only girl there. She has heard about these sort of rides before. After all, the two in the front *are* Murry's cousins. Share and share alike is their code.

'Just gettin' some of Caesar's stuff.'

''Ere. Turn off,' Caesar orders. He is the boss again, just as he was up in front of Crystal's.

The taxi rocks and bumps down the gravel track until it reaches the water's edge.

Caesar leaps out and searches in the long grass until he finds the .303 and the bag. He holds them up and shouts a challenge to the soaring flats and the dancing moon and the cold, white, impassive stars.

The cab screeches back onto the main road, spitting dust and gravel in defiance.

Caesar produces the flagon of riesling. Drunk and happy again, he hands out pieces of jewellery to everyone. He keeps the .303 on his knee and the watch and two earrings in his pocket. He takes a long swig of the flagon, then hands it to Elgin.

'Ya smart little bugger. 'Oo'd of believed it, eh?' Elgin gives Caesar a proper grin. A man-to-man grin for the new hero of the clan.

Caesar aims his rifle at buildings and boats and the occasional bird, Murry and Lynette snuggle up close to one another and take the odd sip of wine from the offered flagon.

Elgin drives, drowning in bitter riesling and his own thoughts.

They will be looking for the cab by now. When they catch him, they will make sure he goes to jail for a long time, if Big Pig Fathers has anything to do with it.

He thinks about his woman, lying alone in their tent out at the camp. Her round, bright eyes and quiet voice, and the gentle smile that can calm his wildness.

A still part of town. A tired sign above a building, flashes blue and red: LAWSON HOT L.

He swings the taxi into the gloom of the parking area.

Two o'clock in the morning. No one around.

The others stare at him in curiosity as he grins around the dark cab.

'We just goin' to break into 'ere an' get some beer. 'Ave one big party, when we get back to camp.'

'Yeah?' Murry, uneasily.

'Nothin' to it, Murry. Wait 'ere a bit, you mob. Be back d'rectly.'

Elgin slips out and scuttles over to the wall. A sharp crack as the window breaks. Protesting squeaks as it jerks open.

A low whistle.

Murry clambers out noisily, not used to this sort of thing.

Caesar floats beside him, holding his .303. Lynette huddles in the cab, with just a cigarette and the riesling to keep her company, feeling terribly alone, without big Murry beside her.

Elgin's head peers out of the window like a fox glancing out of his lair. A sly, thin, black fox, about to grab the fluttering white chickens and make them squawk.

'Come 'ere, Murry, Caesar, keep watch.'

The two coloured boys stand inside the murky lounge, while their eyes become used to the gloom. Elgin leads the way as they sneak into the storeroom.

'We right now, baby,' Elgin whispers, 'Fuckin' Christmas, unna, out at camp, when we deliver this little lot.'

Murry is afraid. It is strange that he is here, in someone else's place, taking all this beer. The pictures on the wall scowl down at him. He passes out the carton to drunk Caesar, who staggers over to the cab.

Carton after carton of bottles and stubbies and cans.

Murry is a criminal now. If he gets caught, it's an end to all his dreams. And all he wanted to do was go home.

'Grab some gnummerai, Murry. Geeze, do ya 'ave to be told everything?' Elgin hisses as he dashes past with an armload of spirit bottles. Murry gets a small cardboard box and quickly fills it up with cigars and packets of cigarettes. His strong hands wrench open the till and he stuffs about $200 in notes into his pockets.

'Come on, Murry, ya ole woman!'

He rushes over to the window and leaps out.

They roll start the taxi. Head for home. Home amongst the gaunt trees, beside the wide river flat.

They weave through the streets, keeping clear of police vehicles and taxis. Out on Guildford Road, Elgin pushes his foot down hard and lets the power and freedom of his body and mind echo in the taxi engine.

Reedy voices crackle feebly over the two-way in a vain search for the cab. Black Elgin is supreme once more. For the second time in his life he has the radios of Perth spread like a spider's web to catch him as he buzzes along.

'What ya reckon they'll say out at camp when we roll up?' he grins.

''Appy birthday,' Caesar laughs.

A train roars past and Elgin tries to beat it.

The only car on the whole lonely road.

Caesar pretends to shoot the people in the train.

Lynette sniggers, 'Look 'ere at Clint Eastwood!'

Caesar turns and laughs with her. All he can do now is laugh. If he stops laughing, he will spew up. He sways and rolls and clutches his .303 even tighter. His smile is a fixed one.

Lynette is only happy-drunk. She leans against broad Murry and his big hand covers her child's breast. He broods about the crime he has committed, then thinks about the money that will buy his woman a lot of joy.

Elgin is remote from the others. Just him and his car and the road.

They are almost at Guildford when they zoom past a speed trap.

Caesar hears the eerie wailing and jerks around.

'Hey couz, bloody munadj 'ave got us!'

Fear settles like a mist over the remnants of the tribe.

''Old tight. When I tell ya to run, ya bloody run – understand?' Elgin says, through clenched teeth.

More cars join in the chase: two blue vans and a CIB car. They bay and howl like hounds after the fox.

'I'll stop 'em!' screams Caesar, and loads the magazine of his .303.

Six bullets.

He leans out the window of the swaying cab so the wind whips his hair back and shrieks through the curls.

He fires the rifle and the bullet whines away. Fires again and again.

On his last shot, the bullet smashes through the windscreen of the foremost van so it slews to an abrupt halt. The RTA car also stops, but the others come relentlessly onwards.

The CIB car comes up alongside them. They think they are Starsky and Hutch, in their olive-green Kingswood. Elgin sees the fat, pale face of Detective-Sergeant Fathers peering in at them.

Slides over to the other side of the road in an attempt to block off the CIB car.

It only comes up on the other side of the road, so Elgin rams the taxi into it.

Twice he smashes the taxi against the car, desperately trying to escape. He has visions of smirking Fathers and his mates, like white toadstools growing on Elgin's black rotting body, down in the forest of Central police station.

The second time he rams the CIB car, Caesar Jackell's arm breaks with a snap like the click of his stolen rifle bolt.

He gives a cry of pain.

Just over the Swan River bridge, Elgin slams on the brakes. The taxi careers up onto the footpath.

'Run! Run!' he yells, and is out sprinting even before the car has stopped. Down over the bank and towards the river.

Caesar stumbles across the road, in the headlights of the pursuing CIB car. He scrabbles painfully down the opposite bank from Elgin, and staggers across the paddock, trailing his .303.

Dull Murry is stunned for three vital seconds and Lynette clings fearfully to him. When he explodes from the taxi, the area is surrounded by police.

He has more to lose than the other two boys. He has his pride at never having committed a crime and his good job and his girl whom he *does* love. He pushes Lynette down the bank after Elgin. Turns to face the approaching horde with the anger of a cornered wildcat.

He lifts one policeman off his feet with a powerhouse right and smashes huge Fathers in the mouth, rocking him.

Six police pounce on the giant Aboriginal and grapple him to his knees with punches and kicks. Hurl him into the van where he crouches in the corner with dead eyes.

'Who's your mates? Who was drivin'? What was the girl's name? How old was she, sonny? Do you know what carnal knowledge is all about? What's your name, arsehole? You 'ad the gun, eh, Jesse James? Well, who did, then? where did you get all this beer and grog, matey? By Christ, you're in the shit now. Tell us who the others were, or we put everything on you. Hey, sarge, one went down along the river. Where'd that bloody girl go? I wouldn't mind arresting her, eh, Billy? ... Hey, sarge, Central want you on the radio: Get every man you can down here, a mob of Abos have split everywhere ... one of them is fucking dangerous ... got a gun ... took a shot at one of our cars ... No, no one is hurt, only shaken ... Listen, Jacky, yer better start talkin' soon, before I belt yer bloody ears off ... How's Mal? Pretty crook, that boong's got a hard punch. Yaaah! They all think they're Baby Cassius.'

Words, words. Going round and round inside Murry's battered head. He drops his eyes and chews on his bottom lip while white faces gaze in at him as though he were a monkey in the zoo, not a human at all. Hard eyes, contemptuous eyes, wondering eyes: slit mouths and Hitler moustaches.

White faces, blue uniforms.

Being the only one caught is such a bitter feeling. The loneliness is more acute. He remembers Caesar joking and Elgin grinning, and Lynette smiling and pressing against him – so close – in a world so far away.

They take him to Midland lockup.

Caesar huddles, moaning, down beside the river. He stares at the blank brown water. His arm hurts now and tears run down his face. He sniffs noisily and wonders if he has killed anyone. The excitement of the chase wears off and he feels sicker then he has ever been. Leans over and vomits all over the ground. Fades among the trees as he hears the droning of a car bouncing over the paddock. Two yellow eyes stare out of the darkness and pick him up, cringing against the tree.

Car stops. Doors open. Feet crunch on the dead grass.

'Look out! He's the crazy bastard with the gun!'

'G'day, Caesar.'

Fathers and company.

'I never meant to kill no one.'

'No one's dead, Caesar. Now, suppose you give me that gun.'

'I busted me arm, ya know.'

The men close in around him.

'Well, we'd better get it looked at, then, hadn't we?'

He is escorted to the car.

The stars watch from above. His people.

They can't help him now.

No one can.

Inside the CIB car, on his way to Midland regional hospital, with the stale fingers of the evening's enjoyment ripping at his small body, he babbles out the truth of everything.

Just as the sun is crawling over the hills to begin a new day, Elgin creeps into the camp. He has run and slipped and swum his way along the river, then over the paddocks.

Safe back at home, in his tent.

His young woman stares at his silhouette in the tent opening with chiding eyes. He is angry, yet ashamed, of her disapprobation.

'Where ya bin, Elgin?' she whispers, tired of asking the same question. Tired of trying to settle her thin husband's turbulent soul.

'Nowhere.'

He throws himself down on the blanket and lights up a cigarette. He cannot meet her dark, all-knowing eyes.

Blood from a rip in his arm where he got caught on a barbed wire fence, trickles down the brown skin like a teardrop.

'Ya badly 'urt, 'oney?' she murmurs.

'No. Go back to sleep, Maydene.'

'It's almost mornin', an' ya been stealin' again. Elgin! 'Ow *can* I go to sleep, with yaself moonin' all over the countryside?' she cries. 'Ya only come out of jail last month, too. Ya *want* ole Fathers to flog ya again, or what?'

And Elgin was going to ride into camp on his white horse and unload all the beer. Everyone was going to gather around, and there would have been jokes and laughter and fun. His woman would have smiled at him and hugged him, and forgiven him – because he had brought some light into the dusty reserve.

He digs his hand into a pocket and pulls out one of Caesar's necklaces. His feral eyes meet her bruised ones.

'I got ya this, Maydene,' he mutters.

'Ooohh, Elgin! What ya tryin' to do to me, boy?' she weeps.

Elgin gets up abruptly, and moves outside. Muffled sobs pierce him like the first shafts of the orange-red sunlight from the new day.

CHRIS TIFFIN

Relentless Realism: Archie Weller's *Going Home*

In his two books, *The Day of the Dog* and *Going Home*,[1] Archie Weller has established himself as the leading chronicler of the lives of urban and fringe Aboriginals. His narratives are searing and depressing accounts of an existence which affords few gratifications and is irretrievably circumscribed by white power. Only very occasionally in Weller's fiction is there any fruitful and productive contact between Aboriginal and white,[2] and even when this occurs the effect is quickly swept away by events. The narratives are almost invariably closed. Where they do not end in actual death they involve either a return to jail or a definitive repudiation of former hopes. Unlike the Maori writers, Patricia Grace and Witi Ihimaera, who often write about incidents in Maori life or Maori-Pakeha relationships which allow for a redirection of attitudes and a future, Weller's stories take the shape of representative life sagas ending in tragedy or stultification whether they are extended account as in *The Day of the Dog* or 'Cooley' or whether they are only a few pages in length like 'Pension Day'. Sometimes the life can even be summed up in an aphorism: 'Cooley, the dreamer. Cooley, the hate-filled and hated half-caste, Cooley, the dead boy.' (p. 212)

Paradoxically, then, Weller views as directed totalities lives which are conceived of by the livers only in fragmentary and very immediate terms. Even in 'One Hot Night' which departs from his normal narrative mode in sharing the focus among a number of differentiated protagonists, the direction of the story is still strongly centripetal. The first three sections show the principal characters in different parts of the city with disparate concerns. In subsequent sections their paths overlap and they proceed inexorably towards confrontation with the police and jail. For some this process is self-induced, but for others it is an inevitability born of their colour and class, no matter how strong their intentions are to the contrary. 'Murry is a criminal now. If he gets caught, it's an end to all his dreams. And all he wanted to do was go home.' (p. 88)

The titles of the two books point up this sense of closure and containment. 'The Day of the Dog' recalls the proverb, 'every dog has its day', which grudgingly celebrates a (brief) period of triumph, but only within an overall framework of ontological inferiority. In Weller's fiction the reality of that inferiority, socially and economically rather than ontologically conceived, is destructively reasserted by the end of the story. Less immediately, the title picks up another traditional saying, 'Give a dog a bad name ...' a piece of pre-Barthesian wisdom suggesting that people will act in accordance with declared negative expectations of them. These two lines of thought fuse in the texture of the world of Weller's stories. Ironically, 'the day' does not come adventitiously to the 'dog'. It is the label of inferiority put upon them by the whites which drives Weller's Aboriginals to try to achieve in white terms. For a while they enjoy the illusion of success and acceptance, but inevitably they learn that they have not really escaped from their racially-determined place in society.

> Perhaps it had always been that way. While Clayton had thought he was getting somewhere in life, he had, in reality, been going nowhere. ... All the time he had thought he was someone – Baby Clay, the champion boxer – and all the people had stared and laughed to see him act the fool. ... He had thought he had found truth but had found only false glory. (p. 30)

The title, 'Going Home', also embodies this causal irony. The story from which the title is taken tells of a white-educated Aboriginal who has succeeded in the white world as footballer and painter returning to his parents' home to celebrate his twenty-first birthday. He learns that his derelict father has been dead for two years, but is still able to make the first steps towards reintegration with his family before he is gratuitously picked up by the police on suspicion of robbery. The story ends with him and his brother in the back of the police van. Instead of being given the key of the door to the white world on his birthday, or even being allowed to rediscover his Aboriginal world unmolested, he is inducted into his 'real home' as society constructs it: police custody and jail. Similar treatments of white society redefining an Aboriginal's home are found in Jack Davis's *Kullark*, and Sally Morgan's *My Place*.

Much of Weller's fiction is devoted to depicting this pressure upon urban Aboriginals and the strategies they adopt to survive and to transcend it. Inevitably, Aboriginals are depicted as holding to some defensive enclave.

The enclave may be metaphorical, like Reg Cooley's 'fortress' (p. 198) or literal, like the caravan the boxers inhabit (p. 29). It may be natural like the night which protects Murry and Lynette (p. 81) or man-made like the car Billy Woodward drives home in (p. 1). The most important enclave of all is the family which is discussed below. Outside their enclaves the characters are awkward and wary. A favourite locational word then is 'corner' combining the senses of marginalisation, the aggression of the boxing ring and being at bay.[3] Whether it is a train, a nightclub, a coffee shop or even the back of the police van, the Aboriginal characters seem instinctively to gravitate to this corner position.

One ambiguous strategy for survival under this pressure is a prudent withdrawal in the face of white harassment. Prudent withdrawal involves avoiding conflict by staying out of the way of whites or making suitable obeisances when confrontation looms. On one level this can be seen as ignoble and cowardly. In 'Going Home', for example,

> Darcy sidles up to the fuming barman.
> ''Scuse me, Mr 'Owett, but William 'ere just come 'ome see,' he whines like a beaten dog. We *will* be drinkin' in the camp, ya know.'
> ....
> 'Well all right, Darcy. I'll forget about it this time. Just keep your friend out of my hair.'
> Good dog, Darcy. Have a bone, Darcy. Or will a carton of stubbies do? (p. 6)

But it is important to ask, seen as ignoble by whom? For this is not the authorial voice, but rather the bitter internal comment of Billy Woodward who had thought he was accepted in white society and who now discovers the hollowness of such acceptance. He is appalled by the loss of dignity he suddenly suffers. But however it appears to the white publican, Darcy's intervention is not from powerless subservience but rather the calculated one of the manipulator of the situation. They *do* get their beer, and as they carry it off Darcy tells Billy, 'Act stupid, buddy, an' ya go a lo--ong way in this town.' (p.6)[4]

Some of the ambiguity of the power dynamics of the situation arises from Weller's use of the image, 'like a beaten dog'. The white publican sees Darcy as 'beaten' in the sense of defeated, and hence is prepared to be magnaminous when he is presented with an appropriate pose of subservience. The reality, though, is that Darcy is 'beaten' only in the sense of being struck, without the concomitant implication that the imposition has been definitive, or that the power lies exclusively with the white man. In a similar way, 'dog' extends some of the ironies noted earlier. Historically, from the nineteenth century the Aborigines in Australia were labelled by the whites as cowardly, because of their curious reluctance to line up and be shot à la Charge of the Light Brigade.[5] Words like 'dog', 'cur' and 'dingo' have been frequently used in such labels. Weller's work engages directly with that sort of thinking, since in depicting the social conditions under which Aborigines live he simultaneously exposes the stereotyping they have endured and continue to endure. Heroism-as-suicide may have been a useful imperial fetish, but Weller makes clear that it has little to recommend it as a practice for modern Aboriginal society.

A similar use of the image of canine evasiveness occurs in 'Cooley' when the protagonist is confronted by a group of white youths who beat him up. 'Once Cooley would have run off like a stray dog, at the sight of all those boys, but lately he had been left alone and his wariness had ebbed. ... Only when they surrounded him and stared silently at him did he realise his danger.' (p. 203) When he is eventually goaded into fighting, Cooley is compared to a dingo, not in the traditional white Australian image of cowardice, but rather in an image of magnificent power and predatoriness:

> All the white boys saw was a thin, weedy half-caste. Then he sprang like a dingo, brown and sleek, into a mob of white sheep, all the more menacing in his silence. (p. 204)

This is a daring reversal of the values of the image. In white Australian discourse, the dingo is the cunning, cowardly and wasteful killer of defenceless, useful animals. Weller rewrites the cunning as disguise, but it is apparent disguise only. In arrogant misapprehension the white youths expect a Clark Kent, but find a Superman. Perhaps, ironically, they were correct in their original apprehension, for it is only when they goad Cooley too far that their taunts call the predatory animal into being. The traditional values of sheep are likewise inverted. While in the Western tradition the sheep/lamb is a symbol of meek gentleness and innocence, from an Aboriginal point of view it is the sheep, as symbol of white pastoral expansion, which has been the major cause of their progressive dispossession. Weller's forceful association of the sheep with the whites who are about to attack the Aboriginal is thus not capricious or arbitrary but historically recuperative.

To varying degrees, Weller's characters are sustained by a sense of racial pride, although it is often a confused and sometimes desperate sense of identity that is left them. At the opening of 'Going Home' Billy Woodward is explicitly isolated from the natural/Aboriginal world, but still instinctively parallels his sense of achievement and belonging with that of his forebears.

> Out into the world of magpies' soothing carols, and parrots' cheeky whistles, of descending darkness and spirits.
>
> The man doesn't know that world. His is the world of the sleek new Kingswood that speeds down the never-ending highway.
>
> At last he can walk this earth with pride, as his ancestors did many years before him. He had his first exhibition of paintings a month ago. They sold well, and with the proceeds he bought the car. (p. 1)

The sense of achievement in a white world is undermined by its reference to an ancestral pride in two ways. In the first place the action of the story shows that not only is his sense of achievement and consequent acceptance illusory but that it is precisely because of his blood link with his ancestors that he is not really accepted. Far from continuing a proud tradition, although in a different sphere of endeavour, he finds that his connection with that older tradition, albeit tenuous, renders his own success nugatory. In the second place there is a more fundamental aporia between Aboriginal tradition and achievement in white terms. It is axiomatic to the discourse of Aboriginal writing in English that Aboriginal identity is valuable and to be preserved and fostered. Hence the abandonment of it is always displayed negatively. In this present story, Billy's achievements and his satisfaction are thus undermined not only by a suspicious and resentful white authority but also by his own guilt at neglect of community and tradition.

Pathetically confused references to traditional beliefs are a constant reminder of the deracination of the contemporary Aboriginal. In 'Saturday Night and Sunday Morning' after robbing a service station, one of the characters outlines his plans:

> 'Yeah, first thing I'm goin' to get is a telescopic rifle,' and the Wolf smiles a secret smile.
>
> To own a gun is the last step in his initiation. *Then* he can own the world. And even when at last he dies, his name will live on like the trees and the rocks and the stars. *That* will be his soul, but it will be more famous than *any* of his ancestors. (p. 64)

In a similar way Reg Cooley mistakes his first sexual experiences with a promiscuous white girl as 'his Dreaming' (p. 161). At other times though, he is more clear-sighted about his inheritance,and is determined one day to reclaim it (pp. 140-141).

Two qualities which are seen in a positive light and which are associated with racial pride are a courageous stoicism, and a strong, even overwhelming community sense. The courage includes schoolchildren hiding their hurt: 'He cried a bit, but he was an Abo so didn't cry for long' (p. 97) which is elsewhere glossed as a refusal to allow the tormentor to see the suffering that he has caused. 'I had to bite back the tears: it would never do for a Nyoongah to cry in front of our number one enemies.' (p. 41) At the other end of the spectrum this stoicism appears as a sort of enthusiastic fatalism which allows for life to continue despite constant repression and intervention by hostile authority. One of the best renditions of this is the short piece, 'Fish and Chips'. In it, a teenager describes the sixteen members of his household and a sample of their activities. What emerges is a series of apparently guileless juxtapositions between an exuberance and sense of enjoyment of life on the one hand and a pattern of violence and criminality on the other. While the narrator makes some general observations, 'We're all Whittys together: there is no hope for us if we don't stick together' (p. 131), most of the power of the story comes from the implicit acceptance as normal of what most readers would find a devastating indictment of social organisation.

> [Jimmy] might not have been able to fight, but he was a solid dancer: his legs were rubber and his body was elastic, so Mum said. You should hear his impersonations of Elvis Presley and Humphrey Bogart.
>
> But he assaulted a policeman who took him up into a back alley to belt him around. (p. 132)

This is skilful use of juxtaposition. The apparent focal point for the naive narrator is Jimmy's dancing ability which is contrasted with his lack of ability in fighting. But the sense of enjoyment of Jimmy's peaceable talents is suddenly cut across by the abrupt statement of his crime. That we have already been told he was not a fighter underlines the disjuncture between the legal term 'assault' and the colloquial 'belt around'. Police may 'belt around' an Aboriginal with relative impunity so long as they are discreet enough to do so out of the public view and the colloquial register asserts both the legitimacy and the casual normality of the occurrence. Resistance to this treatment though is 'assault' which places the action immediately in the socially constructed judicial arena. As for Ezeulu in Achebe's *Arrow of God*, language becomes focally complicit in Jimmy's oppression.[6] A similar back-alley incident is spelled out much more fully and graphically in the story, 'Saturday Night and Sunday Morning' (p. 59), but the implications of this brief 'innocent' narration are more chillingly felt.

The stoical elasticity under oppression is maintained by strength drawn from family and kin. It is a truism of Aboriginal writing that the family is the point of connection both between individual and society and between individual and his/her culture. It is also the basis of a sort of corporate identity. As one character says, 'We've got cousins everywhere; we'd be no one without cousins.' (p. 135) The strength of this bond is grudgingly recognised even by whites who disparage it in an image of flies congregating. 'You bastards stick together like flies on a dunny wall.' (p.11) In 'Violet Crumble' it is an implicit condemnation of Sammy that he can use that image himself.

> My mob used to hang around me like flies. Every prize I'd win, the whole tribe would be in for their share. There'd be none left for me. One day I had a big brawl and told them all to clear off. I shifted over east for a few years and haven't looked back since. (p 112)

Family support is equally necessary in the inter-clan fighting which occupies much of the urban characters' time. Not only money and possessions but quarrels are shared family matters, and as in traditional Aboriginal society, an injury by one member of a family or clan can provoke retaliation against any other member. Thus the laconic response of Lynette to Murry's self-absorbed romanticism in 'One Hot Night':

> 'We'd better go soon, Murry. The 'Owes'll be everywhere.'
> 'They won't bother us,' the giant rumbles.
> The girl realises he is still white, in many ways as well as in his manner of making love. She sits up and takes out cigarettes for them both.
> 'They will if they know ya one of Elgin's people.' (p. 85)

It is the mark of the total isolation of Cooley, the protagonist of the novella which concludes the book, that he has no family support. He lives in an all-white household, since his full brother has left to play football in the east, and his white father has remarried a white woman and clearly regrets his earlier marriage and its offspring. He has no kinship with the other Aboriginals in the area since he comes from further north. While Cooley receives the support of other Aboriginals when it comes to fights with the white youths, at crucial times he realises how alone he is. Significantly he is finally shot not by a white policeman, but by an Aboriginal.

The Aboriginal family is portrayed as imperative as well as supportive. Weller reiterates the belief that no matter how hard an Aboriginal tries to put aside his family it will call him back eventually. Talking to Darcy, Billy Woodward 'suddenly ... has to know all about his family and become lost in their sea of brownness.' (p. 5) Similarly in 'One Hot Night', despite being fostered in a white home Murray James finds that 'the murmurings of his people stirred in his heart and he wandered home again to Lockridge camp.' (p. 78) In 'Fish and Chips' the narrator predicts that his sister, who has disowned the family and married a white, will be back. 'She can't stay away from home forever. No one can.' (p. 133) Even the landscape can take part in this recall. In 'Violet Crumble' the land calls Sam who has deserted his family in order to become a top surfer. 'The thin ragged strip of land in the middle beckon[s] like a crooked dry finger ... asking Sam to come back and be a black man, as he should be. Beckoning and sighing for the sheep to come home.' (p. 121) Neglect of the family in order to succeed in the white world as in 'Going Home', 'Violet Crumble' or 'Fish and Chips' is always seen as a betrayal of responsibilities.

For some – not by any means all – of the repressed characters the natural world offers not only an environment in which white persecution is temporarily lessened, but one where Aboriginals can display skills and feel adequate to their environment and connected to their ancestry. Even at such times, though, white domination remains implicit in the background. The clearest example of this is in 'Cooley' when the hero goes to check his rabbit traps.

> Cooley blended into the swirling shadows of the bush and the black cockatoo's cry echoed in his mind. Back, back to a thousand years ago when a wild, short full-blood had also fled silently into his sanctuary. Cooley's slouch and sullenness were gone, and a rare glint shone in his yellow, evasive eyes. Cooley was home. The wind that sang for him told him this, the leaves that brushed gently against his face told him; and Cooley was free, alone, a man again.
>
> When he was here he could forget all about the troubles that fell upon his sloping shoulders. He could forget Packer with his red face and contemptuous blue eyes, he

> could forget his lying, sneering brood. He could cease worrying about the insults heaped upon him by the white boys in class, or by his family at home. He could forget the teachers with their canes and detentions and more subtle insults. Now he was Yagan. Now he was Pigeon. Now he was king of the universe. (p. 180)

There are multiple identifications here, most obviously with the natural world which communicates with him, emancipates him and restores to him his sense of manliness. Not surprisingly this is accompanied by a sense of identification with an ancestral past and the ability to figure in the mind earlier presences in the terrain. But having established his identity in this way, the passage turns to his relations with the whites showing how constrained he still is. He tells himself that in this natural environment he can forget his white tormentors, and he identifies with some of the heroes of Aboriginal resistance. But ironically in naming them he is inscribing the presence of the whites, and so not really dismissing them at all. Whatever success Yagan and Pigeon had as guerrillas, they did not succeed in driving out the whites, and as talismans of Cooley's new-found independence they are ultimately illusions. Even Cooley's purpose there that day, capturing rabbits, an imported animal, shows how much he remains inside a white-constructed and dominated world.

The authorial voice in 'Saturday Night and Sunday Morning' makes a more mystical identification between the natural world and the Aboriginal Dreaming. Awareness of this identification, however, has been subverted by hatred in the time since the whites came.

> His temper burns behind his sombre eyes while his teeth are a white slash across his dark face. Just like the Milky Way slashing across the sky, showing where his God has trodden in glory, even before white man was thought of. That is how old his people are. Timeless and never dying, like the land they are buried under. Then their bones became the trees and dancing rivers and folding mountains and their souls became the stars. They float to the end of time, yet are the beginning.
>
> Except now his God is the steel and wooden shot-gun he points at the girl. He worships it with his whole hating spirit. (p. 54)

A similar correspondence between the stars and the Aboriginal ancestors is deftly sketched in at the end of 'One Hot Night' as Caesar is arrested. Again the stars have been displaced and rendered useless as sources of strength and as guides to conduct. 'The stars watch from above. His people. They can't help him now.' (p. 91) The stars have been replaced in these stories by the city lights which are constantly seen as hard, hostile and empty, the deracinating parody of the ancestor symbols.

One way back from this twisted impasse of frustrated hate is through love. Several of the stories deal centrally with love, between whites, between Aboriginals, between Aboriginal men and white women. In the case of the last, the white woman is able to replace some of the defensive bitterness of the youth with a hopeful peace. In 'Saturday Night and Sunday Morning' this involves both a Pygmalion motif and an inversion of sexuality. Wolf, a wanted killer and now a kidnapper, records his sense of utter deprivation. '[Wolf is] a good name, unna, cos it all belongs to me, an' is all I got left.' (p. 59) His hostage responds to this *cri de coeur*, is able to communicate her sympathy and rekindles his belief in relationships with people other than hate. She is awed by the power she thus manifests:

> She feels the power she has as she watches the happy brown youth. She created him from a heap of broken hopes and shattered laughter and rubbish. He is all her own, shaped from her hands and peacefulness. (p. 61)

This is not, however, the arrogant claim of a possessor but rather the concerned acknowledgement of responsibility for him. The giving and taking of names is often seen as paradigmatic of the appropriating and control of people. Thus in 'The Boxer' Clayton Little is renamed by the man who eventually comes to control utterly his boxing career and his life. In 'Saturday Night and Sunday Morning', however, Melanie offers her name in exchange for the explanation she had asked of his, and it serves as a token of equality and trust.

> 'Melanie, unna?'
> He rolls the name around between his purple lips. When he speaks her name it is the same as his - a part of him that he can call his own. (p. 61)

The dissolution of power tensions – Melanie represents the macrocosmic dominant white power, but in the microcosm is herself a hostage of Wolf and his brother – is paralleled by a projected resolution of heterosexual tension. An aspect of deracinated Wolf is a brutal misogyny which arises from a fear of making himself too vulnerable. For the first time he trusts sufficiently to offer love, but that the offer is itself an acceptance is stressed by the inverted sexuality in which he envisions their embrace.

> He had never really cared much for girls. Painted faces. Shrill, nagging voices. Giggling to annoy him. Crawling all over him, trying like the police to capture him. The police take away his freedom; the girls take away his soul. But his soul is all he has, so he belts the girls and makes them cry.
>
> ....
>
> That is what he needs most of all – love. To be able to lie beside her and feel her warm white body pulsating, full of life and kindness. Pumping her serenity into his wild brown body. Then he will have no need for anger any more. (pp. 62-63)

Instead of him penetrating her, she is to penetrate him and impregnate him with calm and serenity. The aggressiveness of his anger, displaced on to his male sexuality, is forsworn. With typical irony, however, no sooner is this position of genuine redemption arrived at than the police arrive and Wolf is killed.

Reg Cooley is less misogynist, but he is equally distrustful of getting close to people, and so has to be led to trust and love. Again the text is quite explicit both about the dissipation of his generalised anger and about the girl as maker of the new man.

> The girl's pale fingers wiped away the last shards of hate and mistrust from his slanted, light eyes and her soft murmurs of passion wiped away his tension and hate so that the fortress he had built himself came crashing down and he stepped from the ruins like a prince freed from some evil spell.
>
> ....
>
> The girl's hands, as fragile and white as eggshells, had moulded him into a new being, a peaceful gentle being. (pp. 197-198)

Just as Melanie was envisioned as the sexual aggressor in the previous example so here Rachel is seen as the female knight liberating the imprisoned prince. Defined sex roles give way just as do racial prejudice and its consequent defensiveness.

Such moments of soul meeting soul, of respecting others for more than their prowess at fighting, are, however, bleakly rare in the stories. For the women there is little hope of any enduring fulfilment so sexual relations are declined or entered into on a principle of minimising the damage. Gentleness in men's lovemaking is regarded as exceptional. (pp. 79, 105) Even the more positively rendered relationships start out on a basis of minimal expectation. Thus, in 'One Hot Night' Lynette, aged fourteen, rapidly calculates the percentages of happiness. 'Soon, one day, a boy will grab her and suck what he wants from her, then toss her away. She would rather it was this boy than any other.' (p. 81)

There can be little doubt about the power of Weller's depictions of urban and fringe Aboriginal life which have recently been credited with giving the 'best insight into contemporary Aboriginal views of authority, sexuality, humour and mores,'[7] but equally there is little doubt that they are almost unrelievedly depressing. Weller's novel concluded with the violent death of the protagonist. Of the eight stories in *Going Home* only one, ('The Boxer'), is open-ended. Of the remaining seven, three culminate in violent death, one in alcoholic death, two in capture and jail, and one in the violent (and apparently permanent) rupture of a relationship.

The novel offsets its generally pessimistic action by endowing the characters with a certain energetic verve and capacity for life which made them in some sense dominant over their situation. The stories are more subtle and more relentless in their analysis of the omnipresent dominance of the whites, but in exploring that dominance Weller has toned down some of the raw, if self-destructive, energy. When the narrator of 'Fish and Chips' says at the end of a catalogue of violence, injustice, selfishness, alcoholism, criminality and jail,

> Well, now we've got some money and there's a programme about Charlie Pride on the radio. Everyone is happy and there's a good movie on TV.
> Tomorrow there'll be fish and chips for tea.
> That'll do me. (p. 135)

this reader is less aware of a sense of tenacious and resilient vitality than of the depressingly low expectations of the speaker.

So effectively has Weller teased out the physical and psychological implications of white hegemony under which his characters suffer that he risks compromising the power of his texts for political intervention. If the characters can no longer offer themselves to black readers as models either of resistance or of achievement, and if they are portrayed as too completely powerless and passive to engage the sympathies of white readers then Weller's triumphant realism will have taken him to an impasse.

There are, however, more optimistic scenarios. Colin Johnson, in his second novel, *Long Live Sandawara,* solved a less acute form of this problem by alternating his realistic urban scenes with a non-realistic and highly rhetorical evocation of militant Aboriginal history. Other writers such as Kath Walker and Jack Davis have contrasted the present-day dispossession with favourable representations of traditional Aboriginal life to imply a residual strength and a way back. Weller has made some use of both these strategies within his predominantly realistic fiction and no doubt can exploit them further. But he has a further option, for perhaps more than any other of the Aboriginal writers in English he has explored the power of language itself for subversion and redirection of values. Refashioning his medium offers a way of avoiding the paralysis towards which his social analysis seems to lead. In Weller's hands, the dog will not only again have its day, but find a voice – and a home.

NOTES

1. Archie Weller, *The Day of the Dog* (Sydney, Allen & Unwin, 1981); *Going Home: Stories* (Sydney, Allen & Unwin, 1986). Page references are to this edition.
2. 'Johnny Blue' tells of a white who befriends the Aboriginals at his school. 'Saturday Night and Sunday Morning' and 'Cooley' both include episodes where white girls and black youths overcome their racial prejudice.
3. See, for example, pp. 3, 11, 33, 39, 59, 68, 74, 90, 128, 168, 209, 210.
4. Darcy's action here can be related to subversion through mimicry which has a long history in Aboriginal-white and in slave-master relations. Cooley entertains Rachel with this mimicry of Packer, a talent he has 'inherited from his mother's people'. (p. 184) Cf. also J.J. Healy, *Literature and the Aborigines in Australia* (St. Lucia, U of Queensland Press, 1978), pp. 8-10.
5. There is a potent if rather blurry nexus of ideas coming from the nineteenth century which links guerrilla-like reprisals by the Aboriginals to treachery and cowardice and images these in the secretive hunting of dingoes and the cringing of a maltreated dog. Cf. for example: 'It is generally the women who suffer [in tribal payback killings]: the men being too cowardly, unless under the influence of very strong passion, to attack those of equal strength with themselves.' E.W. Landor, *The Bushman: Or Life in a New Country* (London, Richard Bentley, 1847), p. 214; 'Ingratitude is innate with them, and they drink in treachery from the breast.' Charles H. Eden, *My Wife and I in Queensland; An Eight Years' Experience in the Above Colony with Some Account of Polynesian Labour* (London, Longmans Green & Co, 1872), p. 108. Warrigal, the Aboriginal character in Boldrewood's *Robbery Under Arms* (1882-83) is the most famous example in nineteenth century Australian fiction. He is, however, figured as a blend of domestic and native dog. His name, his treachery and his ability to move through the country undetected indicate the dingo; his 'pluck', his utter devotion to Starlight and his willingness to submit to abuse from him indicate the domestic dog.

6. In Achebe's *Arrow of God* (London, Heinemann, 1964), a young British administrator is perplexed at how to justify imprisoning Ezeulu simply because the latter declined to participate in the Administration's scheme of appointing Paramount Chiefs. The solution comes as a form of words from his superior: 'refusing to cooperate with the Administration' (p. 218), and he mentally applauds verbal skill that permits such realignment of moral authority behind political expediency.
7. Jack Davis and Adam Shoemaker, 'Aboriginal Literature: Written', *Australian Literary Studies*, 14, 3 (October 1988), 43.

Roger Knox Photo *The Northern Daily Leader*, Tamworth, NSW.

We Call it Koori Music

INTERVIEW WITH ROGER KNOX

INTRODUCTION

Roger Knox was born at Toomelah Aboriginal Mission near Moree in NSW in 1948. Six years ago he was badly injured in a plane crash. In 1983 he formed his own band which he named Euraba after the Euraba bush. He chose this title because it was the juice from the Euraba bush, along with goanna oil, with which he was treated after his plane crash and which he believes was instrumental in his recovery.

Today he is not only a major figure in the world of Country & Western music in Australia, he is also a leading spokesman for the aboriginal people. He is deeply involved in the 'Rock Without Grog' campaign and in 1988 toured the Northern Territory promoting alcohol-free concerts. 'Alcohol is a really bad problem for our people', he said. 'We find a lot of hotels won't book our band because they think we will attract drunks. But not all Aboriginal people are drunks and it really isn't as bad as it's made out to be. I'm hoping the 'Rock Without Grog' tour can show people that Aboriginal people don't have to be drunk at a concert'.

Another venture in which Roger Knox is involved is giving free concerts for prisoners in NSW prisons.[1]

Roger's aim is to create a better world for his people and he believes that what is necessary is a greater understanding by white people of aboriginal culture and history. 'White people don't know a lot about Aboriginal history, although I know a lot about white ways. It is important that this balance is changed. I think I can partly achieve this through my music'.

Carolyn Osterhaus

In October 1988 Carolyn Osterhaus interviewed Roger Knox.

I spoke with Roger Knox on the telephone at his home in Tamworth, New South Wales, for approximately one hour on September 14, 1988. When I asked to do an interview, he asked me to wait while he went for a glass of water and pulled up a chair.

The circumstances at my end were not so comfortable. The office was noisy and I cradled the phone hard against my shoulder in order to hear. I typed on the word-processor as he spoke. My concentration was intense and I spoke rarely, interjecting questions only where they seemed appropriate. Roger spoke softly, punctuating his sentences with a deep, exhaling 'wow'.

Roger Knox and his music have been described as country or country and western, partly because he is based in Tamworth, home of Australia's country music industry. When I asked him what he called his music, he said:

WE CALL IT KOORI MUSIC

We call it Koori Music and we just use words that tell the way of our people in song.

On the mission where I grew up the only music I knew was Slim Dusty and gospel music. The gospel songs I learned from my grandmother, from missionaries and people in the community. I didn't realize until I left the mission that this music I knew, the songs I learned from my grandmother, were songs that everybody knew.

Then came people like Slim Dusty, I know all of his songs. I learned them as I was growing up, not from the radio but from other people singing them. Everybody in the community knew him and knew the songs. He would come to Goondiwindi which was close.

I didn't have any big influences until I came to Tamworth at 16 or 17 years of age. I didn't have any dreams up to then. I just sang me songs because people asked me to sing.

I came to Tamworth to work on a farm; the guy I left the mission with invited me up. We went to see a band in one of the hotels here, a live band, the first time I'd seen a live band.

It was country music – a Slim Dusty song. This guy Geoff Brown sounded like Slim as well. Albert Bennet, he knew I could sing a bit. I was asked to get up to sing a song and it was an all white audience. The band was all white. Just going to town was something – to get up and sing was worse. I don't know how I did it, I just got up there and sang an old song. Then everybody started jumping up and clapping. I was shocked. (*He said when he sang in the community people sat and listened. He had never been 'applauded' before, the physical outburst was wholly unexpected*). I was really scared, then when I saw this happen, I thought 'wow', I must be doing it right.

Roger's singing became a regular Friday night event.

I was invited to go into a Talent Quest by John Minson in Tamworth. I didn't realize then it was country music, it was just songs.

I was approached by a guy who had a tour, he would travel around by plane and said, 'I'd like to give you a place', so I accepted the job to sing in a band that used to fly around the central and northern part of the country right into outback settlements. Brian Young was his name. I had to learn to play bass to become part of the band. Because of the size of the plane he could only fit a singer/bassplayer not a singer AND a bass player.

During one of these tours in the early 80s Roger was severely injured in a plane crash and received burns to 75% of his body.

That's how I got my hands. I never played the guitar again, my hands are sort of tender and disfigured. It stopped me from playing the guitar but it never affected my voice. I still have the desire to sing and travel to the communities.

I sing mainly to all Aboriginal audiences, I started that about two years ago. I got involved with some fund raising at the start and from then until now I have been singing mainly to Aboriginal communities. Because of my injuries it's hard for me to get going. (*Besides the physical trauma of the accident, he alluded several times to mental anguish.*) Also, from October to March each year I go into prisons, all the major prisons in NSW, and do concerts. Sometimes we do three shows a day, especially over the weekend. We go to

Grafton, down to Cooma, Tumbarumba and finish up in Sydney's Parramatta and Long Bay. (*Parramatta and Long Bay are jails in Sydney.*)

Aboriginals make up a big proportion of the prison community. Judging by the letters we get from people inside they always look forward to us. There's heaps of talent inside there, a lot of good song writers, a lot of really heavy stuff. We found the majority like country. I've got quite a few songs from them I'm thinking of doing.

I always sort of talk to people and try to really encourage them once they get out. Wow there's so much talent there, everywhere we go we run talent quests inside, not only for Aboriginal people but for everyone. A lot of Kooris in there get really down, they tend to be forgotten.

The topic of songwriting led to one of language. Did he speak or sing any aboriginal languages?

We lost our language. That's gone. That's lost. It's totally destroyed. We did know a lot f words but not enough to speak, not enough to communicate. Growing up on the mission there I remember my mother and father saying they weren't allowed to speak it. 'If you speak it we'll take your children away', they (*white authorities*) said. My mother was taken away when she was twenty-one months old. We were threatened by that. That's why it's gone.

I would like to sing a song in my language but there would be no point. No one would understand it.

The white Australian Country and Western singer, John Williamson, received tremendous acclaim for his album Mallee Boy *and in particular for the song 'True Blue'. It was taken up by the present government and given multi-media exposure to promote a sense of national pride, a unity and the idea that the 'real' Australian is the Australian 'hero' of the period of the 1890s, the 'true blue' Australian who is Anglo/Celt, male, enjoying male corporate life in the outback, an image which excludes Aborigines, women and people of other ethnic origins. What was his attitude to that particular song?*

Shit, I don't go along with that. Who's blue? I'm black. We don't want to be blue. I'm true but they can't accept that fact, that I'm true. 'True Blue', that doesn't do anything for me. Dundee and all that shit (*Crocodile Dundee*).

We've been here for thousands and thousands of years. Today RSL clubs are on about this Asian thing, you go to different parts of Sydney and hear them (Asian people) speaking the language of their own culture, but our thing was wiped out. Our language was wiped out. Aboriginal people fought and died in both wars and fought and died before....

I have a song called 'Our Reserve'. This guy on the radio introduced it as a controversial song. Controversial! It's been called political. I call it true fact. It's about being told Australia was founded by a sailor 200 years ago. We were here 40,000 to 50,000 years ago. I get a bit tired of this. Because I grew up in a tightknit community and I come out and I try to get people to understand and I sing about it and then it gets called controversial or political. I wouldn't call that song controversial. I was talking fact.

Does he see any change, has the 'Bicentennial Year' made any difference?

It's going to start to happen and white people are listening and maybe understanding. They say '200 years'. I can understand them being here 200 years. I can't accept that Australia is only 200 years old. You can't just ignore the real facts. As we were growing up we were told that Blaxland and Lawson were the first people to cross the Blue Mountains. That's taught as a historic fact.

I went to a school yesterday. It was Aboriginal Day and I went up to sing songs to the kids. There were a lot of white teachers. They did everything for them kids. They had artefacts, all kinds of things. But we weren't even allowed to talk about our culture at school. We were not even allowed to mention blacktrackers.

Eighty-eight has been a really good year, it's opened up a lot of eyes, opened up a lot of eyes in different parts of the world. England and parts of Europe now know more about Aboriginal culture than Australians do. It's a crazy situation.

Is there an Aboriginal label?

There's nothing. (No black label, no black studio.) When I first went into a studio I was scared, nobody told me what I should do, if I was doing it right. There's one in CAAMA (Central Australian Aboriginal Media Association) but there's a white person there. I reckon there should be one run by all black people. Because Aboriginal people are shy, we've still got that in our blood from years back, it's still part of you. You still get worried too much about it. I'd love to do a sort of proper recording with all black people running it.

What about his music?

We're learning rock and roll. Chuck Berry, you know, wow. I'd love to learn blues. We do our own business now, we play different songs. We can perform for anyone, white or black.

As long as its a story of understanding, a good ballad-type song, I like to get an understanding across, especially to non-Aboriginal people. It could be about anything, as long as it's for me.

I've been through mental problems, I was really into the drugs, pain killers, because of the accident and I just went cold turkey. I still have problems but I believe I have a strong spirit in me, a dreamtime spirit, some force is there stronger than we are. Aboriginal people were here before Adam and Eve and my god is stronger than that.

We played in a place in Alice Springs, in a hotel, it's a pretty racist town. We thought well, we'll check this out and do something, we'll pick what we'll do and we looked to give them some rock and roll. Everybody really liked it, they even rang up some of their friends and they boogied all night.

What about the country and western image as portrayed in the media?

People tend to know where I stand on issues like that. I do things my way. People can't make me what I'm not. I couldn't stand up in a white coat and be a redneck.

How does he feel about Midnight Oil, *an all white band singing about Aboriginal issues?*

I feel they're doing a good thing as far as getting people to understand our ways. Musically I can't sort of take to it but the intentions are pretty good. Some of the Aboriginal people were shocked by *Midnight Oil.*

(He laughs.)

The band didn't know how to perform to these people. Some people reckoned he was sniffing petrol.

I'm a fighter against alcoholism. That's why I did these 'Rock Without Grog' concerts. The *Midnight Oil* guys did pretty much the same. But give me Jimmy Buffett anytime.

What songs do Aboriginal communities request most?

'Johnny Be Good' and 'Mountain of Love'.

He still finds it difficult dealing with fame.

When I was growing up I wanted to be either a footballer or a fighter. I didn't dream of singing. People keep ringing me up. Maybe one day we'll get fair dinkum. I'd love to go to Nashville just to see how things are done. I reckon it would be great.

NOTE

1. A disproportionately high number of inmates in Australian prisons are Aborigines. See John Janke's article.

Too Many Cooks in the Past

New vantage points, new perspectives, the first fleet flying
Aboriginal flags;
The historians hesitate over the wounded and wrench out nails from
the deck stairs
Leading to the death of the cook swilling in his bowl,
Digging in someone else's earth, sea-flying-sailing
Into areas where of not the right way
Arguments as to that drowning, as to how best to view
Problems of value devalued, overvalued and submerged
The seen is unseen, lost and missed in the swill.
Ought to see not to see the labouring to bring forth
A bloated carcase,
Structured on human beings through unrestrained restraint,
Just lying there, never striding forth to pepper the police station
With too, far too many skeletons in the cook's shall we call
it, broth?
Boiling over, unstressed flesh coming from the bone
At uninstructed attempts to escape a boredom of
Points of view, ideologies of undertakers,
And difficult to sort out burial service professors
Falling over them them them them them themselves
To prevent fashionable accords
Coming forward to propagate discords
Based on higher salary ranges and prestige.

Talking in Hysterical Voices

1

Inviting a penetration, land seen
as a specific feminine
Patriarchal voices, pricks, horses, pistols
invade, enter, explore
Explode, break, exploit, denude, cover
with the well-taken, well-broken.

2

Old people, fish, water hole, drink,
muttering, broken words –
It seems that they were in some
sort of trance –
It may be they had nothing to say –
all said, all long time said –
No more, now; no more; long gone, ever gone.

3

Corridor, structural limitation placed
on land,
Unable to relate to naturalness, gaps,
walls, passageways,
Built up, brick by brick, stone by stone,
plank by nailed plank.

4

Language into the naturalness,
language into the all else –
Police stations, high rises, low rises, mansions
palaces, persons and perhaps –
All words, all languaging
the inability to be natural.

MARK O'CONNOR

Aboriginal Literature Becomes A Force

> You and my people roamed this land
> Thousands of years before
> The booted foot and the cloven hoof
> Came from another shore
>
> Jack Davis 'Dingo'[1]

The usual Aboriginal line on Australia's Bicentennial has been that the 200 years of white occupation are small beer beside the 40,000 to 100,000 years of Aboriginal presence. Yet 1988 may prove an important milestone for modern Aborigines, and may yet justify Oodgeroo Noonuccal's (Kath Walker's) belief that blacks should use the Bicentennial 'to educate, not to celebrate.

It is no secret that Hawke's Labor Government hoped Bicentennial sentiment would create public support for a formal treaty with the Aborigines. But while Hawke has tried to lead public opinion, he has led cautiously. He knows that the conservative opposition, eager for an election-winning issue, is poised to launch a full attack the moment it sees the government put itself too far ahead of public opinion. The conservative parties' line is, predictably, that no Australian should have special advantages over any other.

The result has been a lot of cautious kite-flying and tentative advance-and-retreat towards a goal that now has no hope of being reached in 1988. This has left many Aboriginal activists disillusioned. Yet it may be that in culture,if not in politics, more ground has been won, and more permanently, than they realize. It is not just that whites have altered: so have blacks.

By a co-incidence, the years around the Bicentennial have seen a great weakening of one of the hidden causes of discrimination against Aborigines – a highly effective language barrier. No single one of the hundreds of Aboriginal languages has much chance of becoming a national language. Yet till recently many Aboriginal groups were slow to master standard English, even though all advancement in Australian society depended on it. But now, within a few years, Australian public life has been entered by large numbers of Aborigines who wield the English language with the full authority of native speakers.

Literary skills are another and perhaps the clearest proof of this new Aboriginal mastery of English. If I had to offer as evidence of the change in just two recent books, I would choose Kevin Gilbert's anthology *Inside Black Australia*[2] and Colin Johnson's verse-narrative, *Dalwurra,*[3] the first as showing a new breadth and the second a new complexity in Aboriginal literature in English.

First a glance at the past. The European invasion robbed many Aborigines not only of land but of language. Quick though they were to improvise compromise languages or Pidgins, they were soon swamped in most regions by an influx of monolingual whites. Later, as the Aborigines were driven from home and imprisoned in reservations with people from different language-areas, their children came to speak various kinds of Pidgin-influenced English which many whites found unintelligible.

For later generations the price of acquiring standard English might be years of commitment to a racist education system – one that openly aimed to replace their culture. Thus Aborigines in their own continent suffer many of the problems of non-English speaking migrants. Throw in the fact that they had no tradition of written literature, and that to sell well an Aboriginal author has to appeal to white readers, and it is no surprise that Aboriginal literature had been slow to appear.

According to Kevin Gilbert, the first complete published work by an Aboriginal was David Unaipon's *Native Legends* in 1929. Oodgeroo Noonuccal (the known as Kath Walker) published the first book of poetry, *We Are Going*, in 1964; and the first Aboriginal novel, Colin Johnson's *Wild Cat Falling*, followed in 1965. The 1970s saw a proliferation of Aboriginal newsletters and broadsheets, in which poetry was prominent.

Now in 1988 Gilbert has produced a national anthology of Aboriginal poetry. This important anthology may well be read in different ways by Koories and non-Koories. Poets from Homer to Burns have long been vital in creating a sense of nationhood. Koories may see their poetry as primarily about defining themselves as a people, about expressing their sense of injustice, and about sinking tribal difference in the vision of a common

Aboriginal nation. White readers may sympathise, but they will lack the Koori's aching need for personal and racial (or national?) identity. They are more likely to ask 'How *good* are these Aboriginal poets?' and 'Can they write about other things beside being Aboriginal?'

An anthology whose main catchment is 'the last twenty years of limited access to white education and education in the alien English tongue' is bound to be mixed in quality. But beside the obvious talents of established Aboriginal poets like Jack Davis, Colin Johnson, Oodgeroo Noonuccal, and Gilbert himself, there are impressive newcomers like Vickey Davey:

> I saw Death take my friend into his arms
> Like a satisfied lion, they disappeared into the darkness

Maureen Watson's performance pieces like 'Female of the Species', though not designed for the page, show obvious quality, whilst W. Les Russell does a fine parody of Queensland's right-wing former Premier, Joh Bjelke Petersen, on rainforests:

> What use are they? well I'll tell you:
> the Japanese – I know they're a funny mob of people -
> but they make paper out of trees, see...

Harvard-educated Bobbi Sykes, though sometimes more preacher than poet, in her poem 'One Day' captures the relief of being greeted by another black person while 'lost' in the USA: 'Moving along Main St. / Whitesville / Diggin all them white faces / Staring or 'not staring '/ Until I felt surrounded...' In a moving poem called 'Final Count' Bobbi Sykes tries to think of the black children who die from poverty as martyrs to the revolution: 'We must count them / We must count them / For if we do not / They will have died in vain.'

Colin Johnson too feels the bitterness, yet looks beyond polemic:

> Don't tell me who I am:
> A child cries in me too often,
> To have many illusions
> My mouth curves
> In sadness these days.

Archie Weller, perhaps the most talented of the younger poets, gives a tribesman's view of Cook's landing:

> A bird with many wings as white as gulls
> sits upon the waters of your bay.
> A wingless baby from her breast is born...
> Wurarbuti, your warriors wonder
> for from the baby strange ghosts appear.

But for me, the outstanding find was the work of Robert Walker who died in custody in Fremantle jail in 1984, aged 25. Walker's death from head injuries followed a struggle with warders after he tried to slash his wrists. He was a natural poet whose imagery combines surprise and certainty:

> The rose among thorns
> may not feel the sun's kiss each mornin'
> and though it is forced to steal the sunshine
> stored in the branches by those who cast shadows
> it is a rose and it lives.

His complaints of injustice are the more forceful for a note of self-knowledge: 'Okay, let's be honest: / I ain't no saint / but then again / I wasn't born in heaven... / Just another non-identity / fighting to be Mr Tops.' There is more force in his swift reference to watching '...my brothers smashed, / thrown into dog-boxes, drunk, crying for the dreamtime' than in the long diatribes others offer.

A poet of such talent who dies young and martyr to his people's cause, is likely to be mythologized. This process seems to be underway in Grandfather Koori's line: 'Never blood / so red so red / never blood so red / as blood of the poet/ the Kokatha poet / who lay in the pool / so dead... / in Fremantle gaol so red'. One wonders if other poems by Walker, beyond the four Gilbert includes, have survived.

It is difficult to comment on the selection of poems in this ground-breaking anthology. No doubt it was a matter of some diplomacy to represent different Aboriginal groups and regions; the result is that some very bad poems are included. I was disappointed to find only two short and undistinguished poems from the promising Selwyn Hughes. The brilliant and mysterious 'Munganje' (whose full name and racial background are still to be clarified) is also missing.

Inside Black Australia does not include all types of poetry dealing with Aboriginal experience. It omits work by white poets, eg. Judith Wright, however talented or sympathetic. More importantly, it omits the rich and ancient oral tradition of Aboriginal sacred and secular songs – perhaps because this might involve using the transcriptions of white anthropologists. The 'black Australia' it reveals is that of dispossessed Aborigines trying to survive in a 'white' society – or perhaps rather in an advanced capitalist multi-racial society which reserves its worst prejudice for those who refuse to 'get ahead'.

Gilbert's notes reveal that many of his poets have had only an interrupted secondary education. when they fail as poets, their faults are not related to Aboriginal culture, but are precisely the ones found in under-educated white poets: outdated poetic licences and archaic phrases of the 'warriors of yore' variety, thumping rhymes and rhythms, McGonagail-style fluctuations of tone, and above all the reliance of abstract declamatory statements. Good poetry tries to convey even its more abstract ideas through concrete images – something the great Aboriginal song-cycles illustrate perfectly.

Jack Davis is one of the few who knows how to use images rather than abstractions:

> The neon lights flicker: 'Kia-ora Saloon'.
> The kangaroo comes from the shop on the corner.
> My brother, my sister, you are dying too soon.

Most of these poets belong to what Gilbert calls 'the stolen generation' - Aboriginal children, often from very large families, who were forcibly removed from their parents and fostered out to white families. The cry of 'Please mista do'n take me chilen, please mista do'n' was widely ignored under a policy of assimilation. children were removed from four generations of the family of the poet Joy Williams, including one of her own daughters whom she is unable to trace. Many such children continue to long for the warmth of their lost Aboriginal families – a recurrent theme in their poems.

Gilbert's preface and his shorter biographical introductions to individual writers turn the whole book into a powerful plea for justice to Aborigines. Yet his concluding remarks suggest some nervousness about the anthology's repetitive harping on themes of injustice. Perhaps some of his poets do need to learn the same hard lessons as conservationist poets: viz. that the answer to resistance is not to 'turn up the volume', and that in poetry a platitude remains a platitude, even though there may be red-necks or self-servers who vehemently deny it.

Yet to develop a personal voice you need to trust your audience. For many poets this anthology may be their first introduction to a large non-Koori audience. They may be surprised to find how generally white poetry-lovers sympathize with their struggle; and in future work one can hope they will feel freer, even when they choose to write for the white reader, to develop their own poetic voice and range.

I suspect this anthology is firmly aimed at a hungry educational market, both inside and outside Australia. Gilbert's eloquent introduction covers many of the issues students will want explored. If its historical facts are coloured by an angry rhetoric, yet students may take both rhetoric and anger as primary source material. Even if only one race's viewpoint is represented in the book's introduction and notes, few readers will be unmoved by the horrors Gilbert recounts. I thought I knew most of the kinds of beastliness Aborigines suffered, but Gilbert managed to surprise me with the sport of 'Lobbing the Distance' which apparently involved trying to kick the heads off live Aboriginal children.

Inside Black Australia is not a substitute for history, indeed the book leans out so far to assault 'white racism' that, when studied abroad, it may risk overbalancing from sheer lack of conservative opposition. Abroad, too, there is more risk that sympathetic readers may be bored into apathy by some of the low-grade repetitive material which dilutes the collection. But at least and at last we have an anthology which states the Aboriginal view of white society – with a vengeance.

Colin Johnson's *Dalwurra* is a new development in Aboriginal literature. Its hero is the black bittern *Dalwurra*, and the book's shape is derived from the traditional East Arnhem Land *manikay* or song-cycle celebrating the travels and adventures of a clan's ancestral heroes.

The black bittern, Johnson remarks, 'is a non-migratory bird, and this explains some of his anguish at leaving his home'. But leave home he does. Swept north from the Australian coastline by the Asian monsoon, he is deposited in modern Singapore. 'From there he flies on to India and the Eastern Himalayas where he is magically ingested by the White Dragon (*Karpo Druk*). He undergoes an identity change and becomes for a time the national bird of Nepal, the *Duva*, and later the Indian blackbird. In Calcutta he 'suffers a psychosis' connected with his mother, then regains health. But the epic journey is far from over. He flies on to Edinburgh (where Johnson himself attended the 1986 Commonwealth Writers' Conference), reflects on sanctions against South Africa, observes a grouse-shoot, moves to Brixton, experiences Britain's racial hatreds, learns West Indian street- talk, and finally returns (partly transformed by a mid-air spiritual experience) to Australia.

Colin Johnson (he seems not to insist on his Aboriginal name Mudrooroo Narogin, though it appears in brackets on the cover) is well aware that this is no traditional *manikay*. But as his editor Veronica Brady points out, 'in following the story-lines, trading in stories, adding his stories to those current where he travels and adding theirs to his, *Dalwurra* is following the traditions of his people, singing each step of his journey into position, widening his sense of himself and his world...'

Many episodes require a prose explanation almost as long as themselves, eg. 'Poem 16 begins and ends with the mantra to *Tara* or *Dolma,* a female Buddhist deity of compassion equated with the Green Parakeet...' Johnson has kept the terse, rather flat narrative style of the *manikay*, and has not tried to match the complexity of his story with a corresponding richness of language. Many passages read like translation:

> Into the clouds I fly
> Through the clouds I fly.

Ahead lies the hills and valleys
Of the rain pouring down,
Pouring down on my wings.

The ideal reader for *Dalwurra* might be someone deeply immersed in Aboriginal legends, a traveller, knowledgeable about Asia, and perhaps even, like Johnson himself, one who has spent time as a Buddhist monk. The book is bound to attract a thesis or two, though probably not a large readership. But its importance cannot be measured by popularity. In his awareness of Asia Johnson is far beyond most other Australian poets. By linking up with the belief-systems of other indigenous peoples of the region he has altered and expanded Aboriginal horizons; yet he has also found a way for contemporary Aboriginal writers to express even the most personal and agonized search for identity in a semi-traditional form. *Dalwurra* is a book that may one day be seen as starting a new strand in Australian literature.

NOTES

1. Jack Davis, *John Pat and Other Poems* (Dent, Australia, 1988). Jack Davis recently won the BHP Award for Pursuit of Excellence in Literature and the Arts.
2. Kevin Gilbert (ed), *Inside Black Australia: An Anthology of Aboriginal Poetry* (Penguin, Australia, 1988)
3. Colin Johnson (Mudrooroo Narogin), *Dalwurra: the Black Bittern*, (The Centre for Studies in Australian Literature, University of Western Australia, 1988)

JULIE MARCUS

The Journey Out to the Centre. The Cultural Appropriation of Ayers Rock[1]

It is well-known that the term 'Australian' referred originally to the indigenous peoples of Australia, not to the settlers of 1788. The transformation in the meaning of the word was linked to a growing need to develop an identity[2] for settlers[3] who could never go 'home' to Europe, and the change seems to have been complete by about the end of the eighteenth century. The transformation of meaning has had important results for Aboriginal Australians – they have lost the identification of themselves with their country while through it, settler Australians have legitimated their own claim to Aboriginal land. The processes by which meanings are transformed within a political hierarchy, I refer to as cultural appropriation. It is a process which is continuous and one now gathering considerable momentum in Australia.

Cultural appropriation can be seen in a great many areas, for example in the rash of new folk-songs celebrating authentic Australian outback values. John Williamson's song written in 1986, 'Raining on the Rock' is an interesting example, for not only is the appropriation very clear, but it refers specifically to Ayers Rock which, I shall argue, is becoming the sacred centre of a rapidly developing settler cosmology.

> Pastel red to burgundy and spinifex to gold
> We've just come out of the mulga
> Where the plains forever roll
> And Albert Namatjira has painted all the scenes
> And a shower has changed the lustre of his lands.
>
> *And it's raining on the Rock in a beautiful country*
> *And I'm proud to travel this big land like an Aborigine*
> *And it's raining on the Rock. What an almighty sight to see*
>
> *And I'm wishing on a postcard that you were here with me*
>
> Everlasting daisies and beautiful desert rose
> Where does their beauty come from, heaven knows
> I could ask the wedge-tail but he's away too high
> I wonder if he understands it's wonderful to fly?

And it's raining on the Rock in a beautiful country....

It cannot be described with a picture
The mesmerizing colours of the Olgas
Or the grandeur of the Rock
Uluru has power!

And it's raining on the Rock in a beautiful country
And I'm proud to travel this big land like an Aborigine
And it's raining on the Rock. What an almighty sight to see

And I'm wishing on a postcard that you were here with me

In Williamson's song, the claim to be 'like an Aborigine' is particularly effective, I think, when it comes after the final verse and the reference to Ayers Rock. The statement that 'Uluru has power' is not only an expression of the widely-held view[4] that Aboriginal Australians draw power from 'the Rock' but a statement that such power really exists and is knowable to settler Australians like the singer. The singer then claims to be travelling around the countryside 'like an Aborigine', a claim that utilizes the imagery of Aboriginal Australian 'travelling' and its links with the Aboriginal Dreaming Tracks.[5]

The writer's intention could well be to validate, legitimate or celebrate the power of Aboriginal law and ways. Yet there is no doubt that the claim that settler Australians can be 'like Aborigines' is a very clear attempt to appropriate an identity which has now become a source of power. The same theme is presented strongly in the popular film 'Crocodile Dundee'. The hero, Dundee, is shown as having access to the hidden part of Aboriginal life, and to the power that those hidden secrets convey.

In 'Crocodile Dundee', however, while it is never clear whether Dundee is of Aboriginal stock, it is perfectly plain that he grew up in mystically close contact with Aborigines and the land.[6] Within the imagery and narrative sequence of 'Crocodile Dundee', there is a very clear expression of the idea that settlers who grow up on the land 'like Aborigines' can also sometimes have access to the power that such closeness to the land brings. Within a context of struggle over land-ownership, such claims are far from benign and they reproduce those made publicly in the community and the print and television media. In Alice Springs, for example, settlers who have a basic knowledge of local Dreaming Ancestors, are quick to point out that they too have 'birth rights' in the Yiperinya Caterpillar Dreaming sites of the town. The irony is that Aboriginal Australians in the town who wish to conciliate, are led to acknowledge such claims, even if only at a very superficial level. It is at this point that the relations of power governing the nature of knowledge become very clear. T.G.H. Strehlow[7] used 'his' conception totem to bolster his right to hold sacred objects that were shown only during secret ceremonies,[8] despite the fact that he was not an initiated adult. And in the case of Ayers Rock, the slogan used to oppose the hand-over of the Rock to its 'traditional' owners was 'The Rock Belongs to Everyone'.

The present force of the current of appropriation arises both from the partly successful moves to legitimate Aboriginal claims to land during the nineteen seventies, and from the conscientious fabrication of a national identity taking place in the nineteen eighties in response to the incorporation of Australia into the periphery of a world-economic system. As national boundaries become economically insignificant, as national governments become less and less able to influence national economic forces, there seems to be a reaffirmation of the cultural reality, value and autonomy of the nation state.

The Australian bicentennial events have provoked a plethora of nationalistic activities at glorifying the achievements of the last two hundred years. These events are taking place within an economy deteriorating into stagnation, a society in which unemployment and falling wages are becoming very common and in which the values of the nineteenth century petit-bourgeoisie are increasingly stressed. Initiative and enterprise are the key-words and the emphasis is on exploiting all and every available resource. In the nineteenth century, economic exploitation was largely of the natural world – Europeans mined and cleared and re-planted the globe at a fantastic rate. Foreign cultures were collected up, ordered and named as part of the first wave of classifying the expanding colonial world. In the 'post-industrial' world, culture itself is considered as simply another resource, and is being mined and exploited accordingly. But collecting and naming are no longer sufficient. Other knowledges are being transformed rather than classified, perhaps in order to support an illusion of the reality of nationality. It is the conjunction of the exploitation and sale of cultural assets with a desperate search for a national identity, that produces the pace and intensity of the current wave of cultural appropriation. It is distinctively Australian than an indigenous settler culture of 'Australian-ness' focuses constantly on the desert, on the centre of the land, and within such an ideology it is clear that the Aboriginal Australian must occupy an ambiguous position. This is a point I shall return to shortly.

With the unification of economies and the obsolescence of national boundaries within the world capitalist-system, and with the changing structures of the world-economy, comes the increasing prominence of tourism. The commodity 'Australia' is now to be defined in terms of its distinctiveness or difference from the rest of the world, an increasing problem as western capitalism tends toward an international homogeneity of culture which is especially evident in urban Australia. Aboriginal Australians become a critical aspect of difference but they do so in a particular way. They become part of difference expressed through the natural world, and are perceived once again as natural curios along with the platypus and Ayers Rock. This aspect of Aboriginality is enshrined in Australian understandings through the presentation of Aboriginal life and culture in museums where Aboriginals jostle for attention beside whale skeletons, large gold nuggets and kangaroos. It is not only that Aboriginal Australians are consistently rendered as 'natural', timeless and unchanging, but there is also a claim to present this land as 'ours' 'together', just as 'we' *all* 'own' Ayers Rock.

Just such a claim is expressed vividly on the cover of a glossy tourist brochure advertizing Kakadu National Park.[9] It shows two young men sitting under a rock shelter, looking amicably out over the park. One young man is a settler Australian, the other an Aboriginal. However, it is the settler youth who is the taller, who sits higher in the picture and who holds the spears. The Aboriginal Australian sits cross-legged, presumably in a 'traditional' manner, and holds the didjeridoo. It is an image in which the power is clearly in the hands of the settler, with only the trappings of traditional culture in the hands of the Aboriginal. It places that settler in command of an Aboriginal environment with control of Aboriginal weaponry. Given the struggle over ownership and use of the Kakadu region between miners, conservationists, pastoralists and Aboriginals, the structure and symbolism of the image is far from neutral.

As I noted above in connection with the slogan 'The Rock Belongs to Everyone', the most recent movement towards appropriation is characterized by just such egalitarian claims. It is now common to hear settlers explain that 'We are *all* Australians' and to continue by saying that 'We *all* have equal rights in these places, not just Aborigines. We want our children to be able to see and understand their heritage.' This then is the new racism, a racism which is expressed and practised through doctrines of egalitarianism. Its soft but critical edge is seen in the forms of cultural incorporation and appropriated meanings used to control and express once again settler and Aboriginal perceptions of Aboriginal society and culture. In other words, it is through particular forms of cultural appropriation, those embodying notions of equality, that knowledge of both Aboriginal culture and the relations of that culture to settler society, is represented not only to settlers, but to Aboriginal Australians themselves.

But it is also important to note that within the long-standing notions of 'the Bush' and 'the Outback', the most authentic manifestation of bush values and actions is located at 'the Centre'. It is in the outback that one finds the real Australian, the bearer of authentically Australian values and skills. Central to the authenticity of the inhabitant of the outback, the 'bushman', the drover, the pastoralist, is the ideology of egalitarianism and it follows that if the most authentic bush values are found at the centre of the outback, then the most egalitarian of fraternal values and behaviours will be found there too. This is a universalizing form of masculine equality, and it is this which is sought by those leaving the cities for the Centre. The Australian

NORTHERN TERRITORY

AUSTRALIAN KAKADU TOURS

1986/87

PACKAGE HOLIDAYS

1985
NATIONAL
TOURISM AWARD

NORTHERN TERRITORY

Ansett.

AUSTRALIAN
AIRLINES

'Centre' is characterized by its harshness, its redness, its space and emptiness.[10] At the centre of the Centre of 'the outback', lies Ayers Rock. Ayers Rock has developed both an international and a national significance as a pilgrimage site.

As a relatively new nation (created in 1901) suffering an abrupt rupture in their history, settler Australians have lacked a sacred centre for their symbolically constructed social and cultural world. There has been no single, central, place at which the universal values that characterized aspects of nationalistic ideologies and rites could be located and made manifest. While settler Australians built a plethora of shrines to death and masculinity inside the towns (war memorials, R.S.L. Clubs), attempts to create a distinctive national identity have lacked the legitimation of a primordial origin myth that celebrates what Victor Turner[11] calls the anti-structural, universalizing, unifying values of society.[12] While the Anzac myth works well for the structural domain of the social and is the basis of a flourishing structural cult, its central shrine, the War Memorial in Canberra is also set firmly within the city, just as were the great shrines of the Greek city-states. But it is at shrines that are located outside the towns, outside social and spatial structure, outside the interests of kin, political and economic groups, that the over-arching values which are said to characterize society as a 'whole' become visible. The 'Muslim World' has Mecca as a primordial place of origin; the European landscape is dotted with great pilgrimage shrines set up outside the spatial and temporal constraints of social structure (Lourdes, Our Lady of Fatima and, in an earlier era, St James of Compostella and the other way-stations leading to Rome and Jerusalem) and the Indian religions all have important anti-structural shrines. But no prophet led Australians into their promised land, they were banished. There was no place at which the law that would bring order out of chaos was proclaimed authoritatively by the gods, there was no cosmic revelation, and there is no place set apart to which one can journey in search of the source, no place at which the meaning of life can be revealed. There is instead, the grim order of an all too mundane nature that characterizes a military colony, an imposed and unwanted régime of terror coupled with an inner emptiness and the fear that perhaps Australians have, in reality, no nature, no culture[13] at all. It is perhaps the absence of a central site of generation that helps to account for the continuing uneasiness that characterizes Australian identities and which requires Australians to expend so much energy on telling themselves who they really are. If it is true to say that 'authority once achieved must have a secure and usable past',[14] then we must analyze the ways in which the bicentennial celebrations of 1988 are being used to rewrite the past of the new nation of 1901 in response to the changing nature of the state.

Given the symbolic and structural significance of the Centre in Australian histories, literatures, folk-lore and advertizing; given the challenge to manhood offered by the rigours of that Centre, it is perhaps not so surprising that Ayers Rock, a spectacular monolith, should have come to assume an increasing importance to settler Australians. Ayers Rock can be said, with only a slight empirical quibble,[15] to lie at the heart of the Centre and at the centre of the Australian landscape. The Rock itself is a magnificent sight at any hour of the day. When Finlayson[16] first saw it on the horizon, he was nearly one hundred miles and still three days away from it by camel; today, even the rapid and easy approach by car on sealed road cannot destroy the impact of that first sight. Ayers Rock, then, has natural qualities which lend it value as a symbolic site, but it is important to recall that such spectacular qualities are by no means a prerequisite for the successful development of a sacred site. The black rock which is the focus of the mosque in Mecca is very small, indeed, and there is nothing obvious about the natural qualifications of many Aboriginal sacred sites. The significance of a successful site or shrine comes not from its natural characteristics but from its continuing role in connecting the events and symbolism of the past to the present. The great pilgrimage shrines of the world, some of which lie in magnificent natural settings and some of which do not, are characterized by the access they provide to the gods, by a primordial event, and by the ways in which, through ritual, visitors are able to shed the constraints of the world, gain access to the gods, and reach a momentary union or loss of self beyond structure.

Ayers Rock as yet lacks a stunning intrusive cosmic event, but the stealing of baby Azaria by the Dingo and the subsequent sacrifice of Lindy Chamberlain to the male gods of Australian society may have the dramatic qualifications for a national super-natural intervention.[17] But to some extent the Rock's extraordinary size and shape so counteract popular images of nature that its existence could itself be understood as proof of a divine and incomprehensible intervention. This empirical 'proof' or sacred origin need not be closely linked into the symbolic structures of meaning that operate within the cults that are growing around the Rock. Again, I refer to Mecca, as it offers a clear example of the disconnection of the focus and legitimation of the site from the specific cult practices which operate at it. Over the millennia, a folklore has grown up around the properties of the sacred black stone, but this has not been substantially incorporated into Muslim doctrines or dogma, even if it may be of more significance to pilgrims than it is to theologians. Meccan pilgrimage rites focus on the Kaaba with the sacred stone located at one of its corners, yet the rites do not make much play on the stone at all. It provides a pivot for the circumambulation, and it legitimates the location. One should touch the stone or kiss it, but these acts are not incorporated into the actual rites of pilgrimage as set out in the various pilgrim handbooks. In the past, the Meccan stone supported a solar calendrical cult. Pilgrims circumambulated the stone in a clockwise direction, a direction which is usual at shrines - one circulates with the right shoulder to the sacred centre. Muhammed changed the direction of flow by decree, and Mecca remains the only major shrine at which pilgrims turn the left side of the body to the centre and move against the sun. Muhammed is thought to have made this change in order to sever the new religion from its predecessor, yet his act provides us with an example of the way in which quite different cults and meanings can be built upon the same natural base.

It is quite possible, then, for a cult not to have a close initial relationship to the focus of the place at which it settles. While not wanting to suggest that cults are only ethereal creatures in search of embodiment, it seems to me that Australian settler nationalism and ideologies of identity can indeed be thought of as a cult in need of a central and suitable location. Furthermore, the transformations of time and space that can be found within Australian settler nationalistic ideologies and symbolism are so related to origins and social structures that Ayers Rock, standing alone at the centre of the great Australian 'emptiness', is a peculiarly suitable candidate for attaching *this* myth to *that* place. If this argument could be sustained, it would indicate that Ayers Rock is on the way to becoming one of the great pilgrimage shrines of Australia and there is now sufficient empirical evidence to suggest that this is precisely what is happening.

The rapid development of the Centre as a tourist destination, the paving of roads and the up-grading of accommodation and other facilities means that now as never before, the 'average settler Australian' is able to make the journey out to the centre, to throw off the constraints of social structure, live the authentic Australian outback life, and to recreate the egalitarian frontier myth. The number of tourists to the centre of the outback has increased dramatically during the last decade, and it would be unwise to ignore the crucial importance of Ayers Rock to current cultural representations concerning national identity and authenticity. A great many tourists, particularly those equipped with four-wheel drive vehicles and their accompanying paraphernalia, bear some of the pilgrim's sociological characteristics.[18]

The modern-day stockmen and drovers, re-creating the conquest, the hardihood and the egalitarianism of the frontier through recreation, are also recreating and affirming the essential masculinity of that frontier and its way of life. As one would expect in an increasingly integrated world-economy, Ayers Rock is of significance beyond the political boundaries of Australia. The last decade has seen a world-wide boom in the sales of distinctively Australian paraphernalia in Europe and America. The Akubra drover's hat and the 'dry as a bone' stockman's oilskin coat sells well overseas (in America) and within Australia. Ayers Rock has been developed as an international tourist resort and the number of tourists visiting it is increasing rapidly.

Pilgrimage, tourism and trade have always gone hand in hand. In the ancient world, the peace of the annual market was guaranteed by the feast days of the local saint or god. Mecca was one such trading town and the Black Stone was the marker of the town's sacred protector. Pilgrims covered the costs of their journey through trading as they travelled, and the result of the processes by which pilgrims stepped outside of the constraints of daily life can be seen in the jollity described by Chaucer. To be a pilgrim was by no means a purely pious experience. Contemporary pilgrims are just the same and in a self-consciously secular world, the tourist on tour to the Centre, in search of enlightenment through visits to secular[19] sources of knowledge, carries many of the attributes of the pilgrim.

The settler Australian tourist to Ayers Rock plays out pilgrim and tourist roles in varying combinations and degrees. There are a variety of ways of making the journey out, just as there are a variety of ways of getting to Mecca (organized tour, independent travel, by plane or bus or on foot, with visits to way-stations or without); but the move to get 'out' of the city and into the 'Outback', to divest oneself of the trappings of civilization, and to live a simpler, more independent and more *authentic* life, is, I think, very strong. It is a theme that is widely expressed in the pseudo-exploration literature and in magazines catering to the leisure market, particularly those aimed at the 4-wheel drive, 'off-road', market.

Those who move out towards the centre, adopt new, more authentically Australian, garments (rough clothes - the felt hat, the boots, the tough trousers or ripped shorts, often ex-army gear); a new language of mateship and equality with a distinctive vocabulary and accent, and new attitudes to those whom they encounter. People wave at passing traffic, passers-by may even stop and come over for a 'chat' or a 'yarn', particularly if there is a warning that can be passed on. 'Watch out for the patch of "bulldust" up ahead' or perhaps, 'the road's washed out, and everyone's bogged up to the axles down there'. The language and the roles and norms can be heard both in the crowded, treeless, campsites which cater to the new mass tourism and among those who wish to camp alone, as all indulge in the authentic pleasure of yarning. The journey out to the centre is characterized by an immediate friendliness, a dropping of the social barriers of class and status between men, a willingness to help those in trouble, and also, by a desire to struggle against the rigours of a harsh land and to conquer. The desire for conquest is a matter I shall return to in discussing the gendered space of the Australian symbolic world.

There are a number of parallels that indicate the way in which Ayers Rock might be considered as a developing pilgrimage shrine. These include the spatial structure of the site, the ritual and symbolism evident in tourist behaviour, settler concepts of the sacred-ness of the Rock, and the ways in which the Aboriginal presence at the Rock feeds into settler dreams of their authentically Australian identities.[20]

The ritual aspects are perhaps rudimentary as yet, but they are regular and recognizably those of pilgrimage sites even if at present those acts are more generally thought of as secular rather than religious. To begin with, Ayers Rock, like Mecca, is surrounded by a discrete area (administered by the Mutitjulu Community in conjunction with the National Parks and Wildlife Service), an area in which no life may be taken – visitors may not take any life nor cut any blade of grass within the sacred precinct, nor may any buildings, apart from those of the local Aboriginal Australian community, be erected near the Rock. On reaching the Rock, visitors can only stay at the tourist resort which lies 14 kilometres from the Rock itself, and they are not permitted to be in the area surrounding the Rock after nightfall. In many respects the Aboriginal keepers of the Rock who live within this forbidden realm come to act as guarantors of its authenticity, an ancient priesthood which knows the secrets of the Rock and its power, with more in common with the Meccan Eunuchs than they have with the settler pilgrims.

Then, the climbing of the Rock and the walk around its circumference are both characteristic of pilgrim behaviour at shrines elsewhere. In Knock (Ireland) and at Lhasa in Tibet, pilgrims climb the holy mountain, sometimes on their knees, and frequently expire on the way. At Ayers Rock every early visitor from Gosse to Finlayson to the members of the scientific parties organized by the South Australian Museum, all struggled manfully to the top. Those who now come as tourists do so, too, the climb also taking its toll on the elderly and foolhardy. The number of deaths at the Rock is steadily rising. The way is now marked by a hand-rail and the number of climbers of all ages is vastly increased.

Ayers Rock is known to settler Australians for its size and for its dramatic colouring. Each visitor goes to watch the Rock at sunset with the hope of seeing the vivid red of the daytime Rock change to the deep violet of its evening incarnation. The more enthusiastic go also at dawn, where they see the goldness redness of Rock rise from the blackness of the desert night. The redness of the Rock is part of a potent colour symbolism in which settlers see the central landscape as characteristically red. Visitors look for the redness as an indicator that they are entering the Centre, and it would be interesting to plot the red sand zones onto the map and see where the tourist destinations lie in relation to it, where the 'outback' might begin. The redness is evident in literary texts, paintings and film and is closely linked up with the centre's dryness and danger. The redness of the Rock and its pulsing transformations of colour give it a very special place in this imagery and those colour transformations act as a challenge to man's control of nature. Here is nature, primaeval and pristine, and man[21] is but as an ant upon its surface.

The circumambulation of the Rock by settler Australians also has a long history. In the past, the track lay close to the base of the Rock, and visitors moved through a series of Aboriginal sacred caves and water-holes. With the closing of some of these sites and the establishment of a new track which makes the walk even longer (about 7 miles), the contact of the walkers with the Rock and its Aboriginal sites has been reduced. Evidence from other developing shrines, however, suggests that the new route around the Rock will eventually become more clearly linked in to the Rock's surface and mythology and the tour guides with their explanations and commentary should assist this process. Ayers Rock has indeed been transformed from an Aboriginal sacred site to an 'Australian' one which belongs to all by birth-right.

Information on the Rock and its significance comes to visitors mainly through settler Australians - through commercial tour guides and through the activities of the resort and National Parks employees. The Mutitjulu Community has some input through their liaison with the National Parks and Wildlife Service, but a great deal of the guiding is done by people who are quite independent of any Aboriginal control. This process ensures that the view of Aboriginal culture and nature that is obtained by tourists is essentially a settler view, one which uses Aboriginal Australians as exemplars of prehistoric society who have access to an ancient knowledge of the land. The reproduction of these images is important to Australian politics of race but it is a theme which is also taken up, elaborated, and appropriated by those pilgrims who see Ayers Rock as part of a global system of sacred sites.

AYERS ROCK AND THE NEW AGE PILGRIMS

In addition to the flow of foreign and local tourists, Ayers Rock is now regularly visited by an international membership of mystics. Australian sacred sites are listed in the New Age 'Pilgrim's Guide to Planet Earth',[22] a handbook which gives a brief synopsis of Aboriginal spirituality and a list of Aquarian communities and festivals all over the world. Other sites of significance to the New Age movement are the Egyptian and Mayan pyramids, Stonehenge, the megalithic 'astronomical' site at Callanish in the Outer Hebrides, the Easter Island statues, and Mt. Fuji. There is an international mystical circuit on which Aboriginal Australians and Ayers Rock have gained a secure place.[23]

The popularity of Ayers Rock among mystics seems to be a relatively recent phenomenon, however, and the number of international pilgrims is low but growing. The foreign pilgrims at Ayers Rock are part of a world-wide mystical tradition which draws on a multitude of sources for inspiration. Mayan and Hopi Indian traditions have been prominent, as have the variety of forms of Hindu and Buddhist beliefs, Theosophy, Druidic beliefs and the Jewish mystical tradition. These religious ideologies feed into and mingle with Aquarian New Age and other alternative life-style philosophies. The numbers of those becoming aware of Ayers Rock through their participation in one or more fractions of the western mystical tradition is, I believe, increasing very rapidly. The emergence of Ayers Rock into this world consciousness is of great significance as the number of potential pilgrims is very high.

At present international pilgrims who fall into this category are known to have come from America, Britain, Germany and Japan. These foreign visitors to the Rock do not think of themselves simply as tourists; they are people who think of themselves as seeking contact with mystical forces through the journey out to sites of particular power. Yet, as I noted above, tourism and pilgrimage have always gone hand in hand and the roles are interchangeable and interactive, distinguishable only partly through emphasis. The visitors who are at Ayers Rock who define themselves as pilgrims are, in my view, pilgrims in the full sense of the word. They have all the sociological qualifications of pilgrims as the Turners[24] would describe them and they share the characteristics and aspirations of pilgrims to Mecca or to Our Lady of Walsingham in England.

The understandings of these pilgrims, in common with those of their Australian counterparts, are expressed in purely cultural terms. The Aboriginal Dreamtime and the travels of the Dreaming Ancestors are understood as creative and originating forces, and Aboriginal ritual is a method of reaching that primal world. In interpreting Aboriginal religion, the works of Mircea Eliade are often referred to, so that the universal features of the spiritual path come into focus.[25] Of the anthropological texts, Elkin's *Aboriginal Men of High Degree* (1945, reprinted 1977) is important, as are some of Strehlow's writings. Aquarian writings on Aboriginal religion have two important characteristics. First, in the understandings of these texts that are presented,[26] there is no sense of any relation between a cosmology and a particular social structure, no sense of the politics of religious beliefs, but rather, a feeling of the timelessness and essential universal truths that such beliefs offer. And second, Aboriginal beliefs are homogenized so that it is possible to speak in generalities and to use a word or concept from here and another from there, without having to consider how widespread such ideas or practices were.

THE NEW AGE IN AUSTRALIA

Some settler Australians are part of this international mystical movement. The significance of Aboriginal religion[27] and Ayers Rock for Australian New Age believers is developing rapidly. Ayers Rock is prominent in Australian Aquarian philosophies, it is sometimes held to lie on a line of power which connects directly with St. Michael's Mount in Cornwall[28] and it is at the Rock that the initial spark that will infuse the world network with light, will strike.[29] In Australia, it is common to find the same people influenced by a variety of philosophical traditions and committed to the same range of political causes. The range of small alternative religious and life-style groups in

Australia alone is very great. The groups tend to be small, unstable, but linked into a loose network. They must not be underestimated as taken together, they contain and influence very large numbers of people. Adelaide, a city of about one million people, contains at least five well-stocked esoteric bookshops which cater to this market.

Among the Australian groups involved are the Rainbow Group,[30] the Fountain Group and a range of meditation and therapeutic groups.[31] The Fountain Group, for example, in common with many others inside Australia and out, is particularly interested in the lines of the magnetic grid encompassing the world. Sites on the intersections of nodes of this grid are particularly powerful access points and ritual concentrates on getting the magnetic structures or forces of the body into a more natural alignment with those of the earth. Crystal therapy and magnetic therapies aim at this. There are also techniques for locating and making magnetic forces and lines visible, and techniques of intervention which aim at making the black forces of evil recede until they are replaced by white.[32]

The Aquarian pilgrim to the Outback and its Centre is very active. One contributor to *New Age News* writes of her trip to the Northern Territory: 'We were on a metaphysical journey seeking ways, by the use of Australian Bush Flower Essences, to help heal negative human emotions.... While we were in the north, I realized that the physical world has been very largely mapped and is known; but *now* the real pioneer work is in the area of "inner" space and in the growth of consciousness.'[33] Although I have separated New Age pilgrims from those tourist-pilgrims whose interest in Ayers Rock originates in more mundane concerns, this passage indicates the ways in which alternative cosmologies are very closely linked to the rationalities and concerns of mainstream settler Australians. The language and the mode of the search vary, but the underlying concern with identity and authenticity, and the use of pioneering and outback metaphors are common to all Australian pilgrims. The frontier is still there. In addition, the use of specifically Australian essences rather than the more traditionally known herbal remedies and scents, combines the belief that the Australian landscape is the oldest, with the belief that Australia was also the most isolated of the continents. It is when one goes out into 'the bush' that one can find the most ancient of essences preserved from interference and pollution by the physical and cultural isolation of the Australian continent from the rest of the planet. Timelessness and isolation are the key factors, factors which are potent in Australian race politics.

What I want to address, though, is not the detailed content of the beliefs and rites of these groups, but the universalizing claims they make and their implications for Aboriginal Australians. Let me begin with a paragraph from Selleck's booklet of visions and predictions for the coming of the New Age in February 1988.

> For ten years I have had a vision of a gathering of people at Uluru.[34] They are there to take part in an awakening of deep mystery from within the Earth. They hold hands in a circle. A didjeridoo plays. A Great Light emerges from beneath the Earth at Uluru. It grows larger and larger until it encircles the Earth. All the people can then see. We are one. We are one. We are one.[35]

In one sense, these are the age-old sentiments of transcendent unity everywhere, but in the Australian context, they carry quite specific, local, meanings. Although there is a clear hope that the Aboriginal owners will join in, the 'they' who will all hold hands around the Rock are largely settler mystics. The unity that is sought is a unity which transcends all local differences and encompasses all religious traditions. In such a unification, Aboriginal Australians would, of course, lose their identity, their singularity, their difference. A great light will emerge, and Aboriginal religion will become united with everyone else's, that is with a settler mysticism that has already incorporated Aboriginal mysticism. Note, too, the use of the didjeridoo, a musical instrument not found in central Australia, but used to indicate the ancient secrets of Aboriginal Australian religion.

A crystal is thought to lie beneath Ayers Rock, and the Rock is held to be welded into the same web of power that supports the other sites of significance within this cosmology.[36] The significance of crystals in Australian Aboriginal ritual as described by Elkin[37] is a happy confirmation of the powers of crystals, for the most recent phase of crystal therapy arose from Hopi crystal imagery and the mining of Hopi Crystals by the Utah Mining Company.[38] A universal cosmology which originated in America, largely on the west coast, is therefore being used to provide an explanation of the spiritual power of an Aboriginal sacred site. This explanation supersedes those offered by Aboriginal cosmology and is used to explain the sacredness of the site to Aboriginals themselves. In addition to replacing the origin and cause of the power of the place, mystical explanations also point to links with other equally powerful places. Such explanations have the effect of negating local knowledge and reducing Aboriginal religion to a variation of a universal, often shamanistic, religion which is being defined and explored by settlers and which origùinates in western mysticism. Bits and pieces are taken from a variety of religions and traditions and are welded into something quite foreign. The Mutitjulu[39] analogy with quarrying is very apt, particularly so given the move away from material exploitation and towards cultural exploitation to which I referred earlier.

In addition to incorporating Aboriginal concepts into a new religion, the new mystics have their own rites, derived from non-Aboriginal sources, which they carry out at the Rock. They use their crystals to get at the power of the crystal under the Rock; they use their magic to produce global and local harmony, and so forth. They attempt to put the power of the Rock at the service of their own universalizing and egalitarian aims. Yet the response from Aboriginal Australians is often far from welcoming.

Aquarian claims to be in telepathic or 'direct' communication with the Aboriginal law men of Ayers Rock are not verified by those who are learned in Aboriginal ritual who live at the Rock. Settler attempts to tap into the power of the Rock are seen by local Aboriginals as simply more of what has gone before - now settlers are mining Aboriginal culture rather than the body of the land itself. And there is opposition to mystics who want to meditate at or on the Rock and perform their own rites during the night, as the sites of greatest power to Aquarians are those already identified as being most powerful by Aboriginals. These are precisely the sites that are forbidden to tourists and protected by settler law. The fear that Aboriginal secret sites will be violated yet again is very great, and well-founded.

At the time of the Harmonic Convergence of 16-17 August 1987, an event widely reported in the media,[40] park rangers had to blockade the entrances to Uluru National Park and make special searches of Ayers Rock and the Olgas to ensure that all settlers left the park at dusk. The Harmonic Convergence was an event originating in American entrepreneurial mysticism[41] which was understood in varying ways by the groups and individuals concerned with it. In Australia, Ayers Rock was the site of greatest significance and there were attempts to organize a large gathering of pilgrims there to, among other things, encircle the Rock with a human chain. One pilgrim describes the time as 'clearly marked as the long awaited quantum point in humanity's re-evolution ... the long promised Millennium of Universal Order will be heralded in...',[42] while another expects the transformation of the genetic blueprint of all living cells.[43]

Formal applications to hold a major gathering at the Rock were resisted by the local Aboriginal community, as were applications by pilgrims to camp together with their Aboriginal 'brothers'. Park rangers managed to intercept some of the convergers and prevented intrusions into the Aboriginal community. Yet one Aquarian[44] claims to have spent the night at the rock, despite being specifically warned off by the rangers, and claims that others did likewise, in order to conduct dawn rites in the Rock's large caves. Zable's claims may be spurious, yet others also say that they went in at dawn and the intent is there - the intent to put into practice the dictum that 'the Rock belongs to everyone', in this case, everyone who really understands. Aboriginal sacred sites are secret and to be protected from all but the settler mystics who also understand the eternal truths of Aboriginal religion. In other words, the universalizing and egalitarian sentiments of mystical doctrine are used to deny the specificity of Aboriginal belief, to disregard entirely the wishes of Aboriginal custodians, and to insert settler Australians into the very heart of that secret Aboriginal knowledge on which their only recognized claim to land rests.

In addition to settler attempts to incorporate the Rock into their own cosmologies, there are also the ambiguities posed by settler understandings of the nature of these particular Aboriginal sacred sites. These ambiguities arise partly from the ready analogies drawn by settler mystics between Aboriginal concepts and those of settler cosmologies. For example, the Rainbow Serpent is linked to other serpentine symbols like the Loch Ness Monster; the notion of the spiritual links of individuals with the land is extended to give settlers their own 'dreamings', and the Harmonic Convergence rites in Sydney took the form of building a 'Rainbow Serpent' of sand on Bronte Beach. The 'Dolphin Dreaming' of the eastern coast is an example of a settler 'dreaming' that is very popular – the dolphin links into a set of beliefs about the mystical nature and speech of dolphins, their relations to the rainbow, and so on.[45] There were several 'Dolphin Dreamers' at Ayers Rock for the Harmonic Convergence. In addition, some therapy or healing groups offer courses in aspects of Aboriginal Australian cosmology.[46] Aboriginal social structures have been crucial for the Australian communalists right from the start when the first communes and festivals tried to organize themselves as 'tribes'[47] although they have a place in Australian settler beliefs that is generally unrecognized. In its present form, interest in Aboriginal Australian religion grew out of the attempt to peel away the corrupting structures of materialism and to resurrect earlier forms more suitable to the human psyche and body. In its Theosophical form, it derived from the search for the pre-Atlantan islands of Lemuria. 'A New Age group in Perth has published detailed accounts of Lemurian sites said to be found in Western Australia and throughout the other Australian states...' and early Theosophists thought that the Aborigines were the descendants of the ancient Lemurians.[48]

Yet the understandings of Aboriginal religion that are propagated are, of course, related to purely settler concerns. One of the other ambiguities which arises from such an engulfed cosmology, concerns the relation of Aboriginal sacred sites to gender hierarchies. Questions of gender are of importance not only to feminist mystics and New Age philosophies but to settler Australian 'tourist-pilgrims' to the Centre of the Outback. These latter are recreating the unrelentingly male ethos of the Australian frontier, even if they do so in a very comfortable way. In the case of New Age philosophies, it is important to note that the coming era will be one in which the female essence will triumph. The division and hierarchical structures of today's world will be replaced by a oneness that is essentially feminine and the feminine side of men that is held to be essential to a peaceable world will be able to emerge. As a result, women and men will be able to live together in a new harmony.

In the case of feminism, there are feminist women who are actively seeking to formulate theologies freed from the constraints of patriarchal thought. This difficult task has provoked an interest in comparative religions and in Australia, the rise of a feminist anthropology has provided new approaches to Aboriginal women's rites. The re-evaluation of the anthropology of Aboriginal women has merged with the doctrines and interests of those seeking a distinctively female-oriented religious life.

Some feminist mystics have been concerned to establish the existence of Aboriginal women's sacred sites and to extract from Aboriginal religions some of their important messages for women. It is now rather widely held that Mt. Olga and the surrounding hills are a women's sacred site. The Olgas have come to represent the new, feminine, world. The rounded intimacy of the Olgas is contrasted with the rigid, terrifying masculinity of Ayers Rock. The water-worn patches etched into one section of the Olgas are perceived as being vulvas - again, a symbolism developed by women who were seeking a contrast to the widely reported phallic symbolism that characterizes many religions. Such an interpretation of the Olgas contrasts with that of Aboriginal Australians and, indeed, constitutes a transformation of local understandings.

It seems to me that the rise of the Olgas as a female sacred site goes far beyond the Aquarian cosmologies within which it seems to have originated. It is connected to the same factors which are leading to the immense tourist activity at Ayers Rock. The significance of both places derives from their location within a settler cosmology in which Australian-ness and authenticity are worshipped in 'the Outback', in 'the Bush'. In the context of the cult of frontier masculinity which characterizes Australian society, a cult which has its structural, urban, focus on the Anzac myth and memorial shrines, the gender separation evidenced at the 'centre' of the outback makes a lot of sense. The blood-red Rock, its severity and harshness, epitomize 'the heart of the centre'. There is nothing soft or feminine about it. The Olgas, on the other hand, are held to be quite different and they are secondary. One goes to visit the Rock, and sees the Olgas if time and energy permits. Their ovoid form, their multiple curves, their vulva-like crannies - these are the feminine element writ large.

If it is indeed the case, that the Australian cult of frontier masculinity is at last developing an anti-structural sacred site at 'the centre', then we are faced with a site that carries radically independent sets of meanings for different social groups. A dramatic Aboriginal site is being converted into a site of significance to several opposed groups of settler Australians. The new values attached to it have nothing to do with Aboriginal religion, much of which is devalued into 'art' or entertainment. The new values building up around Ayers Rock have instead everything to do with the bonding of settler society through race and the hierarchical division of that society through gender.

There are, then, at least four sets of cosmologies circulating around Ayers Rock and the Olgas. The first of these is Aboriginal and is, of course, partly secret. In this cosmology, however, Ayers Rock carries sites of significance to women and to men, while the Olgas is a powerful and predominantly male place even though female ancestors travelled to it and left the insignia of their genitalia in passing. The second cosmology is the international mystical tradition with which the Australian movement shares much, especially its origins.[49] In this cosmology the Rock and the Olgas tend to be less overtly engendered, perhaps because of the universalistic sentiments and the explicit privileging of a notion of the eternal feminine enshrined in their beliefs. The crystals and power of the site on an international magnetic grid and network predominate in this group of beliefs. The third is the specifically Australian settler mysticism that contains many feminist aspects. It is this latter cosmology that defines the Olgas as a female sacred site. Ayers Rock is central to each of these, but it has also become immensely prominent in the cosmology of a much wider settler public through the massive increase in tourism, and it is this I see as referring to a mushrooming nationalism – to the gender structures of Australian society, to the struggle to develop some sense of identity and authenticity in a homogenizing world, and as receiving a terrific boost from the nationalist emphases of the bicentennial activities.

In the bicentennial process, through the re-creation activities of recreation, through the commissioning of new conservative histories,[50] through reprinting and re-issuing the earlier colonial literatures,[51] and through the redefinition of the authentic in terms of the landscape and outback in art and film, Aboriginal Australians are being pushed back to where they used to be, back into the primordial time and no-place of myth.

I now want to return to my opening remarks in which I stated that the term 'cultural appropriation' refers to the processes by which meanings are transformed within specific hierarchical structures of power. It is important to note that cultural appropriation refers not just to any meanings and not to meanings taken out of their political contexts. It is the place of meanings within a structure of power, in this case, within the structures of race, that renders them into sites of struggle.

In the case of Ayers Rock, a site of significance to Aboriginals has been incorporated into several distinct settler cosmologies in such a way that settler claims to land and settler versions of Aboriginal meanings are legitimated. In this case, settler nationalism marches hand in hand with its alternative, settler mysticism, so that in the bicentennial nationalist fervour of 1988, there can still be no place and no comfort for Aboriginals.

The political processes which have forced settler Australians to recognize and re-value Aboriginal culture have led to successful Aboriginal claims to land. These are the material bases which keep reconstituting the symbolic and cultural frontier at the centre of Australian race politics, the frontier which is critical to the rampant settler nationalism which glorifies that frontier, the conquest of the land and the particular form of masculinity that goes with it.

Yet Aboriginal claims to the land are still contested, and the nature of Aboriginal society and culture is a matter of fierce popular debate. That struggle for the land and the struggle to enforce existing race and gender hierarchies will come, it seems to me, increasingly to focus on Ayers Rock. As more settlers make the journey out to the Rock as tourists and mystics, more live out the Outback myth of Outback egalitarian mateship. The rise of the Rock in settler cosmologies accompanies a conservative movement in Australian politics, one seen in many aspects of daily life, but one seen most clearly in the pace of the cultural appropriation of Ayers Rock.

NOTES

1. Research for this paper was funded by the University of Adelaide. Unless otherwise stated, all information derives from the author's field-work at Ayers Rock and in Adelaide. I am particularly grateful for the assistance of Hilary Tabrett in suggesting further examples of appropriation and for explaining many aspects of Australian mysticism to me; and also to Annette Hamilton for a stimulating seminar on media imagery which indicated the direction and dimensions of the challenge.
2. R. White, *Inventing Australia. Images and Identity 1688-1980* (George Allen & Unwin, Sydney, 1981), p. 15.
3. I use *settler* and *Aboriginal* as adjectives to describe categories of 'Australians' to avoid the use of the categories of race, colour or culture.
4. A newspaper report on the hand-over of Ayers Rock to the Pitjantjatjara people was titled 'Centre of Power', for example, and begins with the statement that 'Ayers Rock is saturated with symbolism', R. Davidson & P. Tweedie, 'Centre of Power', *National Times,* 25 April – 1 May 1982, pp. 12-16.
5. Bruce Chatwin's novel *The Songlines* (Jonathan Cape, London, 1987) also plays on the notion of travelling across the land, setting it in an evolutionist perspective.
6. A. Hamilton, 'Media, Myth and National Identity', unpublished paper delivered at Macquarie University, Sydney, 1986.
7. Linguist and anthropologist, born of mission parents at Hermansberg Lutheran Mission west of Alice Springs, who worked in conjunction with the University of Adelaide and the South Australian Museum. See W. McNally's biography *Aborigines, Artefacts and Anguish* (Lutheran Publishing House, Adelaide, 1981) and Strehlow's partial autobiography *Journey to Horseshoe Bend* (Sydney, 1969).
8. J. Morton, 'In Search of Lost Law: A Preliminary Study of T.G.H. Strehlow and his Presentation of the Aranda' (unpublished paper, Macquarie University, Sydney, 1987).
9. 'Australian Kakadu Tours 1986/87 Package Holidays', Ansett & Australian Airlines.
10. There are dozens of titles of books that play on this symbolism – Ernestine Hill's *The Great Australian Loneliness,* J. Kirwan's *An Empty Land,* Sydney Upton's *Australia's Empty Spaces,* H.H. Finlayson's *The Red Centre. Man and Beast in the Heart of Australia,* C.T. Madigan's *Crossing the Dead Heart,* Mrs A. Gunn's *We of the Never Never,* and so on.
11. Victor Turner developed his notions of structure and anti-structure in relation to African cults, and then applied them to European pilgrimages in V.W. & E. Turner, *Image and Pilgrimage in Christian Culture* (Columbia University Press, New York, 1978).
12. The Anzac myth carries some of the meanings and functions of a national origin myth, but at present remains set in historical time.
13. The reference is to Marilyn Strathern's influential paper 'No nature, no culture: the Hagen case' in C. MacCormack & M. Strathern, eds., *Nature, Culture and Gender* (Cambridge University Press, Cambridge, 1980).
14. J.H. Plumb, *The Death of the Past* (Boston, 1971).
15. The actual centre of the Australian landmass lies at Central Mount Stuart, north of Alice Springs.
16. H.H. Finlayson, *The Red Centre* (Angus & Robertson, Sydney, 1936), p. 40.
17. I refer to the disappearance of Azaria Chamberlain from the camp-site at Ayers Rock and the subsequent prosecution of Mrs Lindy Chamberlain for murder. The body of the baby was

never found and Mrs Chamberlain was imprisoned in Darwin. Her husband was charged as an accessory to the murder. Mrs Chamberlain claimed that a dingo stole her baby from the tent. Media reportage was scandalous, and police investigation incompetent. After a series of investigations, Mrs Chamberlain was eventually released from prison, but she served over four years, a sentence that would never have been imposed had she been willing to plead post-natal depression. A film is now being made of the incident, with Merryl Streep in the leading role. There is already an extensive literature commenting on the case.

18. The sociological aspects of pilgrimage are developed much more fully in a forthcoming paper, 'The Creation of an Australian Dreamtime', an early version of which was presented at the Anthropology Seminar, University of Sydney, April 1988.
19. I use *sacred* and *secular* as empirical native categories only.
20. This factor is played on increasingly by the advertizing industry. An image of Ayers Rock is used to advertize everything from car batteries to women's clothing.
21. I use 'man' not in a generic sense, but as a reproduction of the form of discourse used. The bush is a male domain and women have no place in it. In a separate paper, I argue for the maleness of Ayers Rock and the essential relation of the discourse of the bush to gender hierarchies.
22. P.S. Khalso, ed., *A Pilgrim's Guide to Planet Earth* (Wildwood House, London, 1981).
23. Cf. R. Grossinger, *Planetary Mysteries, Megaliths, Glaciers, the Face on Mars and Aboriginal Dreamtime* (North Atlantic Books, Berkeley, 1986) and Adelaide Fountain Group's newsletters.
24. V.W. & E. Turner, *Image and Pilgrimage in Christian Culture* (University of Columbia Press, New York, 1978).
25. P.S. Khalsa, op. cit., p. 252.
26. *Understanding Aboriginal Culture* by Cyril Havecker (Cosmos Periodicals, Sydney, 1987) and *Crystal Woman. The Sisters of the Dreamtime* by Lynn V. Andrews (Warner Books, New York, 1987) both illustrate this point.
27. J. Newton, 'Aborigines, Tribes and the Counterculture', *Social Analysis,* forthcoming.
28. *Adelaide Fountain News* 25: 6, 28 April 1986.
29. V. Selleck, *Winged Serpents Dancing* (Shekinah Foundation, Thora, 1987), p. 21.
30. Rainbow, unicorn and butterfly - seen as being the three fundamentally important symbols of the magic movement. Wika, referring to new life and potentiality, sexual power and soul or spirit.
31. EST (Erhardt Seminars Training), JEL (Joy, Energy, Life) and Insight, for example. Channel 10 in Sydney ran a New Era Programme for some time.
32. In Adelaide these techniques have been applied to Glenelg, a site of drunkenness and to Mt. Barker Road at a corner notorious for traffic accidents.
33. K. White, 'Mapping Inner Space', *New Age News,* 1 (9) (1987), p. 7.
34. The Aboriginal name by which Ayers Rock is known.
35. V. Selleck, op. cit., p. 22.
36. Aunt Millie Boyd is quoted as saying that a crystal also lies beneath Mount Warning in N.S.W. in *New Age News* 1 (9) (1987), p. 6.
37. In *Aboriginal Men of High Degree,* op. cit.
38. I am indebted to Hilary Tabrett for this information.
39. Mutitjulu Community is located at Ayers Rock.
40. 'Mayan Hopes for Harmony', *The Weekend Australian,* 15-16 August 1987; 'Gathering was so Harmonious', *Central Australian Advocate,* 19 August 1987.
41. From the teachings and visions of José A. Argüelles, 'Harmonic Convergence, the Last Call' in a newsletter distributed by Planet Art Network, Boulder, Colorado, 1986; and see also *Adelaide Fountain News* 39, 9 October 1987: 7. Other meetings were held at Mt. Warning (N.S.W.), Bacchus Marsh (Victoria), Victoria Square fountain in Adelaide, and at Bronte Beach in Sydney.
42. R. Bee, 'Harmonic Convergence Playback', *Maggies Farm* 37, December, p. 26.
43. *Adelaide Fountain News* 39, p. 8.
44. B. Zable, 'Report from Uluru', *Maggies Farm* 37, December, p. 26.
45. Dolphin symbolism comes from America, too, and Lynn Andrews gives them a pivotal place in her account of the path which brought her to Australia in order to do battle with the forces of evil which are sapping the strength of Aboriginal Australians. One therapy group

offers seminars on dolphins and whales, Dolphin Dreamtime meditation tapes, dolphin whale products (*Nexus New Times* 3 (Summer 1987) page 49).

46. For example, Natural Living Potential Centres in Cairns offers various therapeutic techniques plus 'Multilinguals, Aborigines, Psychologists, Medicos', *Nexus New Times* 3 (Summer) 1987, p. 47.
47. J. Newton, op. cit.
48. N. Drury & G. Tillet, *Other Temples,* Other Gods (Methuen, Sydney, 1980), pp. 10-11.
49. J. Newton, op. cit.
50. Like Molony's (1987) *The Penguin Bicentennial History of Australia* and the reappearance of Manning Clark's *Short History of Australia* in a Penguin illustrated edition plus a new children's version.
51. Particularly the exploration narratives, the diaries and so on; but also the new editions of the works like those of Mrs Anaeas Gunn and Mary Durack which are now considered to be classics.

WESLEY HORTON

AUSTRALIAN ABORIGINAL WRITERS:

PARTIALLY ANNOTATED BIBLIOGRAPHY OF AUSTRALIAN ABORIGINAL WRITERS 1924-1987.

FOREWORD

Aboriginal Studies is an area that is expanding each year, with more and more courses being offered to the student. Resource material for these courses is important. Until quite recently (the 1960's), all material on the world of Aboriginality was compiled, written and produced by white writers. Since the 1960's, a large amount of Aboriginal writing on a wide range of topics has appeared. These texts provide us with a valuable resource of authentic Aboriginal material, the value of which is not just its content but that it offers a comparison to the white literary production and its ideological perception of Aboriginality.

Apart from a few exceptions, Aboriginal texts are highly critical of this white perspective. For the student and researcher, access to such material is an advantage but to date little bibliographical compiling has been done. The locating of various Aboriginal texts is often difficult. This bibliography (although not exhaustive) hopes to overcome that problem to some degree.

The bibliography provides a listing of over 180 *Aboriginal Writers*. It gives the titles of works by authors within categories. Kevin Gilbert for example appears under Poetry and Politics. All entries are numbered and the author index gives these numbers. Annotations have been included where the works have been sighted.

As stated, the bibliography does not draw on ephemeral material, such as newsheets and periodicals for titles of works by authors. However the writers listed are for the most part the contributors to all other forms of publications, and represent the social and political force of the Aboriginal people.

CONTENTS

AUTOBIOGRAPHIES

1. BARKER, Jimmie
The Two Worlds of Jimmie Barker; As told to Janet Mathews. Canberra, Australian Institute of Aboriginal Studies, 1977, xiv, 218pp., illus.

The story of life on Missions. Covers the social conditions, and contains a lot of local information. Although the author was 70 at the time of relating his life to Mathews, he had an excellent memory. Mathews spent about four years on his life story. Barker was historically minded, and worked hard to produce a valuable piece of work.

2. BROPHO, Robert
Fringedweller; Sydney, Alternative Publishing Co. Ltd., 1980, 153pp., ports, illus.

Life as a fringe dweller in and around Perth, W.A. The reality of Aboriginal urban living that still exists in Perth. This text was produced with the assistance of Catherine Berndt. The author insisted on a direct transcription of the tapes and as such there is some repetition, but it provides an authentic text in Bropho's own words.

3. CLARE, Monica
Karobran; Chippendale, NSW Alternative Publishing Co., 1978, 96pp.

Written as a novel it may be the first novel by an Aboriginal woman. The author died before it was completed. It tells of her childhood and the separation from her father, and then her brother through forced social conditions. She searches throughout her life for her lost father, and becomes a political activist.

4. CLEMENTS, Theresa
From Old Maloga; The Memories of an Aboriginal Woman. Victoria, NSW, Fraser and Morphet, (not sighted).

5. COHEN, Bill
To My Delight; Canberra, Aboriginal Studies Press, 1987, photos, 163pp.

The autobiography of the grandson of the Gumbangarri tribe of the Northern Tableland. As with the Sally Morgan (1987) this provides an insight to lifestyles of part Aboriginal people in a dominant white society.

6. DHOULAGARLE, Koorle
There's More to Life; Sydney, Althernative Publishing Co. Ltd., 1979, 125pp., illus., 22cm.

The story of an alcoholic who gave up drinking and found a new life. This is an unusual book in that it is not involved with Aboriginals in a white society, but with the problem of drinking, and how one may overcome it. Written in an emotive style.

7. KENNEDY, Marnie
Born a Half-Caste; Canberra, Australian Institute of Aboriginal Studies, 1985, 70pp., illus., maps, ports, 21cm.

8 LAMILAMI, Lazarus
Lamilami Speaks; Sydney, Ure Smith, 1974, 273pp., illus., plts.

The autobiography of an Aboriginal of the Maung tribe at Goulburn Island who became a carpenter and went on to be a Minister of the Church. Gives a good account of the life style, culture, and customs of the Islanders, and life on the missions. Also includes the war period.

9 McKENNA, Clancy / PALMER, Kingsley
Somewhere Between Black and White; Melbourne, Macmillan Co., 1978, ex, 143pp., maps, 22cm.

The story of McKenna as told to Kingsley Palmer. Taken from tapes over a one year period. Covers the social conditions of Aboriginal life in a white dominated world.

10 MIRRITJI, Jack
My People's Life; N.T. Aust, Milingimbi Literature Centre, Milingimbi, 1976, 76pp.

Recollections of traditional life in Arnhem Land.

11 MORGAN, Sally
My Place; West Australia, Fremantle Arts Centre Press, 1987, 358pp.

This auto and biographical text covers the lives of the author, her mother, grandmother and uncle. A very moving story of the problems faced by a part-Aboriginal family. In its first six months nearly 60,000 copies were printed.

12 NEIDJIE, Bill / DAVIS, S. / FOX, A.
Kakadu Man; Queanbeyan, NSW, Mybrood Pty. Ltd., 1985, illus., photos.

Looks at the traditional life of the Kakadu people, story Neidjie, text Davis, photographs Fox. Text is in free verse. Large format, very attractive presentation.

13 NGABIDJ, Grant / SHAW, Bruce
My Country of the Pelican Dreaming; As told to Bruce Shaw. Canberra, Australian Institute of Aboriginal Studies, 1981, 202pp., 2 maps, illus., ports, 23cm.

The life history of Grant Ngabidj compiled by Bruce Shaw. Covers history, geography and customs.

14 PEPPER, Phillip / DE ARAUGO, Tess
You are What you Make Yourself to Be; Melbourne, Hyland House, 1980, 144pp., illus., photos, tables, ports, 25 cm.

The story of an Aboriginal family in Victoria. Produced with assistance from Tess De Araugo, a researcher. This is a well-detailed piece of work. Includes many photographs and provides a good Aboriginal perspective of black and white relationships. Gives a superb picture of the local area and living conditions.

15 PERKINS, Charles
A Bastard Like Me; Sydney, Ure Smith, 1975, 199pp., illus., plates.

Autobiography of Perkins; his rise to sports fame and to the position of assistant secretary in the Department of Aboriginal Affairs. An insight into an often controversial political figure. This work also in a way marks the era of Aboriginal activism.

16 ROUGHSEY, Dick
Moon and Rainbow; The Autobiography of an Aboriginal. Artarmon, NSW, A.H. & A.W. Reed, 1971, 168pp., illus.

Autobiographical but contains many dreamtime legends, customs and rituals from the Mornington and Bentinck Islands. An important text because although it is a transcription by a white co-author, the narrator is Roughsey. A valuable insight into Aboriginal culture by a full-blood Aboriginal.

17 ROUGHSEY, Elsie
An Aboriginal Mother Tells of the Old and the New; Victoria, McPhee Gribble, 1984, 245pp., map, illus., 20 cm.

The life of Elsie Roughsey born into the Lardie tribe on Morning Island in 1923. A good portrait of the social life of Aborigines between two societies.

18 SIMON, Ella
Through My Eyes; Adelaide, Rigby, 1978, 189pp.

On Aboriginal social conditions in New South Wales. The story of a woman between two cultures as seen through her eyes. Re-published Collins Dove, 1987.

19 SMITH, Shirley, C., M.B.E.
Mumshirl; As told to Bobbi Sykes. Victoria, Heinemann, 1981, 115pp., illus., ports, 21 cm.

The life of Shirley Smith, MBE, with assistance from Bobbi Sykes. An emotional story of a woman who devoted her life to the welfare of the Aboriginal people of NSW. Covers the welfare of prisoners and other socially deprived Aboriginals.

20 SULLIVAN, Jack
Banggaiyerri; As told to Bruce Shaw. Canberra, Australian Institute of Aboriginal Studies, 1983, 263pp., vii-viii, illus., maps, ports.

Jack Sullivan was born in 1901 and the story of his life is interesting and often very funny, yet very moving. An insight into Aboriginal social conditions.

21 TUCKER, Margaret, M.B.E.
If Everyone Cared; Autobiography of M. Tucker. Sydney, Ure Smith, 1971, 205pp., illus., 32 plates.

This is a moving story of a girl who was forcibly removed from school one day and sent off to a domestic training school, which was the policy at that time of the Aboriginal Protection Board. From there she was placed into service with a white family. The author became politicised at an early age.

BIOGRAPHIES

22 BLAIR, Harold (by) HARRISON, Keneth
Dark Man White World; Melbourne, 1975, 285pp., ports, 22 cm.

The story of the Aboriginal tenor Harold Blair, who was internationally known in the 1950's. The only Aboriginal to date to become a famous singer.

23 FERGUSON, (by) HORNER, Jack
Vote Ferguson for Aboriginal Freedom; Sydney, ANZ Book Co., 1974, 208pp., photos.

Very detailed account of the social/political life of Australia's first Aboriginal political figure. A source of early political information dating back to the 1920's.

24 *FIGHTERS AND SINGERS*
'The Lives of Some Aboriginal Women', (eds) Barwick, Meening, White. Sydney, Allen & Unwin, 1985, xxi, 226pp., illus., ports, 26 cm.

Accounts of the lives of a number of Aboriginal women and their roles in white society.

25 GOOLAGONG, Evonne / COLLINS, B / EDWARDS, V.
Evonne Goolagong a Biography; London, Hart-Davis, MacGibbon, 1975, 101pp., illus.

The story of her rise to fame in the world of tennis.

26 HOGAN, Alan / HARDY, B.
The World Owes Me Nothing; Rigby, Australia, 1979.

The author B. Hardy points out that she is only the recorder of the story and not the author. (Not sighted).

27 NICHOLLS, Douglas, R., M.B.E. (Pastor)
Pastor Doug; 'The story of an Aboriginal Leader'; (by) Mavis Thorpe Clark. Lansdown Press Pty. Ltd., Melbourne, 1966.

The story of a well known sportsman who became a Pastor and a leader of his people.

28 ROBERTS, Philip, (by) DOUGLAS, Lockwood
I the Aboriginal; Adelaide; Rigby, 1971.

This is a biography of Roberts, however the author, Lockwood, has chosen to make him the implied author of the text which results in a text that is not completely authentic. The language used by the implied author far exceeds the ability of any 'Noble Savage' created by Lockwood, yet oddly enough, this is the most reprinted book on Aboriginality there is.

29 ROSE, Lionel (by) HUMPHRIES, Rod
The Biography of a Boxing Champion.

The story of his rise to fame.

30 SAUNDERS, R.W. (by) GORDON, Harry
The Embarrassing Australian; Sydney, Angus & Robertson, 1963, 172pp., plates, 23 cm.

The story of an Aboriginal who became a Commissioned Officer in the Army.

31 THONEMANN, H.E. / BULUDJA, B.
Tell the White Man; The Story of a Lubra Woman. Sydney, Collins, 1949, 190pp., illus., maps, diag., ports.

A biography rather than an autobiography. The implied author is Bunny Buludja, a full blood Aboriginal woman. Contains a great deal of material on customs, culture and the social conditions of Aborigines living on and near stations. It appears to be the first attempt by a writer to take up the Aboriginal perspective and as such is interesting. Possibly the only book written by Thonemann.

32 WEST, Ida
Pride Against Prejudice; Reminiscences of a Tasmanian Aboriginal. Canberra, Australian Institute of Aboriginal Studies, 1984, viii, 113pp., illus., map, ports.

A collection of her experiences on the Furneaux group of Islands.

33 YIRAWALLA
Artist and Man; (by) Sandra Le Brum Holmes, Sydney, Jacaranda Press, 1972, 92pp., illus.

CHILDREN'S LITERATURE

34 ABORIGINAL CHILDREN (collection by)
The Aboriginal Children's History of Australia; Sydney, Rigby Pub. Ltd., (with assistance from the Australian Arts Board), 1977, 150pp., illus., col., plates.

A superb publication written and illustrated by Aboriginal children from all over Australia. This is a very rich source of fascinating material for anyone involved with children.

35 CONNOLLY, Stan
'The Echidna and the Marsupial Mole', in *Folktales from Australia's Children of the World*; Sydney, Ure, Smith, 1979.

36 GULPILIL, David / MCLEOD, N.
Birirrk; Australia, Edward Arnold, 1983, 32pp., illus., 30x21cm.

37 *Kwork Kwork The Green Frog and other Tales*; Canberra, Australian National University Press, 1977, 48pp., illus., 22x29 cm. (Aboriginal Legends).

A collection of 15 legends from Queensland, written and beautifully illustrated by 23 Aboriginal children. Large format.

38 MARAWILLI, Wakuthi
Djet; Dhu Walny Dhawn Djat Puy; Melbourne, Nelson, 1977, 16pp.

A story about a boy who became a sea eagle.

39 MAYMNURU, Narritjan
The Milkyway; Sydney, Harcourt, Brace, 1978.

40 SIMPSON, Richard and Maureen
Mindi; 32pp., illus.
Daydreamer; 40pp., illus.
Friends; 44pp., illus.
Bush Holidays; 48pp., illus.
The Runner; 64pp., illus.
The Girl Who Loved Football; 72pp., illus.
Milton, Jacaranda Press, 1984, illus.

Six books written in a simple style for reading by primary students.

41 TJILARI, Andy
Going for Eyros
Chasing Kangaroos
Going for Dinjar
Killing Emus
Hail
Alice Springs, Institute for Aboriginal Development, 1974-75, illus.

Bilingual texts, English and Pitjantjatjara.

42 WALKER, Kath
Stradbroke Dreamtime; Sydney, Angus & Robertson, 1972, 120pp., illus.

A book of stories based on the author's recollections of growing up on Stradbroke Island and of Dreamtime stories. 26 legends and tales. The author's style is appealing to children as well as to adults. Has been translated into Japanese.

DRAMA

43 BOSTOCK, Gerry
'Here Comes the Nigger', (excerpts). *Meanjin*; April, 1977, pp. 479-493.

This play has not to date been published. It was first performed in Sydney in 1976 and had a good reception. The manuscript is in the possession of the author.

44 BOSTOCK, Gerry
'Black Theatre', in *Aboriginal Writing Today*, (Eds) Davis & Hodge, Canberra, Australian Institute of Aboriginal Studies, 1985, pp. 63-74.

45 DAVIS, Jack
Kullark; The Dreamers; Sydney, Currency Press, 1982, xxii, 146pp., illus., 21 cm.

Kullark, brings together the two historical figures of Captain Stirling and the Aboriginal legendary figure, Yagan. Colourful, fast moving and very dramatic. *The Dreamers* is set in the present. It deals with the existing social conditions of Aboriginal suburban families.

No Sugar; Sydney, Currency Press, 1986, 116pp., photos.

This play received international acclaim at the Canadian World Theatre Festival in 1986. The play is based on an event that took place in W.A. The forced movement of Aboriginals from the town of Northam and their virtual imprisonment at the notorious Moore River Mission in the 1930's.

Barungin; World Premiere at the Festival of Perth, W.A., 1988 – followed by National tour.

The latest of Davis's work and the third part of his trilogy 1829-1988.

The Bitter Bit; Manuscript in the possession of the author. This is possibly a sketch, and is an earlier work of Davis. Performed in Sydney, 1975.

Aboriginal Writing Today; (Eds) Davis & Hodge, Canberra, Australian Institute of Aboriginal Studies, 1985.

A collection of papers presented at the first National Aboriginal Writing Conference at Murdoch University, W.A., 1983.
An important collection that gives an insight into the direction of Aboriginal writing.

46 GILBERT, Kevin
The Cherry Pickers and Sketches: The Gods Look Down, Evening of Fear, Eternally Eve, Everyman Should Care, The Blush of Birds. Brisbane, Fryer Library, Manuscripts number 1971 B.

All have been performed, though not yet published.

47 MARIS, Hyluss / BORG, Sonia
Women of the Sun; Sydney, Currency Press, 1983, xiii, 234pp., illus., 23cm.
A Television series in four parts.
Alinta, the Flame.
Maydina, the Shadow.
Nerida, the Waterlily.
Lo-Arna, the Beautiful.

The stories of four women of different eras. Alinta is the first to see the white man and Lo-Arna is the present and must face the truth of her origin. (Published as a novel, Penguin, 1985).

48 MERRITT, Robert, J.
The Cakeman; Sydney, Currency Press, 1978, xxviii, 63pp.

A drama dealing with the arrival of whites in Cowra, NSW in 1840. A play in two acts. The first set in 1840, depicts the enforcing of Christianity onto Aboriginals. The second act is set a hundred years later and shows that little has changed and is symbolised by the Cakeman in both acts. Has been staged and was televised on the ABC in 1977.

Pig in a Poke (Sketch)

Little information available on this but it has been performed, possibly in Melbourne. Manuscript with author.

FICTION

49 BANDLER, Faith
Wacvie, Sydney, Rigby, 146pp., illus., 1977.

A novel based on the life of the author's father, Wacvie Mussington, who was taken by force to work on the Queensland plantations in 1883. the novel depicts a life of harsh cruelty inflicted by white owners on their workers, who were virtually slaves.

Marani in Australia; Sydney, Rigby, 1980, 112pp., illus.

A novel based on actual incidents. A young islander goes to Australia to search for his father who was kidnapped to work on the Queensland plantations. This is a sequel to *Wacvie*. This novel is suitable for young readers also.

Welou My Brother; Sydney, Redress Press, 1984, 125pp.

Semi-biographical. The growing up of a boy born to ex-Queensland plantation slaves. His mother's hopes, for his white education, versus his own compassion for the elder ex-slave members of their community.

50 CLARE, Monica
Karobran; Biographical novel. (See autobiographies, Clare 3).

51 JOHNSON, Colin
Wild Cat Falling; Sydney, Angus & Robertson, 1965, xviii, 131pp.

The first of Johnson's novels. Written in 1965, still holds good for the 1980's in W.A. The story of a young man's release from prison and his quick return.

Long Live Sandawara; Melbourne, Quartet Books, 1979, 170pp., 22 cm.

Two stories are woven into one. The story of Sandawara, an Aboriginal leader who dies fighting to save his land from the whites, and then in the present time we have a young man Alan, who sees himself as a modern Sandawara.

Doctor Wooreddy's Prescription for Enduring the Ending of the World; Melbourne, Hyland House, 1983, 207pp., 22 cm.

A historical novel told from the perspective of the Aborigines, and their view of the arrival of the whites. The novel features the last Tasmanians Truganini and Wooreddy. Doctor Wooreddy who is philosophical in his outlook takes up the position of an observer, watching the ending of the Aboriginal world.

'White Forms, Aboriginal Content' in *Aboriginal Writing Today*; (eds) Davis & Hodge, Canberra, Australian Institute of Aboriginal Studies, 1985, pp. 21-30.

52 MARIS, Hyllus, BORG, Sonia
Women of the Sun; Victoria, Penguin, 1985, vi, 177pp.

The novel of the television series. See Drama 43.

53 WALKER, Kath
Father Sky and Mother Earth; Milton, Queensland, Jacaranda Press, 1981, 44pp.

MYTHS AND LEGENDS

53A. WELLER, Archie
The Day of the Dog, Allen & Unwin, Sydney, 1981. (Revised in paperback by Pan Books, Sydney, 1982).

54 BENNELL, Eddie and THOMAS, Anne
Aboriginal Legends; Adelaide, Rigby, 1981, 80pp., illus, col., 29 cm.

A beautifully presented book with attractive illustrations.

55 CAIRNS, Sylvia
Uncle Willie MacKenzie's Legends of the Goumdirs; Milton, Jacaranda Press, 1967, 46pp., illus.

56 *Djugurba; Tales from the Spirit Time*; Canberra, Australian National University Press, 1975, 64pp., illus.

57 GOONACK, Bura
'Why Possum and Porcupine Look the Way They Do', in *North of the 26th*; (ed) Weller, Helen, W.A., The Nine Club, 1979, pp. 183-84.

58 GUBOO, Ted,
Mumbulla-Spiritual Contact; Canberra, Aust. National University Press, 1980, 52pp., illus.

A pictorial presentation of Aboriginal sacred land areas. The author is a leader of the Yuin people at Lake Wallaga. This is a plea for its preservation.

59 GULPILIL, David
Gulpilil's Stories of the Dreamtime; Sydney, Collins, 1979, 127pp., illus., col., plates,

This is a colourful presentation which includes photographs and art work to present the stories of legends.

60 MILINBILIL
Walking by the Sea; The story of Currmirrinju Land, Milingimbi; Milingimbi Literature Production Centre, 1976.

61 MOWALJARLUI, Turkai
'Crocodile Dream Time Story' in *North of the 26th*; (ed) Weller, Helen W.A. The Nine Club, 1979, 182pp.

62 NANGAN, Joe / EDWARDS, Hugh
Joe Nangan's Dreaming; Melbourne, Thomas Nelson, 1976, 64pp., illus.

A book of 20 legends from Fitzroy River, Western Australia, that represent the dreaming of Joe Nangan 'Maban' (traditional doctor) the last of the Nygina Songmen. Transcribed by Hugh Edwards.

63 RAGGETT, Obed
Stories of Obed Raggett; Sydney, Alternative Pub Co., 1980, 116pp., illus., 19cm.

A collection of traditional stories in English and the 'Pintupi' language.

64 REEVES, Wilf
The Legend of Moonie Jarl; Retold by Moonie Jarl. Illustrated by Wadi (Olga Miller), Brisbane, Jacaranda Press, 44pp., illus., diag., col.

65 ROBINSON, Roland
The Man Who Sold His Dreaming; Roland Robinson, Sydney, Currawong Pub. Co., 1965.

Roland Robinson in his collections of Aboriginal myths and legends has always given credit to the oral authors of collected texts, and in doing so has provided us with a historical list of oral authors.

The authors and their stories are as follows:

66 CHARLES, Julia
'The Cicadas' pp. 138-139.

67 CARPENTER, David
'Bundooia the King of the Sea' pp. 24-26.

68 DALY, Lucy
'Dirrangull at Baryulgil' pp. 84-85.

69 GORDON Ethel
'The Sacred Mountain' pp. 101-104.

70 GORDON, Ken
'The Sacred Spring', pp. 35-36.
'Ginervee, the Black Swan', p. 125.

71 KELLY, Thomas
'The Man Who Broke the Tribal Law', p. 105.
'Geerdung, The Maker', pp. 110-111.
'The Brown Jacks', pp. 134-135.

72 LAURIE, Bella
'Dirranguh at Yamba', pp. 86-87.

73 McGARTH, James
'The Flood', pp. 30-32.
'The Native Companion', pp. 117-119.

74 VESPER, Alexander
'The Three Brothers', pp. 40-44.
'The Twin Stars', pp. 51-58.
'The Mountain Beings', pp. 70-75.
'The Battle of the Birds', pp. 76-78

The Feathered Serpent; Sydney, Edwards & Shaw, 1956, 87 pp., illus, 28x20 cm.

Contributors/Oral Authors

75 TJEEMAIREE, Kianoo, of the Murinbata Tribe.
'The Water-Lubra and the Lotus-Bird, pp. 3-4.
'The Rainbow Serpent Kunmanngur', pp. 5-9.
'Kunmanngur and the Flying-foxes' pp. 10-12.
'The Bregla-Men, the Frog-Men and the Stone Coolaman', pp. 12-14.
'The Crocodile-Man and the Heron-Man', pp. 14-15.
'Moitjinka, the Old-Woman of the Ngowaroo Ceremony', pp. 19-22.
'The Dreaming of the Eagle-Men', pp. 24-25.
'Kurraapun and Bull-Roar of Kunmanngur', pp. 27-28.
'Journey of Karkpee the Rainbow-Snake, p. 29.
'The Snake-Woman Narpajin and the Old-Man Padarooch', p. 32.
'Birth of a Man in the Ceremony of Karwadi', pp. 34-35.

76 TJIEMAIREE/Mardinga, of the Muinbata tribe.
'The Flood and the Bird-Men', pp. 16-18.
'Karabulla, the Crocodile Old-Man', pp. 18-19.
'The Four Water-hole and the Milky Way', pp. 22-24.
'Ngalmin and the Water-Lubras', pp. 35-37.

77 PARUNGBAR, of the Djamunjun tribe.
'Tjigarit the Billabong-Bird.'

78 MARDINGA
'The Spirit Children, Ngarit-Ngarit' (i) p. 30.

79 MOITTA, of the Murinbata tribe
'The Spirit Children, Ngarit-Ngarit (ii), p. 30.

80 MUNGI, of the Birrikilli tribe
'Garun, the Greenbacked Turtle', pp. 41-42.
'The Kranga of Weemirree and the Turtle', pp. 51-52.

81 DARWOODEE/Y. KATANI, of the Leagulawulmirree tribe.
'The Two Waugeluk Sisters' pp. 43-47.

82 DAINGUNNGUN, of the Kuppapoingo tribe.
'The Ranga of Kunji the Jabiroo', pp. 46-47.

83 MANOOWA WONGUPALI, of the Jumbapoingo tribe.
'Banumbin, the Morning-Star', pp. 46-47.

84 WELTJENMIRREE, of the Kuppaoingo tribe.
'Barwal and the Maccassars', pp. 53-54.

85 RINJEIKA, of the Djauan tribe.
'Eingana the Mother', pp. 57-58.
'Marrgon the Lightning', pp. 58-60.
'The Old-Man and Marrgon the Lightning', pp. 60-61.
'Nyal warrai warrai, the Daughter of Bolong', pp. 64-66.

86. GOODOONOO, of the Ngalarkan tribe.
'The Old-Woman Marmoonah of Kunappi, p. 63.
'The Two Children', p. 64.

87 NAMATJIRA, Albert (Tonanga) of the Arranda tribe.
'Erintja the Devil-Dog', pp. 69-71.
'The Eagle-Men of Alkutnama', pp. 73-75.
'The Old-Man and His Six Sons, the Namatuna', pp. 85-87.

88 EIWIN, Arranda-Luritja tribe.
'The Old-Man Tullapinja', pp. 71-72.

89 INTAMINTANA, of the Arranda tribe.
'Journey of the Fish-Women', pp. 75-76.

90 TJONBA, of the Arranda tribe.
'Dreaming of the Fish-Woman, Intabidna', p. 76.
'Tjonba the Printi and Looartjarra the Goanna', pp. 80-81.
'Jlia the Emu-Man', pp. 82-83.

91 PALENGNA, of the Luritja tribe.
'The Sons of Lungara, the Blue-tongued Lizard Men', pp. 77-78.

92 MINYANDERRI, of the Pitjantjarra tribe.
'Keepeva the Scrub-Turkey-Man and the Firestick', pp. 78-79.
'Yoala and the Seven Sisters', pp. 84-85.

93 ROUGHSEY, Dick
The Giant Devil Dingo; Sydney, Collins, 1973, 32pp., illus.
The Rainbow Serpent; Sydney, Collins, 1975, 16pp., illus., col.
The Qunkins; Sydney, Collins, 1978, 29pp., illus., co-author Trezise, Percy.
The Flying Warriors; Sydney, Collins, 1985, co-author Trezise, Percy.
Banana Bird and the Snake Men; Sydney, Collins, 1980, 28pp., illus., col., 27 cm, co-author Trezise, Percy.

Roughsey's artwork is so appealing that one cannot reference his books as 'young reader only'. All are large format.

94 ROUGHSEY, Labamu/ EGAN, Ted
The Turkey and the Emu; Sydney, Harcourt, Brace, Javanovich, 1978.

95 UNIAPON, David Reverend 1871-1967.
This writer is the first of the Aboriginal writers. His writings begin in 1924 and continue up to 1959. Listed here are his known writings but there are possibly more.

1924, 'Why Frogs Jump into the Water', *Sunday News*, July 27th, p. 22.
1925, 'The Story of the Mungingee' *The Home*, February, pp. 42-43.
Native Legends, Hunkin Ellis and King, About 1929-1930, contains a single legend.
1929-1930 *Legendary Tales of the Australian Aboriginal*; Sydney, The Mitchell Library, Manuscript No. A1929-A1930.
1936, 'Native Poetry', *Aborigines Protection*, Vol. 2.
1954, 'Why All the Animals Peck at the Selfish Owl.' *Dawn*, Vol. 4, No. 4, pp. 16-17. 'How the Tortoise Got His Shell'. *Dawn*, vol. 3, No. 11, p. 9. 'Love Story of the Two Sisters'. *Dawn*, Vol., No. 9, p. 19.
My Life story; Adelaide, Aboriginal Friends Association, 1961.

Believed to be a ms. of only a few pages.

96 UMBAGAI, Elkin
'Pidgeon the Outlaw', in *North of the 26th*, (ed), Helen Weller, W.A. The Nine Club, 1979, p. 178.

LAND RIGHTS

97 OLBREI, Erik
Black Australian: (ed), Olbrei, Erik, Queensland, Townsville, Student Union, James Cook University, 1982, 225pp.

A collection of papers and discussions from the national conference on 'Landrights and the Future' of Australian race relationships. Contributors, O'Neil, Kyle, Geia, and Mado.

98 BONNER, Neville
Australian Parliament Senate Select Committee on Aborigines and Torres Strait Islanders; Canberra, A.G.P.S., 1978, xxi, 314pp.

On the social conditions of Aboriginals.

Australian Parliament Joint Selection Committee on Aboriginal Land Rights; Canberra, A.G.P.S., 1977, xv, 102pp.

Aboriginal Land Rights in the Northern Territory; Report, Canberra, A.G.P.S., 1978, 102pp.

Black Power in Australia

99 DAY, Bill
Uranium Miners Get Off Our Land; N.T. Kulaluk, 1978, 15pp., illus., 20 cm.

A pamphlet extracted from the periodical, *Bunji*.

100 GILBERT, Kevin
'Land Rights' in the H.R. KELLY (ed) *Report of a Seminar on Aborigines in Australian Society*; Melbourne, Centre for Continuing Education, Monash University, 1975.

Because a White Man'll Never Do It;
Sydney, Angus & Robertson, 1973, xii. 210pp., 20 cm.
An important book dealing with the social and political aspects of Aboriginality. Gilbert critically looks at a number of areas, such as the role of Black Power and Land Rights. This was an important book at that time, 1973, and remains so.

101 GIRRABUL, Priscilla
'Kunyuhyungki. Agarrikadjung Mungovh'. *Aboriginal Sites*; Rights and Resource Development, (ed) Berndt, R.M. W.A. Perth, U.W.A. Press, 1982, pp. 27-33.

On Aboriginal Sites

102 LANNUPUY, Wesley
'Aboriginal Perspectives of the Land and Its Resources', *Aboriginal Sites*; Rights and Resource Development (ed) Berndt, R.M. W.A. Perth, U.W.A. Press, 1982, pp. 53-59.

103 LEICHLEITNER, Japananka / NATHAM, Pam
Settle Down Country; Vic, Malmsbury, Kibble Books, 1983.

A research report on country camp movement. Written to give the White Australians an insight into what the movements mean to the Aborigines. Although Leichleitner is not literate in English, Pam Natham points out that he is the co-author in every sense.

104 *The Mapon Story*; (ed) Robert, J.P. Vic, Fitzroy, International Development Action, 1975, illus., maps, dia., photos, documents. This text was initially published as a series of 3 paperbacks. Book 1 *The Mapon Story by the Mapon People*. Book 2 *The Mapon Story According to the Invaders*. Book 3 *The Cape York*.

This book is packed with information and gives an insight to the problems of Land Rights versus Mining. A highly political manuscript.

POETRY

105 BOSTOCK, Gerry
Black Man Coming; Melbourne Fitzroy, Gerald Bostock, 1980.

106 DAVIS, Jack
First Born; Sydney, Angus & Robertson, 1970, xviii, 51pp., 21 cm.

A collection of poems from the Aboriginal point of view. Tells of the experience of the poet and others in the outback. The poems have a large Aboriginal Bibbulmum language content and there is a glossary to cover this.

Jagardoo; Sydney, Methuen, 1977, 42pp., illus.

Poems of Aboriginal Australia.

107 FOGARTY, Lionel
Kargun; Brisbane, Cheryl Buchanan, 1980, 95pp., illus., 22 cm.

Yoogum Yoogum; Victoria, Penguin 1982, xi, 132pp., illus., 20 cm.

This is a large collection of over 70 poems, on a wide range of topics. Fogarty has a unique style of his own, which breaks with conventional rules.

Murrie koo-ee; Qld, Spring Hill, Cheryl Buchanan, 1983.
Kudjela; Qld, Spring Hill, Cheryl Buchanan, 1983.

Nguti; Qld, Spring Hill, Cheryl Buchanan, 1984, 119pp., illus., 12 plates, col., 25 cm.

The theme is Black and White interactions. Has a glossary of 80 Aboriginal words.

108 GILBERT, Kevin
Poems 1970; Sydney, the Mitchell Library, 1970, Ms 2429.

These are poems written while in prison, around 1969-1970. A copy is held under the title, 'Drafts of Literary Works', type script, Canberra; The Australian National Library 1969-1970, Ms 2583.

End of a Dreamtime; Sydney, Island Press, 1971, 42pp., illus., col.

A collection of poems.

People are Legends; Queensland, University of Queensland Press, 1978.

A collection of 69 poems all of which are a strong social comment on the relationship between Black and White Australians. The poems are narrative in form and depict often violent incidents that have occurred to Aboriginals.

109 JIMMI, Jean
'Creation of Nature', p. 2.
'Unrecorded Bloodshed', p. 5.
'Mapon', p. 23.

The Mapon Story by the Mapon People; Victoria, Fitzroy 1975. International Development Action, 250pp.

110 JOHNSON, Colin
Sunlight Spreadeagles Perth in Blackness; A Bicentennial Gift poem.

This is a massive poem of 1500 lines. Manuscript with the author, Perth, W.A., 1985.

The Song Circle of Jacky; and Selected Poems; Melbourne Hyland House, 1986, 112pp., illus.

This is the first volume of poetry by Johnson, 35 poems depicting the values of traditional ways for Aboriginal people. Johnson's Buddhist background shows through.

111 ROBINSON, Roland
Altjeringa and other Aboriginal Poems; 1970, Sydney, A.H.S.A.W. READ, 79pp.

The following list of contributors/oral authors are from the above work:

112 BIGG, Fred
'The Child Who Had No Father' p. 18
'Mapooram' p. 22
'The Star Tribes' p. 25
'The Everlasting Water' p. 35

113 BAMBOO, Billy
'Bamboo Billy' p. 24

114 DONNELLY, Dick
'The Platypus' p. 43

115 JEEMBORALA
'The Water Lubra' p. 4

116 KIAROO, Tjeemairee
'The Water Lubra and the Lotus Bird' p. 47

117 KUWORPITA
'The Flying Foxes' p. 54

118 MANOOWA
'The Two Sisters' p. 44

119 MINYANDERRI
'Yoola and the Seven Sisters' p. 38

120 MUMBULLA, Percy
'Jerrangulli' p. 21
'Bees' p. 28
'The Battle of Wallage Lake' p. 35
'The Surprise Attack' p. 50
'Jacky Jacky' p. 56
'Captain Cook' p. 29

121 NALUL
'One Eyed Nanul Speaks' p. 17.

122 TURNBULL, Mary
'The Sandpiper' p. 24

123 VESPER, Alexander
'The Sermon of the Birds' p. 46

124 WILLIAMS, Charlotte
'The Song of Wao' p. 31
'Song of the Vine' p. 53

125 WILLIAMS, Eustan
'Myth of the Mountain' p. 51

126 SYKES, Bobby
Love Poems and Other Revolutionary Action; NSW, Cammeray, Saturday Centre Books, 1979, 51pp., 21 cm.

A collection of 27 poems.

'A Prayer to the Spirit of the New Year' *Australian Voices;* (ed) Rosemary Dobson, Canberra, Australian National University 1975.

127 *Us Fellas*; (eds) G. Glass & A. Weller, W.A. Perth, Artlook Books, 1981, illus., 250pp.

The following authors and poems are from the above work.

128 ANDREWS, Marie
'Resurrection' p. 222

129 DEBLE, Victor
'For' p. 244
'Against' p. 244

130 DOLMAN, Sylvia
'Poem' p. 199

131 SHAW, Stewart
'Exchange' p. 226
'The Meeting' p. 2
'Back Home' p. 227
'Speechless' p. 228
'The Leaf' p. 228
'A Misty Morning' p. 229
'Rabbit the Cat' p. 229
'Death' p. 230
'The Heron' p. 230

132 WILLIAMS, Sheryl
'Bus Stop' p. 238
'Miller's Cave' p. 238

133 YATES, Reg
'The Black Experience' p. 220

134 WALKER, Kath
We Are Going; Brisbane, Jacaranda Press, 1964, 43pp. 23cm.

The first book of poetry by an Aboriginal. This title was reprinted six times in as many months. 43 poems in all.

The Dawn is at Hand; Brisbane, Jacaranda Press, 1966, 40pp.

My People; Brisbane, Jacaranda Press, 1970, 96pp. illus.

An anthology of 96pp., poems and prose. An important work on the inequalities between black and white Australians.

135 WATEGO, Cliff
'Aboriginal Poetry and White Criticism' *Aboriginal Writing Today*; (eds) Davis & Hodge, Canberra, Australian Institute of Aboriginal Studies, 1985, pp. 75-90.

136 WOOLEGOOJA, Sam
Lalai Dream Time; Sydney, The Aboriginal Art Board, 1975, 35pp., illus.

A traditional story told in a poetic form, translated by Michael Silverstein.

137 WORRUMBARRA, Banjo
'The Man', in *North of the 26th,* (ed) Helen Weller, W.A. The Nine Club, 1979, p. 186.

POLITICAL SOCIAL AND MISCELLANEOUS WRITINGS

138 BANDLER, Faith / FOX, Len
The Time was Right; NSW, Chippendale, Alternative Pub Co. 1983, 201pp., illus, 22 cm.

The history of the Aboriginal Australian Fellowship from 1956 to 1969. This is almost a Who's Who in Aboriginal politics. A good book to start with. Contributions are from members of the Fellowship in retrospect.
'The Role of Research' in *Aboriginal Writing Today*; (eds) Davis & Hodge, Canberra, Australian Institute of Aboriginal Studies, 1985, pp. 55-62.

139 BOYLE, Helen
'The Conflicting Role of Aboriginal Women in Today's Society' in *We are Bosses Our-selves*; (ed) Fay Gale, Canberra, Australian Institute of Aboriginal Studies, 1983, photos, dia, pp. 44-47.

140 BUCHANAN, Cheryl
We Have Bugger All; Vic. Carlton, Race Relation Department, Australian Union of Students, 1974, 26pp., illus.

141 CHESSON, Marlene
'The Social and Economic Importance of the Women in Jigalong' in *We are Bosses Our-selves*; (ed) Fay Gale, Canberra, Australian Institute of Aboriginal Studies, 1983, photos, dia, pp. 40-43.

142 COLBUNG, Ken
'On Being an Aboriginal', *Aboriginals of the West*; eds, R.M. & C.H. Berndt, W.A., U.W.A. Press, 1979.

143 DAYLIGHT, Phyllis / JOHNSON, Mary
Women's Business; Report of the Aboriginal Women's Task Force; Canberra, Australian Government Publishing Service. 1976, ports, photos, 140pp., 30 x 21 cm.

The first Government report compiled by two professional Aboriginal women. A detailed look at women's issues from an Aboriginal perceptive. Covers: Aboriginal women today, women and their children, women and families. An important work.

144 DUNCAN, Pearl
'A Teacher's Life' in *Fighters and Singers*; (eds), White, Barwick and Meehan, Sydney, Allen & Unwin, 1985 pp. 45-54.

145 FOGARTY, Lionel / BUCHANAN, C. / BRADY, V.
The Queensland Aborigines Act and Regulations 1971; Brisbane, Black Resource Centre, illus., ports. 1976, 38pp.

Interpretation of the Act in layman terms.

146 FOLEY, Gary
'Self Determination': *Report of a Seminar on Aborigines in Australian Society*; ed., H.R. Kelly, Melbourne, Monash University Press, 1975.

Foley has written quite widely on Medical care, and Education, particularly in *Identity and Aboriginal News*.

147 GALE, Fay
We Are Bosses Our-selves; Canberra, Australian Institute of Aboriginal Studies 1983, photos, 175pp.

'The Status and Role of Aboriginal Women Today'. Gale is a well known white writer on all aspects of Aboriginal society. This text contains a lot of material on the social position of Aboriginal women, and interviews with them.

148 GILBERT, Kevin
Living Black; Blacks talk to Kevin Gilbert, NSW Allen Lane, 1977, 305pp.

Gilbert talks to Aboriginals on many issues, including the social conditions of Aboriginals. A key text.

'Black Policies' in *Aboriginals Writing Today*; (eds) Davis & Hodge, Canberra, Australian Institute of Aboriginal Studies, 1985, pp. 35-42.

149 GLASS, Colleen / WELLER, Archie
Us Fellas; An anthology of Aboriginal Writing, W.A., Perth, Artlook Books, 1987, photos, 250pp.

The latest collection of 'Social Perception' by Aboriginals, most of which appears to be compiled from interviews and could be termed 'biographical portraits'. Contains 26 bio-portraits and 13 creative writing pieces. (Listed here under various headings). An interesting collection.

150 HERCUS, Luise / SUTTON, Peter (eds)
This is What Happened; Canberra, A.C.T. Institute of Aboriginal Studies, 1986, photos, ports, dia, illus., 341pp.

This is a superb text and is a major attempt to overcome the ambiguity of transcribing Aboriginal oral texts. It does this by providing the original spoken Aboriginal language text with its literal translation in English and then a grammatical standard text. Each text is accompanied by notes, maps, ref., diags., and other relevant material. Texts have been transcribed by a number of white linguists. An important work that covers history, geography, language and literature. A book which through its format recognises the importance of cultural and linguistic interpretation. It contains the following list of authors and their stories:

151 BARANGA, Albert
'Violent Contacts' pp. 165-76

152 BARNABAS, Robert
'Stealing on the Station' pp. 280-91
'Moving into the Mission' pp. 62-68

153 BARRENGAWA
'Macassar Man' pp. 125-27

154 BOXER, Johnny
'The Drowning of Constable McLeay' pp. 233-40

155 CLARMONT, Billy & OMEENYO, Charlie
'The Story of Old Paddy' pp. 193-204

156 CLEGG, Willy
'A Chinaman Provides the Excuse' pp. 133-35

157 COULTHARD, Andrew
'Boning Each Other' pp. 227-32

158 DAY, Stan
'A Chinaman in the Shearing Shed' pp. 136-38

159 EJAI, Tudor
'The Killing of the Bilikin Brother' p. 140
'Punitive Expedition Against the Bardi' p. 151
'That Game of Guns' p. 271

160 FLINDERS, Johnny
'Land Rights' pp. 326-30

161 GOETZ, Harry
'Conflicts with Native Police' pp. 205-216

162 HARRIS, Dave
'The Origin of Cobar' pp. 77-81

163 IRINJILI, Mick
'The End of the Minidiri People' pp. 182-92
'A Garden' pp. 69-76

164 JACK, Joker
'Just a Put-On' pp. 266-70

165 JOSHUA, Isaac
'Massacre at Hodgson Downs' pp. 177-81

166 KARNTIN, Jack Spear
'Dutchmen at Cape Keerweer pp. 82-108

167 KENNEDY, Eliza
'Government Clothes' p. 297
'Fanny Brown's Nugget' p. 301

168 KERWIN, Benny
'The Way It Was' pp. 16-40

169 KULAMBURNT, Harry
'Strange Food' pp. 47-61

170 KYNGAYARI, Long Johnny
'The Wave Hill Strike' pp. 303-11

171 LINGIARI, Vincent
'Vincent Lingiari Speech' pp. 312-16

172 MALIWANGA, Jeffery
'Yard Building at Mainoru Station' pp 317-25

173 MOSES, Robert
'The First White Man Comes to Nicholson River' pp. 41-46

174 MURRAY, Ben
'Dhirari Story' pp. 128-32
'Paradise Crossing' pp. 292-96

175 SOMMER, Bruce A.
'The Bowman Incident' pp. 241-64

176 WURRAMARRBA, Charlie Galiyawa
'Macassar Story' pp. 111-124

177 KARTIWYERI, Doreen
'Recording Our History' in *We Are Bosses Our-selves* (ed) Fay Gale, Canberra, Australian Institute of Aboriginal Studies, 1983, photos, dia. pp. 136-157.

178 LANMDS, Merrilee
Mayi; Some Bushfruits of Dampierland; W.A. Broome, Magabala Books, 1987, illus.

179 McGUINNESS, Bruce
'Black Power in Australia', Racism; *The Australian Experience*; ed, F. Stevens, Australian & New Zealand Book Co., Sydney, 1972, pp. 150-58.

180 McGUINNESS, Bruce / WALKER, Denis
'The Politics of Aboriginal Literature' in *Aboriginal Writing Today* (eds) Davis & Hodge, Canberra, Australian Institute of Aboriginal Studies, 1985, pp. 43-54.

'The National Aboriginal Congress' in *Report on Seminar on Aborigines in Australian Society*; Melbourne, Monash University Press, 1975.

181 McGUINNESS, Joe
Conference on Aboriginal Affairs; A report, Melbourne, F.C.A.A. & T.S.I., 1966, 45pp.

A report on that Conference. McGuinness is a well known political figure and contributes to many publications.

182 McLEOD, Isabelle / REID, Billy
Shade and Shelter; Brisbane, Jacaranda Press, 1982 58pp., illus.

The story of Aboriginal resettlement, and the services of the F.R.A.C. available to Aboriginals. Well illustrated.

183 MARIARTY, John
'Development in South Australia' in *Aboriginal Progress* (ed), D.E. Hutchinson, W.A., Perth, U.W.A. Press 1969, pp. 89-105.

184 MILLER, James
Koori; A Will to Win; Angus & Robertson, 1985, xvii, 302pp., maps, illus., ports, plates, dia., appen., bib.

Miller's book is to date the most professional piece of work by an Aborigine. The research is detailed and there are 80 pages of appendix, notes, etc. The text is on the Koori people. Miller traces the last 200 years of his family and tribal history in the Hunter River Valley, NSW. Beautifully researched work.

185 NANDAJIWARE, Amagula
'The Northern Territory' in *Aboriginal Progress*, (ed) D.E. Hutchinson, W.A., Perth, U.W.A. Press 1969, pp. 133-37.

186 PEPPER, Philip / ARAUGO, Tess De
The Kurnai of Gippsland; Volume 1; Melbourne, Hyland House, 1985, biblio, index, illus.

The story of the Kurnai people and their destruction by the whites and their law - a shocking account of early colonisation - and one which was repeated across the country. Well researched and documented.

187 PERKINS, Charles
Road Traffic Accidents; Aboriginal Development Committee Australia.

The role of alcohol in accidents.

'Economic Imperatives as far as Aboriginals are Concerned' in *Aboriginal Sites, Rights and Resource Development*; (ed) R.M. Berndt, Perth, W.A., U.W.A. Press 1982, pp. 157-177.

188 PERKINS, Neville
Aboriginal Australian Yesterday and Today; Adelaide, Aboriginal Rights Community Council, 1973.

189 ROE, Paddy / BENTERRACK, K. & MUECKE, S.
Reading The Country; Fremantle, W.A. Fremantle Arts Centre Press, 1984, photos, col. plates, 250pp., 27 x 21 cm.

As the title suggests the book is on reading the country and particularly the northern part of Western Australia. The text contains 30 segments or short chapters covering such topics as: Nomadic Writing, Key to the Country, Making Rain, Interviews.

A valuable resource on the North of W.A. as experienced by Aboriginals.

190 ROSSER, Bill
This is Palm Island; Canberra, Australian Institute of Aboriginal Studies, 1978, 91pp.

An account of the social poverty and racial conditions existing on Palm Island, as of 1976.

Dreamtime Nightmare; Canberra, Australian Institute of Aboriginal Studies. 1985 191pp., maps, photos.

A collection of interviews with Aboriginals. Reprinted by Penguin in 1987.

191 SILAS, Robert
'The Northern Territory: Aboriginal Opinions' in *Aboriginal Progress*; (ed) H.E. Hutchinson, W.A., U.W.A. Press, 1969, pp. 137- 142.

192 SYKES, Bobbi
'Aboriginal Women' in *Women Cross-Culturally: Change and Challenge*, Rohrlich Leavitt, (ed) The Hague, Mouton, 1975, pp. 56-80.

Black Power in Australia; Vic, South Yarra, Heinemann, 1975, illus., 93pp.

Incentive, Achievement and Community: An analysis of Black viewpoint, on issues relating to Black Education. Sydney University Press, 1984. 138pp., illus., 22 cm.

193 TATZ, Colin
Black Viewpoints; Sydney, Australian and New Zealand Book Co. 1975, 126pp. Contributors include well known Aboriginal writers and activists.

194 THAIDAY, Willie
Under the Act; Queensland, Townsville Black Publishing Co., 1981, illus., maps, tables.

Autobiographical - early life spent on Darnley Island and removal to Palm Island and then to Woorabinda. Covers the social and political elements, also the 1957 strike.

195 UNGUNMERA, Miriam Rose
Nature of Aboriginal Children; Dept. of Education, Northern Territory, 1976, 16pp.

This is a teachers' aid for the understanding of Aboriginal children.

196 VALADIAN, M.
Aboriginal Education; Aboriginals in Australian Society; Melbourne, Centre for Continuing Education, Monash University, 1975.

An Untitled Address; proceedings of the First National Conference of Teachers of Aboriginal Children, Adelaide, South Australian Education Dept., 1977.

197 WATSON, Len
From the Very Depths; A Black view of White Racism. NSW, Surry Hills, Quaker Race Relations Committee, 1973, Pamph., 6pp.

198 WALKER, Denis
'The Politics of Aboriginal Literature' in *Aboriginal Writing Today* (eds) Davis & Hodge, Canberra, Australian Institute of Aboriginal Studies, 1985, pp. 43- 54.

Contributor to many publications. Writes on social and political issues.

SHORT STORIES

199 GLASS, Colleen / WELLER, Archie
Us Fellas; W.A. Perth, Artlook Books, 1987, photos, 247pp.

The following authors are from the above anthology.

200 ALGER, Yvette
'Changing Times' p. 231.

201 DEBLE, Victor
'The Kid Was Okay All the Time' pp. 240-42.

202 IRVING, A.
'Meearnie' p. 197.

203 MORICH, Noel
'The Great Australian Supermarket' pp. 218-19.

204 VANDENBERG, Rosemary
'The Old Place' pp. 216-17.

205 WILLIAMS, Sheryl
'Joey Takes a Walk' pp. 234-36.

206 WINMAR, Daryl
'The Way It Was' pp. 206-15.

207 GORDON, Tulo
Milibi; Canberra, Australian National University Press, 1980, col., illus., maps, 23 x 29 cm., 59pp.

Aboriginal tales from Queensland Endeavour River.

208 JOHNSON, Colin
'A Missionary Would I Have Been' *Westerly*; 1975, pp. 5-11.
'Long Live Pidgeon' *Meanjin*; 1977, pp. 36-40.

209 MOWALJARLUI, Turkai
'Crocodile Dream Time Story'
'Yulum' in *North of The 26th* (ed) Weller, Helen W.A. The Nine Club, 1979, 182pp.

210 ROBINSON, Roland
The Man Who Sold his Dreamings; Sydney, Carrawong Pub. Co., 1965

The following list of contributors / oral authors, are from Robinson's above work.

211 FLANDERS, John
'The Aboriginal Jesus' pp. 37-39

212 MUMBULLA, Percy
'The Whalers' pp. 21-23
'Gold and Grog and Pretty Stones' pp. 91-94
'The Bugeen' pp. 108-109
'The Surprise Attack' pp. 129-130
'The Little People' pp. 136-137.

213 SAMBO, Daniel
'The Native Bears' pp. 61-65
'The Lover of the Mountain' pp. 66-69.

214 SIMS, Mary
'Left-Hander Ferguson' pp. 95-96.

215 TURNBULL, Bob
'The Man Who Killed the Porpoise' pp. 27-29.

216 UTEMORRAH, Daisy
'Cry of our Ancestors' in *North of the 26th;* (ed) Helen Weller, W.A., The Nine Club, 1979, pp. 177-182.

217 VESPER, Alexander
'The Three Brothers' pp. 40-44
'The Twin Stakes' pp. 51-58
'The Mountain Beings' pp. 70-75
'The Battle of the Birds' pp. 76-78

218 WHADDY, Tom
'The Frog Who Was a King' pp. 33-34.

219 WILLIAMS, Charlotte
'The Fairy Emus' pp. 46-47
'The Song of the Vine' pp. 59-60

220 ROE, Paddy
Gularabulu; Compiled by Stephen Muecke, W.A. Fremantle, Fremantle Arts Centre Press, 1983 xii, port., 22cm., 98pp.

A collection of 9 short stories told in the unique style of Paddy Roe. They are mostly of the Ghost Genre and are open ended. None of the mysteries are solved. The author lets his reader believe or reject them. Linguistically the text is of interest and worth reading. An innovative text.

221 *Visions of Mowanjum*; Aboriginal Writings from the Kimberley, Sydney, Rigby, 1980, illus., maps, ports, 110pp.

This is a collection of stories by Aboriginal writers, who are well known as Aboriginal story tellers in the Kimberleys. As follows:

222 ALGARRA, Buruwola
'The Possum and the Porcupine' p. 82.
'The Baler Shell and the Rock Cod' p. 83.
'When I Was a Girl' p. 85.

223 MOWALJARLUI, David
'The Native Cat and Blackheaded Python' p. 100.
'The Story of the Sun' p. 102.
'Body Language' p. 104.
'Yaada' p. 108.
'Death is Nothing' p. 108.

224 UMBAGAI, Elkin
'Tumbi the Owl' p. 74.
'The Mountain of Initiation' p. 76.
'The Disobedient Children' p. 78.

225 UTEMORRAH, Daisy
'Wodoi and Djungu' p. 43.
'Initiation' p. 43.
'How the People were all Drowned' p. 46.
'The Whirlwind and the Little Girl' p. 48.
'The Blue Tongued Lizard' p. 51.
'The Journey of the Two Dreamtime Dogs' p. 32.
'The Boy and the Wild Honey' p. 53.
'A Boy's Lesson' p. 55.
'A Boy's Dilemma' p. 56.
'The Harvest Spirit-Men' p. 57.
'The King Fisher' p. 58.
'My Early Days' p. 61.
'A Worord Woman' p. 63.
'In This Strange World' p. 65.
'Chains' p. 66.

'Longing for the Old Days' p. 68.
'No Clock. No Calendar' p. 70.

This large collection by Daisy Utemorrah, gives some idea just how much material is contributed by Aboriginal authors to the production of texts by white writers such as Robinson, and others. She contributes to other publications, newsletters etc. and is the major writer of short stories.

226 WUNGUNYET, Jean
'A Promise-Marriage' 96pp.
'The Women Who Destroyed the Old World' 90pp.
'The Trap' 91pp.
'The Wanderer' 93pp.
'The Husband and Wife Who Were Murdered' 94pp.

227 WELLER, Archie
Going Home: Stories; Allen and Unwin, Sydney, 1986.

AUTHOR INDEX AND REFERENCE NUMBER TO TITLES

NOTES ON CONTRIBUTORS

PHILIP MORRISSEY is an Aboriginal and developed and managed the Bicentennial National Aboriginal and Torres Strait Islander Program.

OODGEROO of the Tribe Noonuccal (Kath Walker). See Interview.

GERRY TURCOTTE is a Canadian who is doing post-graduate studies at the University of Sydney, Australia. He is a poet as well as a critic and has published poetry in both French and English. Several of his poems were published in the last issue of *Kunapipi*

MUDROOROO NAROGIN (Colin Johnson). Leading Aboriginal writer and critic. His published works include *Wildcat Falling, Long Live Sandawarra* and *Doctor Wooreddy's Prescription for Enduring the Ending of the World* (fiction) and *The Song Circle of Jacky and Selected Poems*. He teaches Aboriginal Studies at Queensland University.

STEPHEN MUECKE teaches at The University of Technology, Sydney. He is a leading critic on Aboriginal literature. His publications include *Reading the Country: an Introduction to Nomadology* (in collaboration with Krim Benterrak and Paddy Roe).

TERRY GOLDIE is a Canadian who teaches at York University, Toronto, Canada. He has published widely in the field of post-colonial literature and his book *Fear and Temptation: The Image of the Indigene in Canadian, Australian and New Zealand Literature* will be published by McGill-Queens in 1989.

SUSAN SHERIDAN teaches in Women's Studies at the Flinders University of South Australia. She has recently published a full length study on the Australian novelist, Christina Stead.

SALLY MORGAN. See Interview.

MARY WRIGHT is Promotions Officer at Fremantle Arts Centre Press.

GLENYSE WARD was born in Perth in 1949. She was taken from her natural parents at the age of three. *Wandering Girl* is her own story. She is now writing a book on the life of the children on the mission where she grew up.

KIRSTEN HOLST PETERSEN is poetry editor of *Kunapipi*. She has published widely in the field of post-colonial studies, especially on African literature.

GRAEME TURNER is Senior Lecturer in the School of Communication at the Queensland Institute of Technology, Brisbane. He has published widely on Australian literature, film, and media and is the author of *National Fictions*

(1986), the prize-winning study of Australian narrative in film and fiction. He is the co-author (with John Fiske and Bob Hodge) of a semiotic study of Australian popular culture, *Myths of Oz: Reading Australian Popular Culture* (1987).

J.V.S. MEGAW graduated in prehistoric archaeology from the University of Edinburgh and is currently Head of the Discipline of Visual Arts at Flinders University.

RUTH MEGAW was trained as a historian at the University of Glasgow specialising in American history.

PAT TORRES. See Interview.

CAROLYN OSTERHAUS is assistant project officer at the Australian Bicentennial Authority. She has worked as a teacher, a journalist and an artist.

TRACEY MOFFATT. See Interview.

JOHN JANKE is a journalist who writes on Aborigines and the law, their encounter with the law and the penal system and moves to prevent Aboriginal deaths in custody.

ARCHIE WELLER writes both fiction and poetry. His works include *The Day of the Dog* (novel) and *Going Home: Stories*.

CHRIS TIFFIN teaches at the University of Queensland. He edited *South Pacific Images* and has written on Australian and South Pacific topics.

ROGER KNOX. See Interview.

MARK O'CONNOR is an Australian poet and critic. More than any other Australian poet he has recorded Australia's natural world. He is the editor of the recently published *Two Centuries of Australian Verse*.

JULIE MARCUS has lectured in anthropology at the University of New South Wales and the University of Adelaide. At present she is a Research Fellow with the Research Centre for Women's Studies at the University of Adelaide, where she is working on a biography of Olive Pink.

WESLEY HORTON is from Western Australia and wrote his thesis on Aboriginal literature.

ANNA RUTHERFORD teaches post-colonial literature at the University of Aarhus, Denmark. She is editor of *Kunapipi*, director of Dangaroo Press and the international chairperson of the Association of Commonwealth Literature and Language Studies.